MILDRED BANGS WYNKOOP

Her Life and Thought

Johan Tredoux

THE FOUNDRY
PUBLISHING

Copyright © 2017 by Johan Tredoux
The Foundry Publishing
PO Box 419527
Kansas City, MO 64141

978-0-8341-3651-9

All rights reserved. No part of this publication may be reproduced, stored in a retrieval system, or transmitted in any form or by any means—for example, electronic, photocopy, recording—without the prior written permission of the publisher. The only exception is brief quotations in printed reviews.

Cover Design: Mike Williams
Interior Design: Sharon Page

Library of Congress Cataloging-in-Publication Data
Names: Tredoux, Johan, 1959- author.
Title: Mildred Bangs Wynkoop : her life and thought / Johan Tredoux.
Description: Kansas City, MO : The Foundry Publishing, 2017. | Includes bibliographical references and index.
Identifiers: LCCN 2017021755 | ISBN 9780834136519 (pbk.)
Subjects: LCSH: Wynkoop, Mildred Bangs. | Church of the Nazarene—Doctrines.
 | Wesley, John, 1703-1791. | Holiness. | Sanctification.
Classification: LCC BX8699.N38 W964 2017 | DDC 287.9/9092 [B] —dc23 LC record available at https://lccn.loc.gov/2017021755

All Scripture quotations, unless indicated, are taken from the *Holy Bible: New International Version*® (NIV®). Copyright © 1973, 1978, 1984, 2011 by Biblica, Inc.™ Used by permission of Zondervan. All rights reserved worldwide. www.zondervan.com.

Scripture quotations marked (DBT) are from the *Holy Bible: Darby Translation*.

Scripture quotations marked (KJV) are from the King James Version.

Scripture quotations marked (NRSV) are from the *New Revised Standard Version* (NRSV) of the Bible, copyright 1989 by the Division of Christian Education of the National Council of the Churches of Christ in the USA. Used by permission. All rights reserved.

Scripture quotations marked (RSV) are from the *Revised Standard Version* (RSV) of the Bible, copyright 1946, 1952, 1971 by the Division of Christian Education of the National Council of the Churches of Christ in the USA. Used by permission.

The internet addresses, email addresses, and phone numbers in this book are accurate at the time of publication. They are provided as a resource. The Foundry Publishing does not endorse them or vouch for their content or permanence.

"It was my privilege to know Mildred Bangs Wynkoop personally. Johan Tredoux has done much more than just describe her theology; he has opened the windows of her life to allow the reader to know the preacher, mentor, and missionary as well as the theologian. For those of us who lived and taught our way through the paradigm shift during the 1970s and 1980s of the Holiness Movement, Mildred is *primus inter pares* as the theologian who cut a fresh path toward a viable future for Wesleyan-Holiness theology. Her *Theology of Love* remains a standard required reading if one wishes to understand the movement, and Tredoux's book provides unparalleled insight into the movement's leading woman theologian."

W. Stephen Gunter, PhD
Associate Dean for Methodist Studies
Duke Divinity School

"Dr. Johan Tredoux has done the Holiness Movement a great service in this study. Mildred Bangs Wynkoop is not only a bridge between the founding theological fathers of the movement (having studied with H. Orton Wiley) and its contemporary adherents, but more importantly, she has opened doors for the Wesleyan message to survive into the twenty-first century. Tredoux builds a fuller picture of her life and development for those of us who only know her seminal work in *A Theology of Love*."

H. Ray Dunning, PhD
Professor Emeritus of Theology
Trevecca Nazarene University

"As a faculty colleague of Mildred Wynkoop at Nazarene Theological Seminary from 1976 to 1980, I am pleased to see Johan Tredoux's explication of her understanding of John Wesley's most practical doctrine of Christian holiness. In the process of detailing the growth of her biblical, theological, and philosophical thinking within the larger context of twentieth-century theological thinking, Tredoux also identifies the correlation (or lack thereof) between contemporary holiness theology and John Wesley's eighteenth-century articulation of the gospel."

Morris A. Weigelt
Professor Emeritus of New Testament and Spiritual Formation
Nazarene Theological Seminary

"I will always count it a blessing that I was able to study under Mildred Bangs Wynkoop at Nazarene Theological Seminary during the closing years of her career. Through her teaching and the witness of her life, Wynkoop played a crucial role in grounding me in the Wesleyan tradition and pointing me toward an authentic and winsome understanding of its central conviction—that God desires, and through grace enables, us to live in holiness of heart and life. This book, written by the son of one of my NTS classmates, is itself an authentic and winsome exposition of Wynkoop's life, teaching, and impact on the Church of the Nazarene, the larger Wesleyan family, and beyond. Highly recommended!"

Randy L. Maddox, PhD
William Kellon Quick Professor of Wesleyan and Methodist Studies
Duke Divinity School

"Heiko Oberman claimed that the function of a historian was to be a 'last advocate' for the dead. Johan Tredoux expertly accomplishes this task in his recent work on Mildred Bangs Wynkoop. Remarkably, he allows this scholar–a theologian, a woman–to speak in her own, authentic voice. Wynkoop was someone who desired to interpret Scripture for her hearers in a language they could understand–hence, *A Theology of Love*. She was not well understood by some of her readers. Tredoux enables contemporary readers to reread, relisten, and reinterpret to better see, hear, and understand the Wynkoop voice. For this, he is to be commended. He deserves our respect and our attention."

David P. Whitelaw
Emeritus Professor of Theology
Point Loma Nazarene University

"In a time when the doctrine of sanctification was sounding like a logical construct with Scripture scaffolding, my young heart needed more. As a student at Trevecca Nazarene College, I sat in classrooms under the teaching of Mildred Wynkoop and later worked as her grading assistant. Her teaching, writing, and life inspired a generation of young pastors to embrace a doctrine as experience. Holiness went from stale to central. I am grateful to Johan Tredoux for reminding us of a theology of love that fits the human experience today."

Dan Boone
President
Trevecca Nazarene University

"This masterful work on Mildred Bangs Wynkoop is a must-read for those who desire a clearer biblical, authentic, and Wesleyan understanding of God's love in the context of relationships. The impact can be extremely timely in these days of our seeking to better grasp the theology of love."

Nina G. Gunter
General Superintendent Emerita
Church of the Nazarene

"Reading this book is like dipping your toe into the refreshing streams of authenticity. For those who have ever hoped for a faith beyond appearances and a theology capable of engaging the world in transformative ways, you will find Mildred Wynkoop a kindred spirit and Johan Tredoux highly capable of introducing you to her. Once the introduction is made, you'll find Wynkoop's thought–revolutionary in its day–to be a wonderful challenge to continue exploring the Christian life in terms of God's dynamic love, a reality that has been and remains revolutionary."

Timothy R. Gaines, PhD
Assistant Professor of Religion
Millard Reed School of Theology and Christian Ministry
Trevecca Nazarene University

"Dr. Tredoux does an excellent job of examining Dr. Wynkoop's theology within her twentieth-century context and finding clear alignment with Wesley. He places her understanding of holiness within a Christocentric model that leads us to a hopeful optimism in living the sanctified life. Dr. Tredoux states that 'the key teleological anchor point for Wynkoop is Christlikeness.

This is the controlling principle of her doctrine of sanctification.' Dr. Wynkoop's work was transformational for many young theologians in the twentieth century, and this new work by Tredoux expands our understanding but also leaves us with handles by which to preach holiness in the contemporary context."

Rev. Carla Sunberg, PhD
President, Professor of Historical Theology
Nazarene Theological Seminary

"It is a privilege to commend this volume to all interested readers. Dr. Tredoux has been a good friend over the course of twenty-five years and on two continents. Our association has taught me that he is a clear and careful theologian and a gifted pastor and preacher. Those qualities served him well as he wrote this monograph analysing the theological contributions of the late Dr. Mildred Wynkoop. Those familiar with her thinking through personal acquaintance will share my enthusiasm for this thorough analysis and exposition of her contributions to Wesleyan theological understanding. My own appreciation for Dr. Tredoux's work is founded upon personal experience as a beginning instructor in the department of religion and philosophy at Trevecca Nazarene College during Dr. Wynkoop's last four years on that faculty. We engaged in discussions that arose out of questions I posed to her, and from her voluntary comments to me out of her teaching, research, and writing during those years. I was never a formal student of hers, but she was my teacher nonetheless. It is an honor to recommend this volume to those already familiar with her work and also to those who would like a rich introduction to this great theologian."

Hal A. Cauthron, PhD
Professor of New Testament Language and Literature
Southern Nazarene University

"In this important work, Johan Tredoux has taken measure of the life and continuing legacy of the great Nazarene theologian Mildred Bangs Wynkoop. Tredoux demonstrates that Wynkoop was first of all a careful and committed biblical scholar who sought to discover and communicate scriptural truth. Certainly she did so as a participant in the Wesleyan theological tradition, but it was her overriding desire to be faithful to a biblical vision of God, creation, humanity, sin, and salvation that comes to the fore in this study. Tredoux shows, too, that Wynkoop's sustained engagement with Scripture led her to insights consistent with early, classic, Christian thinkers, especially Irenaeus. Tredoux has done us a profound favor in commending this saintly thinker for our ongoing theological conversations as Wesleyans."

Michael Lodahl, PhD
Professor of Theology and World Religions
Point Loma Nazarene University

"My first encounter with Mildred Bangs Wynkoop was in the reading of *A Theology of Love* as an undergraduate student. It was a bright light to my developing understanding of our doctrine of holiness, and it resonated deeply with how my lay parents guided me into the knowledge and experience of sanctifying grace. I had no idea at the time that Dr. Wynkoop's work was controversial in the Church of the Nazarene. I received it gratefully as an honest and hopeful articulation of our beloved doctrine. In this volume, Dr. Tredoux offers a great service to us, taking us behind *A Theology of Love* to know the development of Wynkoop's own theology.

This text places Wynkoop's work in its necessary historical context. Among the critical understandings that Tredoux reveals is not only Wynkoop's commitment to Scripture but also her clarity on the nature of biblical authority as the foundation of her work. This clarity helped to keep the doctrine of holiness as preached in the Church of the Nazarene from becoming truncated by parochial narrowness. This clarity also gave her freedom to see something deeper than a quantitative understanding of two works of grace but, rather, holiness as dynamic, relational maturation in the likeness of Jesus toward the goal of reflecting the image of God. I urge pastors to study this text and thereby to grow in our knowledge, understanding, and articulation of holiness and particularly of the doctrine of entire sanctification. I am grateful to Pastor Tredoux for the gift of this scholarship."

Jeren Rowell
District Superintendent
Kansas City District, Church of the Nazarene

DEDICATION

I am dedicating this book to my parents, Rev. Gideon and Jeanette Tredoux, whose enduring hearts for relational holiness have engaged a lifelong quest. My parents were pioneers for the work of the Church of the Nazarene in South Africa as well as pioneers in the establishment of the Nazarene Theological School in Lilongwe, Malawi.

CONTENTS

Foreword	11
Preface	15
1. Mildred Bangs: A Brief Biography	19
2. Wynkoop's Journey toward a Theology of Love	27
3. The Role of Scripture in Wynkoop's Theology	47
4. Wynkoop's Theological Anthropology	79
5. The Divine-Human Interaction	119
6. Wynkoop's Soteriology	157
Conclusion	231
Glossary of Terms	235
Bibliography	241

Illustrations 111-18

FOREWORD

Theology does not stand still. That may be a worrying thought for some who are committed to "the faith once delivered to the saints" (Jude v. 3, DBT). If our theology is true, how can it change? Are we not simply to believe what the apostles and prophets wrote in the inspired Scriptures? And, for Nazarenes and others in the Wesleyan-Holiness tradition, did not the great Nazarene theologian Dr. H. Orton Wiley formulate our theology? And are we not all committed to the same theology, particularly in our understanding of Christian holiness? It may have been assumptions such as these that lay behind some of the opposition encountered by Dr. Mildred Bangs Wynkoop.

One must have the greatest sympathy for deeply loyal and committed preachers and laypeople in the Holiness Movement in the 1970s. To begin with, there was the discovery in the mid-twentieth century that there were differences between Wesley's understanding of Christian **sanctification** and that of the nineteenth-century Holiness Movement, which produced an immediate question: which version of our tradition should we go with? But Dr. Wynkoop took it further. It was not just a matter of who—whether John Wesley or Phoebe Palmer—got it right: Wynkoop took her bearings from biblical theology. Her thorough study of the text of Scripture led her to recast many of the ways we had articulated our doctrine. It is quite understandable that her assertions were somewhat unnerving. Was she then a heretic, as some alleged? Or did our treasured formulations of doctrine have to be recast in the light of Holy Scripture? Had we been using ways of thinking and preaching that were actually shaped by our culture? Did we have to reshape the way we articulated our doctrine?

Although this was perhaps not always understood, behind the great debate of the 1970s, which echoed round the halls of learning in Nazarene colleges and at Nazarene Theological Seminary, those were really the underlying questions: Is Christian theology static? Or do we have to think of Christian theology as something that has developed under the guidance of the Holy Spirit and continues to develop through the centuries? And do we all have to state our doctrine exactly the same way? Or is it possible that there can be varieties of expression within the one church and within the one theological tradition?

In the nineteenth century, John Henry Newman wrote his seminal work, *The Development of Christian Doctrine*. That was a century in which people gained a new understanding of history, and one of the aspects of that development was the new understanding that, over the centuries, Christian doctrine had *developed*. The full doctrine of the Holy Trinity—that God was three persons in one being—was not fully articulated until the fourth century. The doctrine of Christ as one person in two natures—divine and human—was not fully articulated until the fifth century. The doctrine of the atonement developed with Anselm, justification with Luther, and (we would want to add) sanctification with Wesley. And we today continue to explore all of these doctrines further.

Newman's point was that development did not mean departing from the faith into theological liberalism (or whatever we want to call it). It did not mean replacing the gospel with some modern, **metaphysical** system or ideology, and it does not mean replacing a Christ-centred faith with one centred on some philosophical notion of love. Not at all: we remain true to the faith of the New Testament and the creeds. We believe in the Father, the Son, and the Holy Spirit. We believe that Christ died for our sins according to the Scriptures. We believe that the Holy Spirit is our Sanctifier. Rather, authentic development could and should mean a deeper understanding of "the faith once delivered to the saints" (Jude v. 3, DBT) as the church is led deeper into the truth of God by God the Holy Spirit. And such development is impossible without faithful and rigorous theological *thinking*.

Mildred Bangs Wynkoop taught the Wesleyan-Holiness tradition afresh the importance of biblically based, theological *thinking*. One danger for the church is that we lose hold of Christ and drift from the gospel. But the other danger is that we will fall into an arid **scholasticism** that merely repeats the cultural stereotypes and categories of our subculture until they become clichés. Theology needs to be challenged again and again by wrestling with the Word of God in Holy Scripture so that our cultural assumptions are challenged. That is how the hermeneutical circle operates, making us come again and again to the text of Scripture so that "the church, having been reformed, must always be being reformed." *Ecclesia reformata semper reformanda*. Only in this way can a tradition be a living tradition and not a dead antique heading for the museum.

Of course, the implication of continual reformation is that Dr. Wynkoop did not write the last word. The development of our theological thinking continues: culture constantly throws up new questions as the modernity still in vogue in the 1970s fades into a new phase, perhaps misleadingly dubbed "postmodernity." Biblical studies have moved beyond the methodology of word studies and captivity to the historical-critical method and have developed a welcome concern with **hermeneutics.** Theology has developed a new concern to recapture its Trinitarian shape and to set personal experience within the corporate experience of the people of God in the "one holy, catholic, and apostolic church." But the work of Mildred Bangs Wynkoop remains a signpost for those of us in the Wesleyan-Holiness tradition. That does not necessarily mean she was always right and her opponents always wrong. But it does mean that it is important for us that each new generation becomes familiar with her thought.

No better guide can be found than Johan Tredoux. His father, Gideon Tredoux, was one of Dr. Wynkoop's students at Nazarene Theological Seminary in the 1970s, and he himself has immersed himself in her writings for years. This immersion finally led him to complete a doctoral thesis at the prestigious University of Manchester, and it is the fruit of this long and thorough study that is now presented in this book. Dr. Tredoux sets Mildred Bangs Wynkoop in her context, beginning with her family's involvement with Dr. Phineas Bresee and her own studies under Dr. H. Orton Wiley in the early days of the Church of the Nazarene. Out of her deep spiritual dissatisfaction with superficial, stereotypical presentations of the way of holiness, she, as a mature woman, undertook academic study in Bible and theology and the study of John Wesley in order to thrash out how to articulate the doctrine in a way that truly brought practical piety and learning together.

Dr. Tredoux's book will be of immeasurable help to those of us who are heirs of the Wesleyan-Holiness Movement to understand the thinking and the passion of this remarkable woman. But more than that, it will help us today in the task of articulating the message of Christian holiness in a way that is biblically based and culturally relevant. This is a book every preacher and thinking layperson in the Wesleyan-Holiness tradition needs to read.

Thomas A. Noble
Research Professor of Theology, Nazarene Theological Seminary
Senior Research Fellow in Theology, Nazarene Theological College in Manchester

PREFACE

• ● •

My father's friendship with Mildred Bangs Wynkoop began in 1975, when he sold everything he owned to make it possible to move from the Republic of South Africa to study at the Nazarene Theological Seminary (NTS) in Kansas City, Missouri, from 1975 until 1977. At that time, Mildred Bangs Wynkoop was the theologian-in-residence at NTS. Crossing paths with Wynkoop's teaching became a pivotal moment in the history of the Tredoux family. Wynkoop not only impacted my father but also impacted my own life.

My father introduced me to Wynkoop in 1980, during the Nazarene General Assembly, which was held in Kansas City that year. I remember meeting Mildred for the first time. I recall a gracious and humble lady who was very present in the moment. Had I known at that time that I would spend six years researching her life and writings, I would have asked her lots of questions.

Having grown up as Afrikaans-speaking citizens in apartheid-era South Africa, a theology of love was not something that would have been a reality in our lives. However, the choice to walk away from prejudice opened up a whole new world to my father, including the opportunity to study under Wynkoop. Under Wynkoop, my father's theological world was opened to the thoughts of John Wesley and to Wynkoop's relational and christological understanding of Christian sanctification. Seeing the impact that Wynkoop made on my family, I became very curious about her life and theology. My curiosity eventually led me to make her lifetime work the focus of my doctoral research at the University of Manchester (UK) under the supervision of Dr. Tom Noble. Part of this research involved spending one day a week for a whole year going through boxes and boxes of her lifetime work that was never published. I especially want to recognize Stan Ingersol, the archivist at the Nazarene Resource Center, for putting together the Wynkoop Collection that made it possible to do this research.

If you met this humble lady, you wouldn't know that Dr. Mildred Bangs Wynkoop was an influential and controversial theologian in the Wesleyan-Holiness Movement of the late twentieth century. In fact, it is through the clarity and urgency with which she set forth her position, particularly in *A Theology of Love*, that Wynkoop became a key figure in effecting a major paradigm shift in the Holiness Movement—to a relational way of thinking about sin and holiness. This relational reading of John Wesley and the American Holiness Movement's theology of Christian holiness raised significant theological debate in the last decades of the twentieth century.

This work breaks new ground in attempting a comprehensive understanding of Wynkoop's passion for a more biblical way of thinking about the Christian life and, particularly, Christian holiness. The research also examines the extent to which Wynkoop's version of Wesleyan-Holiness theology was an authentic interpretation of John Wesley's doctrine of sanctification.

Wynkoop thought that a "credibility gap" existed between the doctrines held in the Wesleyan-Holiness Movement and the way these doctrines were lived out in real life. Through her doctoral work in biblical interpretation and her master's work in theological anthropology, she concluded that the problems causing the credibility gap were present at a presuppositional level and that the solutions would have to be addressed at that level as well. Wesley's emphasis on the living Word and his spiritual reading of Scripture helped Wynkoop to realize that an **existential** and Christocentric reading of Scripture is the primary way to overcome the credibility gap.

The role of the "moral" also became a major hermeneutical principle used by Wynkoop to address the credibility gap. As a key interpretive principle, the "moral" became a way through which she was able to assess whether sanctification proceeded along the lines of moral integrity and moral responsibility. Through her critical study of the *imago Dei*, Wynkoop made a distinction between "image" and "likeness." Building on this distinction, Wynkoop postulates that human potential, freedom, development, and growth are embedded in her biblical understanding of "likeness," which to her is a disposition that remained after the fall. The outcome was that Wynkoop followed the Eastern tradition in its Christocentric reading of creation. This research further affirms that the divine-human interaction, as postulated in her existential theology, is not anchored in the metaphysical world of **Boston personalism** or relationalism but, rather, in the Hebraic, biblical understanding of corporate personality.

Wynkoop's studies and theological reflection led her to see Wesley's understanding of sanctification as dynamic, christological, relational, **teleological**, and socially oriented. Together with Wesley, Wynkoop concludes that holiness is not a withdrawal from society in a posture of indifference, isolationism, or exclusivity. It is, rather, love locked into the true centre, who is Jesus Christ, being lived out in the existential realities of everyday life. Holiness is faith expressing itself in love that bears witness to the enabling grace of Christ and fulfils the royal law to love our neighbours as ourselves.

This work thus explores the sources and development of Wynkoop's theology of sanctification. It will not be possible in the space available to develop a wider evaluation of her thought against the broader theological currents of her time or to assess her influence.

A NOTE TO THE READER

To assist the reader, a glossary of terms is included at the end of the book. Each term's first appearance in the text—including the foreword and preface—is highlighted in bold.

1
MILDRED BANGS: A BRIEF BIOGRAPHY

Mildred Bangs was born on September 9, 1905, in Seattle, Washington, as the first child of Carl and Mary Bangs, emigrants from Norway and Switzerland who became naturalized American citizens.

Her mother, Mary (née Dupertuis), was born in Canton de Vaux, Switzerland. As a six-year-old girl, and one of a family of twelve siblings, she endured tremendous hardship as her father tried to make a living farming on an incredibly steep section of a Swiss mountain. In the spring of 1889, he gathered his family and immigrated to the "grand new world" of North America.

Mildred's father was Carl Oliver Bang, a Norwegian, born in Norway in a drunkard's home (not an unusual situation, then). Carl's mother died soon after his birth, and Carl was shunted from one place to another. Always serious and seeking meaning, he ended up attending the Society of Friends (Quakers). Influenced by the Quaker missionaries, he felt a strong reluctance to enter the military service. To avoid signing up with the army, he signed up with his uncle, a sea captain, on a freighter going to the West Coast of the United States. For reasons unknown, Carl decided to jump ship in Pensacola, Florida. This decision saved his life because the ship went out to sea and sank, and all on board drowned. No one of the family back in Norway knew that he had *not* been in the disaster. He changed his name from Bang to Bangs—never to return to his fatherland. He worked his way on other ships around South America (pre-canal) to San Francisco and then worked on lumber ships going from Washington to California and back. Lonely, hungry, and drinking too much, he finally found a haven in Seattle.

It was only a matter of time before the lively Dupertuis family and the lonely Norwegian met and established a friendship.

It all started when he was on the docks, thinking of signing up on another lumber ship going to Alaska, and he met Mary, who was playing in a Salvation Army band. With Mary as an incentive, he began attending services at the Salvation Army Mission, and there one night he was converted and became a Christian.[1] Carl Bangs and Mary Dupertuis eventually developed a relationship and were married in December 1904. To this union, five girls and one boy (in that order) were added. Mildred was the first child, followed by Bernice, Thelma, Florence, Olive, and Carl.[2]

Nazarene Roots

Mildred Bangs's biography is rooted deeply in Nazarene soil. Her first memories were of the Seattle Salvation Army Mission, the singing and the drama and the beautiful, uniformed soldiers. Given the location of the Salvation Army, Carl Bangs decided to find a safer place for his young family because the streets were dark and the night people rough. This is where the Seattle First Church of the Nazarene came into play. Carl Oliver Bangs found the Nazarene meetings to be more of a family church than the Salvation Army, and they had already connected with P. F. Bresee's Los Angeles church on their honeymoon. When Bresee came to Seattle the following year and organized a class of Nazarenes there, Carl Bangs was one of the three officers appointed. The Bangses thus became pioneers for the Nazarene work in Seattle.[3]

Religious influences constantly surrounded Mildred as she grew up in the Seattle First Church of the Nazarene. One of her earliest memories was hearing Dr. Bresee preach. She remembered, "He stood before us like a Moses!"[4] H. D. Brown, the first Nazarene district superintendent appointed by Bresee, lived in Seattle and was a friend of the Bangs family.[5] Mildred's early exposure to missionaries speaking in the pulpit, eating at their home, and then leaving for the distant, pagan world from the Seattle

---

1. Mildred Bangs Wynkoop, "This Is Mildred Bangs Wynkoop" (article, undated), file 1427-3, Wynkoop Collection, Nazarene Archives, Lenexa, Kansas, 1 (hereafter cited as WC).
2. Wynkoop, "Birth and Marriage" (article, undated), file 1427-4, WC, 1.
3. Carl Bangs, *Phineas F. Bresee: His Life in Methodism, the Holiness Movement, and the Church of the Nazarene* (Kansas City: Beacon Hill Press of Kansas City, 1995), 249–50.
4. Wynkoop, "This Is Mildred," file 1427-3, WC, 1.
5. Ibid.

port gave her a missionary mind-set that would eventually have a profound influence on the way she did theology. She wrote, "I felt called to every country I heard about and contracted to go at the altar, regularly."[6] She would eventually (fifty years later) leave from the same city to go to Japan as a missionary teacher.

Early Years

Mildred remembers her parents' devotion to Christ to be so genuine that not the slightest hint ever came to any of the six children that they had even remotely considered any other way of life.[7] She said of her father: "He taught us how to look past the false front of ideas and to ask probing questions of easy answers. He loved his Bible and talked to us about it. He wanted us to learn to read and understand for ourselves. He taught us to read the classics."[8]

The Nazarene services became a very exciting part of Mildred's young life. As a family the Bangses drove to church in a buggy, pulled by Billy, their milk-wagon horse. She remembered the services being so exciting that she wouldn't miss a single one, especially Wednesday night prayer meeting.[9] Her shy personality surfaced already at this very young age as she came home one night too excited not to awaken her parents: "Mama, Papa," she said, "the people testified about their problems today. They didn't shout—they cried."[10] This was the first hint she had that it was all right to have problems without having to shout it aloud for everyone to hear.

One of the great ironies of this scholar's life was her traumatic experience of going to school for the first time. At age six, her first grade experience was so terrifying to her that her mother brought her home and homeschooled Mildred for two years. She carried this scar with her for the rest of her life, frequently explaining her lifelong reluctance to meet with unfamiliar people as a reflection of her first school experience.[11]

---

6. Ibid., 2.
7. Ibid.
8. Ibid.
9. Ibid.
10. Ibid.
11. Wynkoop, "School (1911–13)" (article, undated), file 1427-3, WC, 1.

College Years

From very early on, Mildred was influenced by her father's desire for his children to be exposed to the classic literature of Europe and early American writings.[12] She remembered getting lost in that treasury of literature on the long streetcar ride from home to grammar school.[13] Later studies in college, university, and seminary sank roots in fertile soil already prepared at a very young age. She reminisced, "I was born a very restless creature, ambitious, impatient, searching. I often scolded God, 'Why don't you talk to me. I don't like you all the time trying to make me guess what you want. You could talk—do it!'"[14]

She wanted to go to college, yet there was no money. She wrote: "I talked to God again. 'You are rich,' I said. 'Send me the money to go to school. You wouldn't miss it.'"[15] Unknown to her at that time, her father took on a second mortgage to make it possible for her to go to college.[16] In 1926 she entered Northwest Nazarene College in Nampa, Idaho. Her most important contact (other than several nice boys) was with its president, H. Orton Wiley.

She joined a collegiate singing quartet that travelled on the weekends and promoted the college from church to church.[17] She remembered how, on one trip to Seattle (they hardly had any money), Dr. Wiley just stopped the car along the road and disappeared down to the river. It wasn't long before he reappeared with a trout in his hand. That was their breakfast that morning.[18] His relationship with the quartet deepened over the year. And when Wiley announced in 1928 that he was leaving Nampa to return to Pasadena College, Mildred Bangs and at least one other student in the quartet followed him there.[19]

Once in college, several nice boys were in her sights, but the one who captured her heart was Ralph Wynkoop. On December 27, 1928, Mildred and Ralph were married at Central Church of the Nazarene (now Aurora Church of the Nazarene) in Seattle, Washington. She graduated twice from

---

12. Wynkoop, "Satisfactions and Regrets" (article, undated), file 1561-32, WC, 1.
13. Ibid.
14. Wynkoop, "Mid-Course Corrections" (article, undated), file 1427-2, WC, 1.
15. Ibid.
16. Wynkoop, "Birth and Marriage," file 1427-4, WC, 1.
17. Stan Ingersol, "The Woman behind the Words" (article, undated), WC, 3.
18. Wynkoop, "Notes on My Life" (article, undated), file 1427, WC, 1.
19. Ingersol, "The Woman," file 1561-32, WC, 3.

Pasadena College—in 1931, with a bachelor of arts degree, and in 1933, with a bachelor of theology degree. In 1934, she was ordained as an elder by Dr. John Goodwin in the Los Angeles First Church of the Nazarene.[20] Her decision to attend seminary came many years later, in the late 1940s.

The Influence of H. Orton Wiley

Stacked away in Wynkoop's 1940 edition of H. Orton Wiley's *Christian Theology* are extensive "write-ins" in the margins and notes of comments she took, both as a student and as a teacher. One of the notes simply says: "In a sense I am a Wileyite, not in a blind guru type of dedication, but as a goad to fresh, released, in-depth, biblical dependence that nourished a searching mind."[21] She met Wiley when she was fifteen years old and became one of his students at about eighteen or nineteen. His impact on Wynkoop can be seen in the way he took her outside of her small world, theologically, and helped her see that she was part of the church universal, linked with the cloud of witnesses from Christ and the early Catholic Church, through the Reformation and, closer to home, through the Wesleyan movement.

Wynkoop went through Wiley's three-volume *Christian Theology* with him, first as class notes when it was in duplicate form and helping him to run it off in the print room, and then she taught from it five times in five years in a seminary on the West Coast.[22] Wynkoop's classroom experience with Dr. Wiley, along with other students, was one of being thrown into the deep sea of church history and the development of church doctrine.[23] Wynkoop could relate very well to the conversation she overheard between her brother, Carl Bangs, and Wiley.

Carl said, "When I began to study theology under you, I was so sure of everything. Now, [after one year,] I'm not sure of anything."

Dr. Wiley laughed and answered, "Think things over and rest good over the summer, you'll come out all right."[24] And so they did.

Wiley's biblical, christological, and Wesleyan presentation of the doctrine of holiness, related as it was to the church, began to challenge

---

20. Wynkoop, "Birth and Marriage," file 1427-4, WC, 1.
21. Wynkoop (handwritten note, February 13, 1991), file 2228-6, WC.
22. Wynkoop, "The Foundations of: *A Theology of Love*" (monograph, 1975), undated, file 2227-11, WC, 3.
23. Ibid.
24. Ibid.

Wynkoop and finally erode some theories that had slipped in from other theological streams. When she first entered the field of theology, she inherited Wiley's theological agenda. According to Stan Ingersol, Wiley was recognized as the leading exponent of Arminian theology within American evangelical Protestantism, and was so identified by Carl F. H. Henry, the founding editor of *Christianity Today*.[25]

It is, then, not a surprise that Wynkoop and her brother, Carl, joined Wiley in the defense of Arminianism. Carl became the leading scholar on Arminius with his publication of *Arminius: A Study in the Dutch Reformation*.[26] Wynkoop's book *Foundations of Wesleyan-Arminian Theology* also shows the deep influence of Wiley on her work as she recognized the Calvinist inroads into the thinking of Nazarene pastors and laity. Wiley opened Wynkoop's eyes to her own denominational, segregationist prejudice. She said, "Born as we were in a very narrow, provincial concept of gospel and church, Wiley with his tremendous grasp of what the gospel and church really were, led us step by step into the high country of vision and understanding and mission. I have much to thank Wiley for; I am indelibly marked by his inspired and inspiring ministry."[27]

Lifetime Work

Mildred Bangs Wynkoop spent most of the 1930s and 1940s travelling with her husband as evangelists and as pastors of small Nazarene churches. Her simple impulse at the age of forty-four to study Greek and Hebrew opened up a whole new academic world to her. She decided to go back to college and earned a master of divinity degree at the Western Evangelical Seminary (now George Fox Evangelical Seminary) in 1952, a master of science degree at the University of Oregon in 1953, and culminating in 1955 with a doctorate of theology from Northern Baptist Theological Seminary.

Wynkoop started her teaching career at Western Evangelical Theological Seminary in Portland, Oregon, teaching theology from 1955 to 1960. She then spent a year teaching in Korea, Taiwan, Hong Kong, and Japan with the Oriental Mission Society. In 1961 she was instrumental in redeveloping theological education for the Church of the Nazarene in

---

25. Ingersol, "The Woman," file 1561-32, WC, 4.
26. Ingersol, "The Woman," file 1561-32, WC, 5.
27. Wynkoop, "Foundations," file 2227-11, WC, 3.

Japan. She became the dean of the Nazarene Junior College from 1961 until 1963 and became the first woman president of the Japan Nazarene Seminary from 1963 until 1966. Upon her return to the United States, Wynkoop became the professor of missions and theology at Trevecca Nazarene College (now University) in Nashville, Tennessee, from 1966 to 1976. She was president of the Wesleyan Theological Society in 1973 and closed her career as theologian-in-residence at Nazarene Theological Seminary in Kansas City, Missouri, from 1976 until 1980.[28]

It is fair to say that the classroom was the most prominent symbol and existential reality of her life. She wrote:

A classroom presents to me a peculiar romantic psychological reaction. A silent empty room, chairs, a blackboard and chalk and chalk dust. Empty, cold, echoes, ghosts, dreams, shadows, and silence, little shudders of fear. That has been my world for over two thirds of my life. And then the jangling bell, and a thundering horde of feet crowding in, crackling chairs, a babble of voices, and suddenly, the cold emptiness is gone and Shakespeare comes alive, and the utter wonder of art, of vivid imagination, of philosophical ideas, of startlingly vivid scenes from histories past. Where did the drab room go? It is full of light, and excitement. The windows are opened into eternity. Who needs a carpet or soft chairs and background music to tie us to the earth? We go out beyond the earth into the stratosphere of transcendent existence—magic, miracle. And then jangling bells break in and the psychedelic trip ends, and the cold, drab room is left behind. This miracle occurs day after day, year after year, a miracle that I would not exchange for anything in the world. A world I love.[29]

Wynkoop's published monographs are *John Wesley, Christian Revolutionary* (Beacon Hill Press of Kansas City, 1970); *Foundations of Wesleyan-Arminian Theology* and *A Theology of Love* (both Beacon Hill Press of Kansas City, 1972); *The Occult and the Supernatural* (Beacon Hill Press of Kansas City, 1976); and *The Trevecca Story: 75 Years of Christian Service* (Nashville: Trevecca Press, 1976).

Mildred Bangs Wynkoop died on May 21, 1997, in Lenexa, Kansas.

---

28. Wynkoop, "Biography" (article, undated), file 1427, WC, 1.
29. Wynkoop, "Appreciation Dinner at NTS" (article, undated), file 1426-5, WC, 1.

2
WYNKOOP'S JOURNEY TOWARD A THEOLOGY OF LOVE

It is essential that we understand the theological and sociological tensions triggered in Wynkoop as she engaged the Holiness Movement[1] during the twentieth century. She did not know it at first, but several tensions were created as she became exposed to the much bigger picture of the body of Christ at large. Her deep desire was to understand the basis for her own faith, especially as it related to the Wesleyan doctrine and experience of entire sanctification. The object here is to show her reaction to multiple hybrid Wesleyan streams that flowed outside the orthodox turf of classical Wesleyan theology. The questions generated in these crossroad experiences had a profound effect on Wynkoop's life and called for paradigm shifts existentially, theologically, ethically, and ecumenically.

The first tension arose in the way the Holiness Movement had chosen to make the doctrine of entire sanctification the very *raison d'être* of the movement. Could this doctrine stand all on its own, without affecting the rest of the dogmatic framework of the greater tradition? This tension came to light specifically in the way the Holiness Movement chose to use experience as a source for establishing the authority of Scripture. Classical Wesleyan theology stood in line with the Reformers in the classic

---

1. The term "Holiness Movement" refers to that group of denominations and congregations in North America who affiliated with either the Christian Holiness Association or the International Holiness Convention. The largest of these groups are the Salvation Army, the Church of the Nazarene, the Wesleyan Church, and the Free Methodist Church.

doctrines of *sola scriptura* and *sola gratia*, keeping tradition and Scripture in balance as checkpoints for experience. The burden laid upon Wynkoop was to think through the Holiness Movement's claim to be Wesleyan when, in reality, their approach was somewhat different.

An exploration of Wynkoop's encounter with these streams will help us understand why she chose to focus on an existential[2] interpretation of Christian holiness. As she travelled during the 1930s to the 1950s, she encountered the Holiness Movement as formed in the nineteenth century. These encounters on the front line of evangelistic campaigns created tremendous tension in Wynkoop's journey of faith. The intellectual conflict came in the way that the experience of entire sanctification was interpreted. Therefore, it is important to look at the way the late-nineteenth-century American Holiness Movement read Scripture primarily through the lens of the experience of entire sanctification.

The Experience of Entire Sanctification in the American Holiness Movement

The theological climate for the American Holiness Movement spanned all the way from the nineteenth-century Oberlin perfectionists, like Charles Finney and Asa Mahan, to post-World War II theologians, like H. Orton Wiley, S. S. White, J. Kenneth Grider, and Richard S. Taylor. Coming out of the nineteenth century, anticipating the new century, the trumpet call was for everyone to experience again the outpouring of the Holy Spirit as received by the apostles on the day of Pentecost. William Greathouse described the theological climate as such: "The nineteenth-century Holiness Movement was the peculiar product of a developing revivalism among persons in whom the principles of Wesleyan perfectionism, Puritanism, and Pietism were at work. Although the doctrine of Christian perfection as understood within the movement did indeed

---

2. Wynkoop uses the concept **"existentialism"** in a very general sense. She seeks to emphasize the essential, vital involvement of a person in his or her theological affirmations. It is Christian truth incarnate in the dynamic flow of everyday, ordinary, human life. This existential focus is primarily anchored in the way she interprets Scripture, especially demonstrated in her exegetical interest in the **Sitz im Leben.** However, Wynkoop also has much in common with **existentialist** philosophers like Buber and Heidegger. They share the ideas of human freedom and responsibility and equally reject the abstract ideals that ignore the situated-ness of human life. However, Wynkoop rejects the atheism and lack of moral standards common in some of the contemporary, existentialist philosophers of her day.

stem from Wesley's teaching, the American milieu gave it an entirely new mood and shape."[3]

Although the Holiness Movement in America was a recognized revival movement, it was represented by many divergent doctrinal positions on Christian sanctification. There was a general promotion of the Wesleyan doctrine, yet that didn't mean the preachers, evangelists, and leaders spoke with one voice. The theological impact of people like Charles G. Finney (1792—1875), Asa Mahan (1799—1889), and Phoebe Palmer (1807-74) shaped most of the nineteenth-century Holiness Movement, and it came into the twentieth century with significant momentum.[4]

Although not Wesleyan in his understanding of original sin or the nature of Christian perfection, Finney's revivalism was welcomed across a broad evangelical spectrum, and there developed from his writings what has become known as Oberlin perfectionism. Finney found Oberlin College in Ohio in 1836 and, along with Asa Mahan, promoted revivalism and a brand of perfectionism that emphasized entire consecration to God.[5] With his Calvinist background, Finney brought with him the urgency for a definite crisis-datable experience as a second work of grace to make sure that one was numbered among the elect. This encounter with the Holy Spirit was then also liturgically linked to the **altar call**.[6]

Asa Mahan (1799—1889) shows in the progression of his own writing, from *Christian Perfection* in 1839 to *The Baptism of the Holy Ghost* in 1870, a major shift in his understanding of Christian perfection. Mahan's book on the baptism of the Holy Spirit was the most comprehensive exposition of this new understanding that had yet appeared. Donald Dayton identified six major shifts that took place in Mahan's own writing from 1839 to 1870. He observed a shift from Christocentrism to an emphasis on the Holy Spirit that was quite radical in character. In *The Baptism of the Holy Ghost*, the fundamental question became "Have you received the Holy Ghost since you believed?" Mahan based his view on the conjunc-

---

3. Paul M. Bassett and William M. Greathouse, *Exploring Christian Holiness*, vol. 2: *The Historical Development* (Kansas City: Beacon Hill Press of Kansas City, 1985), 298.
4. Ibid., 299–302.
5. Ibid., 302.
6. Paul M. Bassett, et al., "A White Paper on Article X," *Didache: Faithful Teaching*, 10:19 (June 2010). The altar was the mourners' bench used to invite people to come forward and pray at the conclusion of the pastor's message. Robert Coleman in "The Origin of the Altar Call" places the beginning of this practice in the year 1789 in a Methodist church in the southern United States, overseen by Francis Asbury.

tion "since" in the Authorized Version. There was a shift in terminology. In *Christian Perfection*, salvation history is divided into covenants—the old covenant of the moral law and the new covenant of grace. In *The Baptism of the Holy Ghost*, salvation history is divided into dispensations, with Pentecost as the pivotal point between the dispensations. Another shift comes in the arena of exegetical texts used. In *Christian Perfection*, Mahan relies on texts similarly used by Wesley, but in *The Baptism of the Holy Ghost*, almost all the key texts are taken from the book of Acts, especially Acts 2. Making Pentecost normative for all believers brought with it the added focus on the gifts of the Holy Spirit, with a focus on power, prophecy, and divine healing. By the time we reach the twentieth century, the shift from Christian perfection to baptism of the Holy Ghost was so engrained that the experience of entire sanctification moved from an ethical journey of love to a focus on cleansing and the episode, or event, itself.[7]

Phoebe Palmer (1807-74), however, was the most important figure in the American Holiness Movement. Phoebe Palmer brought with her a simple way to appropriate John Wesley's focus on entire sanctification. In her 1843 book, *The Way of Holiness*, she described "a shorter way" to the experience of entire sanctification. This shorter way is best described as her "altar theology," using Paul's language in Romans 12:1–2 of placing oneself as a "living sacrifice" on God's altar to represent consecration. The altar was Christ, the Sanctifier himself. Since the New Testament declares that "the altar sanctifies the gift" (Matt. 23:19, paraphr. in *Way of Holiness*), the Christian who is fully and consciously placing all on the altar may at that moment claim the blessing of entire sanctification.[8] The experience of entire sanctification, which to John Wesley was the crown of the Christian life, became for Palmer almost the beginning. She was convinced that God can sanctify his people *now*, and she incorporated the idea of claiming the experience as a present reality with no evidence needed other than the biblical text itself.

One can then see how this opened the door to an intensified focus on the instantaneousness of the experience of entire sanctification. The attainment of entire sanctification was reduced to just three simple steps,

---

7. Donald W. Dayton, "Asa Mahan and the Development of American Holiness Theology," *Wesleyan Theological Journal* 9:1 (1974): 11 (hereafter cited as *WTJ*).

8. Thomas C. Oden, ed., "The Way of Holiness (1843)," in *Phoebe Palmer: Selected Writings* (New York City: Paulist Press, 1988), 165–79.

namely, (1) entire consecration, (2) faith in the written Word, and (3) confession.⁹ Whereas Wesley had taught that entire sanctification is evidenced by the witness of the *Spirit*, Phoebe Palmer taught that it is evidenced by the witness of the *Word* (the Word meaning, in her case, a written statement found in the Scriptures).¹⁰ It is thus clear that she has set the table for the altar call, this time not for salvation but for a "second work of grace" instantly brought by the baptism of the Holy Spirit. Not only did she follow John Fletcher in his identification of entire sanctification with the baptism of the Holy Spirit, but she also developed Adam Clarke's suggestion and linked holiness with power.¹¹ Her insistence on this shorter way was widely welcomed by thousands who read her books and listened to her preaching, but this shorter way brought with it a propositional, stereotyped formula that has been described as **syllogistic holiness**.¹² What dominated this approach was a sense of urgency that did not take into account the seeker's own religious, sociological, and psychical history. The allowance for a time of growth in sanctification leading up to entire sanctification is completely absent in Phoebe Palmer. Al Truesdale commented, "Palmer did not simply correct popular Wesleyanism. In important respects she replaced it by setting aside its **reification** of experience and inserting a predictable theological formula that minimized (if not negated) experience and could not fail to deliver certainty. In the replacement there were no experiential patterns to approximate and no hurdles to overcome. Her 'shorter way' arose out of existential frustration, and she eagerly offered it to other weary travelers."¹³

One can now already begin to see why Wynkoop's first major work as a theologian was called "An Existential Interpretation of Sanctification," a major unpublished work, written in 1958.

---

9. Charles Edward White, "Phoebe Palmer and the Development of Pentecostal Pneumatology," *WTJ* 23:1 (1988): 1.

10. Rob L. Staples, "John Wesley's Doctrine of the Holy Spirit," *WTJ* 21:1, 2 (1986), 105.

11. White, "Pentecostal Pneumatology," 1. John Wesley designated John Fletcher (1729-85) to be his successor as the leader of the Methodist Church, but Fletcher died six years prior to Wesley's own death. Adam Clarke (1762—1832) was the great Methodist commentator.

12. Bassett and Greathouse, *Exploring Christian Holiness*, 301.

13. Al Truesdale, "Reification of the Experience of Entire Sanctification in the American Holiness Movement," *WTJ* 31:2 (1991): 117.

The Credibility Gap

Most of Wynkoop's writing is the result of a lifelong attempt to answer the practical problems arising in the tension between doctrine and life. This quest became a scholarly venture resulting in a 300-page, mimeographed book titled "An Existential Interpretation of the Doctrine of Holiness," which later was expanded into the 430-page monograph "A Theology of Depth." Two-thirds of this work eventually became her published work called *A Theology of Love*. She described how this all started:

> One day, I said to Dr. Wiley, "I'm in trouble—please write another book explaining your philosophy so we can understand your theology." He laughed as he did so easily and delightfully and said, "Mildred, you know what I mean, you write that book." I did not take him seriously, but in the deep, soul-searching anguish of trying to honestly answer the questions of my students, biblically, I found myself discovering that philosophy and committing that discovery to writing. It became a large manuscript of lectures and, eventually, a mimeographed text.[14]

As Wynkoop began this process of putting her thoughts down on paper, the most basic problem she faced was one of methodology. How should she proceed to bring together two very different approaches to theology and truth? On one side was the approach of the absolutes—systematic with not much room for the tentative, the dynamic, and the historical conditioning. On the other side was the dynamic, empirical, historical, or personal approach. This side was where she saw the greatest need to theologize on a down-to-earth level. She wrote, "There certainly are absolutes, but man is himself a relational person. We know in part. The incarnation is essential to an understanding of revelation. The Word became flesh. It became an empirical matter without reducing truth to historicism or scientism."[15]

It is then important to note a particular methodology taking shape in the progression of Wynkoop's thought as she moved from her master's degree on the *imago Dei*, completed in 1952, to her doctoral degree on biblical interpretation, completed in 1955, and finally culminating in "A Theology of Depth," written in 1958. By the time she wrote *A Theology of Love* in 1972, she was able to incorporate the thought of John Wesley

---

14. Wynkoop, "Foundations," file 2227-11, WC, 4.
15. Wynkoop, "Breakfast Club" (article, undated), file 1426-2, WC, 4.

as well as other contemporary relational views as an expression of where she was at that point. What is obvious is that she decided not to take the route of the absolutes. She struggled to come up with a title for this book. At first she thought she would call it *A Pre-Theology Prolegomena*, but her ongoing openness to Wesley's thought suggested that love should be the key concept to relate theology and life. She then thought about a title *Toward a Theology of Love*, but the publishers did not want tentatives, so eventually she landed on the title *A Theology of Love*.[16] It is important to note that this work is not a systematic theology but, rather, an expression of her keen interest to understand humanity's involvement in God's grace. This interest was especially noticeable in the tension raised between crisis and process in the call for sanctification. The earnestness with which she dealt with this problem is captured by this honest question: "How do you make provision for human fallibility and its need for growth and maturation, without sacrificing moral decisiveness?"[17]

At the forefront of Wynkoop's passion is to make sure that the moral and rational interaction between God and humanity is accounted for, especially moral responsibility. She called this dualism between idea and life the "holiness credibility gap," and thought this to be one of the greatest problems faced by the theology of the Holiness Movement.[18] She observed that theological concepts and terms had been abstracted from dynamic living situations, which were caught up in the words.[19] She wrote, "When the historical drops away, the words can almost be used as mathematical units and pave the way for logical structures to be built."[20] Wynkoop, then, did not believe that "words alone" had the ability to preserve orthodoxy. It was, rather, the situation that made the words meaningful that would have to be recovered.[21]

We see John Wesley also paying attention to the credibility gap with his followers, with his desire to communicate on a level that they would understand. In his preface to his *Standard Sermons*, he wrote, "I desire

---

16. Ibid., 1–3.
17. Wynkoop, "A Theology of Depth" (monograph, undated), file 1431-15, WC, 29.
18. See Mark Quanstrom, *A Century of Holiness Theology: The Doctrine of Entire Sanctification in the Church of the Nazarene, 1905 to 2004* (Kansas City: Beacon Hill Press of Kansas City, 2004). Quanstrom addresses the credibility gap and gives a historical analysis of what he felt was the impact of Wynkoop's thought on the American Holiness Movement.
19. Wynkoop, "Breakfast Club," file 1426-2, WC, 1.
20. Ibid., 2.
21. Ibid.

plain truth for plain people: therefore, of set purpose, I abstain from all nice and philosophical speculations; from all perplexed and intricate reasonings; and, as far as possible, from even the show of learning."[22]

Awareness of these problems only surfaced as Wynkoop studied the reality of basic **presuppositions**[23] in her university philosophy classes. This put her whole intellectual and spiritual life into a new dimension. These studies brought about a revolution in her thinking as she realized that there were specific presuppositions at work in the preaching and pastoral experiences in which she participated. The danger she saw was that the words of her faith could become, "like Moses's veil, a cover to hide the fading glory of [her] once shining face."[24]

She was concerned about static concepts of Christian truth being more at home in the world of ideas than being expressed in real life. The need Wynkoop saw was for the Christian words to be baptized with the dynamics of life as well as the vibrant life of the Holy Spirit. What Wynkoop realized was that one of the sources for the static concepts of Christian truth was the Greek Platonist absolutism that characterized some Christian theology. It had a way of placing truth just outside the reach of human experience and isolating people from life.[25] She wrote: "It is our conviction that in the lives of some of our people our 'holy words' have become escapes from thinking and action, substitutes for the vital Christian freedom and holy aggression which belong to the Spirit-filled life and to the holiness message. This escape is a response to a real area of misunderstanding. The Hebrew connotation of 'Word' as personal must in our tradition prevail over the more static and formalized and abstract Hellenistic concepts."[26]

Here she thinks particularly of the pagan dualism in cosmology that had a way of modifying Christian theology. This modification comes when Christians go beyond **Platonism** and embrace **Gnosticism,** which portrays

---

22. Edward H. Sugden, ed., *Wesley's Standard Sermons* (Nashville: Lamar & Barton, Agents, n.d.), 1:30.
23. Wynkoop, "Look Out, Our Presuppositions Are Showing" (article, undated), file 1426-2, WC, 6. Wynkoop here defines presuppositions as mind-sets derived from personal temperament, cultural background, early training, and experiences that are formative for the way humanity responds to all the experiences and decisions made in life.
24. Wynkoop, "The Word Became Flesh" (article, undated), file 1425-21, WC, 3.
25. Wynkoop, "Some Implications of the Existential Doctrine of Holiness" (article, undated), file 1432-7, WC, 3.
26. Wynkoop, "The Word Became Flesh," file 1425-21, WC, 3.

humans as a combination of a divine soul and an evil body. Under this philosophy, all matter is evil, including human nature, and with it comes the soteriological misconception that salvation consists in an escape from this body and from this world.

It was, however, her understanding of human beings' capacity to engage themselves as whole persons to theology that challenged Wynkoop to look for a hermeneutic—a principle of interpretation—by which she could unpack this problem and search for a way to bridge the gap between doctrine and life. She found this critical principle to be the role of the "moral" in the interrelatedness of God and humanity. Her work can then be seen as an attempt to funnel the whole range of theological truths into the range of the whole person. She said: "Christian life is not as simple as Christian theology. The moment clean-cut theological conformations are laid against warm, flesh-and-blood human situations, the lack of simplicity begins to show up. Theology is much like a signpost pointing the way into and through the very rugged country over which a Christian must travel—on foot."[27]

With this in mind, it will be good to take a look at her church and classroom experiences to understand the challenges she faced. It would be easy for us to look only at her ideas written in a book without connecting the real-life story behind the problems she observed and documented. As we will see, these experiences brought a set of presuppositions that we need to take into account in order to understand her passion for the moral relevance of the doctrine of Christian perfection.

Early Church Experiences

Some of the immediate problems Wynkoop identified as contributing to this credibility gap came from within her own circle in the Holiness Movement. She describes these problems as "narrow **provincialisms**."[28] The first was a tendency to make too sharp a distinction between justification and sanctification, considering them not **concomitantly** but, rather, as unrelated. Second, too much confidence was placed in emotional experiences to solve all human problems. Third, preachers neglected to make practical applications in their sermons, especially linking real-life prob-

---

27. Wynkoop, "A Theology of Depth," file 1431-15, WC, 5.
28. Mildred Bangs Wynkoop, *A Theology of Love* (Kansas City: Beacon Hill Press of Kansas City, 1972), 46.

lems to the experience of grace.[29] These issues did not present themselves as coming overnight. Already at age five, Mildred Bangs remembered sitting on the front row of a church (which happened to be in a barn), tossing her long curls around restlessly and praying, "Dear God, why doesn't the preacher say things so I can understand them? When I get big, Lord, if I am a preacher, I'll explain things to people."[30] Little did she know that that uneasiness at a very young age was to become a call with a very specific job description.

The church she attended was a young church with a deep sense of mission and vitality. It was not fighting anybody. It had no tradition to preserve. It had a message to deliver that it believed people needed to hear: holiness of heart and life. The message was something like this: "Christ has come to save people from their sins. This salvation is very real. One can know one is saved. It makes a difference in every part of life. Victory through grace was the promise."[31] Wynkoop recalled that the "saved and sanctified and on my way to glory" formula had not yet crystallized into a pattern. What people said came from the heart, born out of the heat and toil of the day.[32] The gap between doctrine and life seemed nonexistent. This was Wynkoop's heritage growing up. However, through the natural processes of life, a shift came that would give a clue into one of the sources for the credibility gap that surfaced.

The older people died one by one and, of course, no problem in any human institution is greater than the second-generation problem. Suddenly, only those who had been children during those years were left, and the complaints were real. Wynkoop's own voice echoes verbatim the concerns of her contemporaries: "The church is cooling off. Nobody carries a burden anymore. Revivals are a disappointment. Why doesn't somebody do something?"[33] The trap that was set for the second generation was to emulate and continue the traditions of those who had gone before them. This emulation included the language they used to describe their religious experiences, their values and sacred memories. Some of the language that was inherited used terms like "sanctification," "the blessing," "entire sanc-

---

29. Ibid., 47.
30. Wynkoop, "My Heritage and I" (article, undated), file 1427-2, WC, 1.
31. Ibid., 3.
32. Ibid., 4.
33. Ibid.

tification," "cleansing," and "baptism with the Holy Spirit." Out of loyalty to the first generation, evangelists and preachers began to preach doctrinal messages with the invitation to seek "it." Wynkoop includes herself in this:

> In my early preaching life the exquisite logical beauty of theology, its almost mathematical perfection, intoxicated me. I recall often baiting my intellectual trap and at the psychological point of climax in a sermon clinching my holiness argument by "some absolutistic" conclusion that I felt settled forever the opposition. I sat on a high, remote, and glorious mountain peak of self-assurance. In mercy and desperation, I presume, the Holy Spirit often moved on the audience, and there were frequent great moves to the altar. But I did not know what to do with those who came. I began to observe that most of the people were seeking the "absolutes" in order to be released from the debilitating humanness of their daily lives. They were seeking "blessings" (mathematically differentiated) and "it" and "something I will know about" and abstracts such as "sanctification" and "cleansing."[34]

Wynkoop remembered people being surrounded at the mourners' bench by people shouting slogans like "pray loud," "lift your head," "take it by faith," and "are you willing to be a missionary?"[35] Another troublesome observation began to filter through Wynkoop's mind. She began to ask about the kind of persons who came to the altar. She concluded that, usually, they were the same faithful seekers at every preacher's invitation.[36] In the classroom, the same phenomenon surfaced as Wynkoop became aware of the confusion and basic misunderstandings that were attached to theological words and concepts gained in the local churches. She elaborated on this problem:

> Recently a student used the term "cleansing" in his classroom interchange. I caught a strange flavour to his use of the word and asked him what he meant by cleansing. He immediately replied, "Oh, of course I mean purification." When we suggested later that sin is not a thing but a spiritual distortion of God's creation, his inner world of comfortable theology was drastically disrupted. Another felt more at ease with a concept of the Holy Spirit as a sort of invisible ghost "out there in the corner," which at

---

34. Wynkoop, "Some Implications," file 1432-7, WC, 4.
35. Wynkoop, "This Is Mildred," file 1427-3, WC, 2.
36. Wynkoop, "Some Implications," file 1432-7, WC, 4.

conversion travels along with us but which somehow in sanctification gets spatially into the physical structure of the human body.[37]

Wynkoop's Journey of Authenticity

This reification of the experience of entire sanctification confronted Wynkoop squarely in the spiritual challenges she faced as a young evangelist's wife and a preacher herself. From 1930 a new generation of Nazarenes arose, nourished now by the plethora of fundamentalist rigidity and emotionalism in many publications.[38] She discovered that not all woman preachers were well accepted, and she did not want that prejudice to knock on her door.[39] The people were critical of her in their small Nazarene church, and no one recognized the sacrifice of talent and education she brought to the table.[40] This criticism caused the pendulum to swing in Wynkoop's own heart from blessing to bitterness.[41] She wrote, "If I could count the number of times I have poured tears on some worn altar rail seeking for holiness, I would be ashamed of it. Excellent early training plus the thrilling early Nazarene services in which the 'glory came down' conspired to set a 'norm' in my thinking of what religion ought to be and could be, and kept me everlastingly trying to abolish the vast chasm between my own experience and that norm."[42]

Time and time again she placed what was known as the "unknown bundle" on the altar. What was interesting is that she could not recall anyone ever following up with her to find out how she was doing spiritually. Her journey to the altar went on for several years, every time seeking that which she already professed, that she was saved and sanctified and going all the way. She had a page in her Bible on which she entered the dates and the places that she went to the altar to seek entire sanctification. She wanted to be able to testify the day she was sanctified, but she had so many entries that she could never decide which one of them to use at any given time. At last count, she had forty entries in her Bible when, one day in humiliation, she tore that page out of her Bible and destroyed it.[43] This

---

37. Ibid., 6.
38. Wynkoop, "Our Presuppositions Are Showing," file 1426-2, WC, 2.
39. Wynkoop, "My Heritage and I," file 1427-2, WC, 3.
40. Ibid.
41. Ibid.
42. Wynkoop, "What Holiness Means to Me" (article, undated), file 2227-14, WC, 3.
43. Ibid.

preoccupation with the when and the how—essentially ceremonial holiness—did not deal with the content of holiness in her heart. She wrote: "I tried to look a piety I couldn't feel. I shouted when it seemed the right thing to do. I prayed loud when the preacher said we ought. And rather suddenly the whole unsavoury farce broke around my head, leaving me an almost full-fledged sceptic, cold-blooded and adrift. The divine formula upon which I had pinned my faith, didn't work."[44]

This conflict broke her health. She became tubercular and had to be left in California while her husband took a new church in Oregon.[45] Here she was, twenty-nine years old, the product of a Nazarene home, two Nazarene colleges, a part of H. Orton Wiley's circle, and a Nazarene pastor's wife—yet she felt she needed to get as far away from an evangelical church as she could.[46] She met some Episcopalians who convinced her to attend their services. Unexpectedly, the cool beauty of the Communion services and the words and form of the liturgy gripped her heart and became like a "life belt" thrown to her in her most desperate hour.[47] She wrote:

> No other local Episcopal church could have done what this one did for me, because both rector and people were in the grip of a spiritual awakening through the Oxford Group, which transformed their sanctuary services from dead formalism to spiritual grandeur. It was that which I felt. I attended the group meetings and heard doctors and lawyers and bricklayers and housewives, never before in a religious atmosphere, tell about the same kind of problems I was facing, and the change that Christ wrought. The utter frankness and the complete absence of any stereotyped expressions helped to freshen the truth to me. It was not salvation, but the beginning of my road back to God.[48]

At this same church, she made the decision to go through the confirmation class, which probably lasted for a year. This period in her life was the beginning of a new quality of Christian experience for Wynkoop. The new was not measured in emotions and sentiment but in genuineness and depth. No longer did she pray in generalities, hiding behind terms

---

44. Ibid.
45. Ibid.
46. Ingersol, "The Woman," file 1561-32, WC, 6.
47. Wynkoop, "What Holiness Means to Me," file 2227-14, WC, 3.
48. Ibid. It is important to note that Wynkoop not only attended the Episcopal church but also became an Episcopalian and remained so without doing anything overt about it. They did not then ordain women.

like, "Lord, bless me," or abstract, theological terms like, "Lord, sanctify me," but now her long-divided heart began a journey of authenticity with God.[49] We can see in Wynkoop a deep desire to live life existentially in touch with God and her neighbour. Coming out of her individualism, with the ability to confess her brokenness and emptiness without being judged, was in a sense a reaction against hollow orthodoxy, icily correct doctrine, and an empty religious profession. It was making her Christian faith her own by bringing together her heart and mind in the bigger picture of God's kingdom. It is no surprise that Wynkoop's style as a theologian is saturated with the existential. She is not a stranger to this painful journey of authenticity.

Relational Theology and the Asian Mind

Wynkoop's journey took an unexpected detour for the six years that she spent in Japan as a teacher and president of the Japan Nazarene Theological Seminary. This experience expanded Wynkoop's understanding of the significance of a relational understanding of holiness. After the primary stimulus for understanding the credibility gap, her thinking about relational holiness was clarified by her missionary service in Taiwan and Japan. She had just completed a five-year teaching contract at Western Evangelical Seminary when an Oriental Mission Society leader came to campus pleading for an academically prepared teacher to spend a year in Asia teaching in the schools to raise the status of the schools before the government. Wynkoop was not interested, but seventy students began to raise money for their professor and one day handed her $1,400 and a new camera.[50] It was the year 1960, and she was fifty-five years old when she said yes and embarked on her first missionary journey to Japan.[51]

She described the initial experience: "Taking the long 18 hour trip in a 'prop' plane did not 'bless me.' But finally looking down on Japan and the islands melted my heart. The Japanese Missionary Fellowship and the

---

49. Wynkoop, "My Heritage and I," file 1427-2, WC, 10.
50. Wynkoop, "NTS Appreciation Dinner," file 1426-5, WC, 6.
51. Jeremy Bangs (son of Carl Bangs), email to author, January 18, 2017, gives us the background as to why she left Western Evangelical Seminary. He says: "When she left the West Coast to go to Japan, the change came about through necessity. She had just been forced out of her job because of informal charges and suspicion of heresy, when members on the board of Western Evangelical Seminary didn't like her opposition to **fundamentalism**."

Nazarene missionaries made the whole trip a door into a new world."[52] Her initial commitment of one year stretched into six years of teaching theology to Asian students. During these years in Japan Wynkoop finalized her primary work, *A Theology of Love*.[53]

Wynkoop, of course, did not walk into a vacuum as far as Japanese Protestantism was concerned. Paul M. Bassett indicates that there was a Protestant stream flowing in Japan long before World War II, primarily fed from Reformed theological anthropologies and soteriologies: "Japanese Protestantism had discovered modern European theology long before World War II and under the long tutelage of Kigawa and the influence of the kingdom of God and Mukyokai 'no church church' movements had developed quite sophisticated forms of Christian faith. . . . Emil Brunner had been teaching in Tokyo on a permanent basis since 1953. And Japanese theological students tackled Barth's theology as well."[54]

To Wynkoop, what was needed was an Arminian-Wesleyan "optimism of grace," and yet, as will be pointed out by Wynkoop, its old rationalistic forms did not work. It did not take long for Wynkoop to realize that there was a huge difference in the way Asian students learned and the traditional language of the theology of the Holiness Movement that she had used all her life. As she saw it, the Western filter, with its overriding Aristotelian categories, did not connect with the Asian minds steeped in Shintoism, Buddhism, and Confucianism.[55] The challenges she faced in the Japanese tendencies of thought helped Wynkoop affirm and clarify the way she communicated and lived out the Christian message of holiness. She was amazed by the excessive tolerance demonstrated in the way theological students wanted to hear many sides but did not want to choose a specific belief system.

Another tendency of thought she noticed in her Asian students was to include everything. No contest of thought ever resulted in a new school of thought. For the Japanese, it was very difficult to understand that Christianity excludes ideas and philosophies contrary to its own. Their tendency was to just add Christianity to what they already believed. She noted that

---

52. Wynkoop, "My Life" (article, undated), file 1427-2, WC, 1.
53. Wynkoop, "Birth and Marriage," file 1427, WC, 5.
54. "Papers Presented at the Mildred Wynkoop Career Celebration," February 1992, file 1561-32, WC, 17.
55. Wynkoop, "A Critique of Japanese Thought" (notebook diary, undated), file 1440-18, WC, 3.

for the Japanese, Shinto was the religion of life; Buddhism was the religion of death, to which one turned in one's final hour; and Confucianism was for ethics.[56]

Even with these distinctions, there was no conflict between these streams of influence. Wynkoop commented, "It was very confusing to a Japanese [person] to ask him if he belongs to the Buddhist religion or if he is a Shintoist."[57] The Japanese tendency was never to join anything and a total reluctance to distinguish one faith from another. Wynkoop wrote, "The Shinto philosophy did not see the need for a God separate from creation, and yet when you take a closer look, you discover that they had no problem worshiping the spirits of their dead ancestors."[58] This unique **philosophical pantheism** of the Shinto religion also saw the earth as divine and its people as gods. Wynkoop noted, "In this context, sin is foreign for a divine people, and a Saviour is taken as an insult."[59] Again, with Buddhism, sin was not seen as rebellion against God but, rather, as rebellion against absolute metaphysical unity. Wynkoop wrote, "Experience, which looms large in Buddhism, is not a personal relationship with God, but a profound discovery of the self as it resolves all contradiction and dualism into itself. Salvation is not a gift from another, even from God, but freedom from the illusion of dualism. Buddhist salvation is not salvation from sin, but transcendence over right and wrong, good and evil, sin and righteousness. It is a state, which includes all contradictions and excludes nothing.[60]

To exacerbate the problem, Wynkoop experienced Buddhism imitating the Christian approach by revivals, hymn singing, youth work, Sunday schools, conversions, and self-renunciations.[61] The question of the Japanese people was then: "What do you have that we don't have?" They were able to take Christian doctrine out of context and mix it with similar Buddhist and Shinto concepts.[62] Christian missionaries faced a tremendous challenge in Christian education. Finding inroads into this pagan

---

56. Wynkoop, "Educational Problems in Japan" (article, undated), file 1387-74, WC, 3.
57. Ibid.
58. Ibid., 5.
59. Ibid., 6. See also Kosuke Koyama, *Water Buffalo Theology* (Maryknoll, NY: Orbis Books, 1929). Now in its twenty-fifth edition, Koyama gives important background to the theological challenges Wynkoop and other Christian missionaries faced in Japan. Koyama would have affirmed Wynkoop's assessment.
60. Wynkoop, "Educational Problems," file 1387-74, WC, 8.
61. Ibid.
62. Ibid., 9.

philosophical religion and creating spiritual language out of pagan words to convey biblical meanings so necessary to the proclamation of the gospel was at the heart of this challenge.

It was a particularly exhausting task for Wynkoop to bring across to the Asian mind the idea of the love of Christ, which is so essential to the gospel and especially to Wynkoop's theology. What stood in the way, she observed, was the ideology of the family system that essentially conveyed a one-way concept of love. The family law was written with the purpose of serving the political hierarchy of the nation. She quoted Taka-aki Aikawa: "It is the organization of the parent-child relationship into a stabilized system of rule, making the father-centred family a 'branch family' of a larger 'head family' ultimately forming a 'state family' called Japan, whose father is the Emperor himself and all his subjects are faithful children."[63] In such a family system there was little room for individual autonomy and decision. The problem in this context was that the Japanese who lived under the family system were not permitted to love Christ more than their fathers, unless their fathers themselves loved Christ. Love in this family system became a thing of duty and was not mutual.[64]

Wynkoop's view was that the barrier of the Eastern mind-set especially manifested itself in the inability of the Japanese to deal with Western logic. In a letter to her sister Thelma, Wynkoop states, "Our problem is the total inability of the Japanese to analyse with reference to relationships. I mean logic. They can classify, but not relate. This means that analogies are impossible. There is nothing about 'this' that helps to understand 'that.' I sat with a group of Japanese who were trying to explain Buddhism to me. I said: 'Why, this point is the age-old problem of such and such.' I almost mortally wounded them."[65]

Given the immensity of these presuppositions underlying the Japanese culture in general, the challenge Wynkoop saw was to find connecting points with the Japanese person buried under a mountain of values totally foreign to the message of Christ. In her diary, written in Japan on September 8, 1963, she reflects on the common misconception that orthodox language and Western logic are sufficient to ensure understanding of the Christian message. She came to the conclusion that communication

---

63. Wynkoop, "Why the Gospel Has Failed" (article, undated), file 1440-16, WC, 1.
64. Ibid., 2.
65. Wynkoop to Thelma Bangs (correspondence, July 8, 1962), file 1427-12, WC.

to the Asian people cannot be on the word-grammar level but, rather, must be on the people level: "Real communication requires profound humility of mind and teachability of spirit. It requires a mutual, sympathetic sharing of experience. One cannot stand outside of the communication experience as a performing theorist. He must be a participant in the experience. And Christian communication can only take place in this kind of an atmosphere."[66]

In this context, Wynkoop's existential **relational theology** was able to become a bridge to find a place for the gospel to stick. In her six years in Japan, she came to the conclusion that it was the human element that made divine revelation accessible. It was not rigid, formal, and unimaginative biblical interpretation that caused the breakthrough but, rather, the dynamic interplay of revealed truth and human experience. It was then essential for Wynkoop to be able to enter into the thought forms and experiences of the Japanese people, which she was able to do by stressing the natural*ness* of Christianity, as distinct from natural*ism*. She stressed the at-homeness of the gospel in the human heart and emphasized that Christ does not stand against nature but against natural*ism* as a substitute.[67]

How effective was she? Stan Ingersol recalls a conversation with a missionary couple from the Wesleyan Church who taught at a college in Hong Kong: "They asked if I had ever met Mildred Wynkoop. I said I had been her student. Is she still living, they asked? Indeed, I replied, and she lives in a Kansas City suburb. They were thrilled. Then they told me that at their school, their Chinese students would read the canon of Wesleyan-Holiness literature and say, we don't understand this. This theology doesn't make very much sense to me. Then they would read Wynkoop's *A Theology of Love*, and say: holiness theology makes sense now."[68]

Given this context at the time of the writing of her primary work, *A Theology of Love*, it is not a surprise to find a whole chapter on the credibility gap. We come to understand statements like "It has to be personal," "Faith has to be incarnate in real life," "It has to be historical." It is then important to note that *A Theology of Love* was not just shaped in an American context but was battle-tested on the front lines by an Asian mind-set as well. It was a book that was shaped by a missionary's effort to com-

---

66. Wynkoop, "A Critique," file 1440-18, WC, 4.
67. Wynkoop, "Tendencies of Japanese Thought" (article, undated), file 1440-17, WC, 1.
68. Ingersol, "The Woman," file 1561-32, WC, 9.

municate the message of Christ's holiness in a way that bridged the gulf between a reified spiritual world and an existential life, as well as an attempt to bring Asian and Western cultures together through the incarnate Word. After serving six years in Japan, Wynkoop concluded that only broken hearts, filled with love, communicated by living experience, patience, and prayer could find a connecting point to advance the gospel in Japan.[69]

---

69. Wynkoop, "Tendencies," file 1440-17, WC, 1.

3
THE ROLE OF SCRIPTURE IN WYNKOOP'S THEOLOGY

Wynkoop's doctrine of Christian holiness is directly connected to the way in which she interpreted Scripture. The focus of the Reformers on the living Word, and Wesley's focus on the sufficiency of Scripture for salvation as the basis for its authority, helped Wynkoop to formulate a Christocentric understanding of Christian holiness. H. Orton Wiley served as a critical mentor to help Wynkoop come to grips with her own Wesleyan theology, as interpreted by the Holiness Movement, especially as it related to her scriptural reading of experience as a factor for doing theology. Wiley and her reading of Wesley helped Wynkoop in her quest for an existential interpretation of sanctification.

In 1955 at Northern Baptist Theological Seminary, Wynkoop wrote her doctoral thesis titled "A Historical and Semantic Analysis of Methods of Biblical Interpretation as They Relate to Views of Inspiration."[1] The fact that she tackled biblical interpretation as the theme of her doctoral thesis is a commentary on the importance she gave to biblical interpretation in the formulation of her doctrine of Christian holiness. Knowing that her doctoral dissertation was written in the wake of fundamentalism's influence on the evangelical Protestant life in America, including the Church of the Nazarene, her response to fundamentalism, both experientially and theologically, is of special interest to this research. The intent is to show the effect fundamentalism had on her existential interpretation of ho-

---

1. Wynkoop, "A Historical and Semantic Analysis of Methods of Biblical Interpretation as They Relate to Views of Inspiration" (doctoral thesis, Northern Baptist Theological Seminary, 1955), file 1237-27, WC.

liness and to examine what she thought would happen when attention was diverted away from the incarnate Word to the written Word. Along the way, we will be able to assess whether Wynkoop operated within a traditional, evangelical-Protestant tradition in her doctrine of Scripture and evaluate whether Wesley's and Wiley's influences were decisive in her understanding of what constituted the nature of Scripture's authority and its sufficiency.

The Reformers' Approach to Scripture in Historical Perspective

LUTHER

According to Larry Shelton, Martin Luther believed that the Scriptures had been given to us under the inspiration of the Holy Spirit. This was not mechanical in the form of dictation by the Holy Spirit, but he believed that the writers were able to do historical research and then organize their material under the guidance of the Holy Spirit.[2] Especially notable in Luther, according to Wynkoop, was his strong emphasis on the internal testimony of the Holy Spirit as a basis for trust in the authority of Scripture. Wynkoop wrote, "Luther's theory of inspiration did not end in the words of the text but in the living Word that stood as the criterion of the validity of the written record. Interpretation was not a mechanical and arbitrary thing, but was very personal and very much dependent upon the ministry of the Holy Spirit."[3]

Wynkoop recognized that, for Luther, there was always this open door toward the spiritual life. The authority of Scripture to Luther was found in its ability to accomplish the work of salvation in the hearts of those who heard it. There was a power at work in the written Word, and its power, to Luther, was the living Word, Christ himself, being revealed to the hearer by the Holy Spirit. The written Word then served as a "cradle for the living Word," Christ himself.[4] Even though Luther was unfamiliar with modern fundamentalism, for him, Jesus Christ was the one who was infallible and without error; he alone was the essential Word of God.[5]

---

2. Larry Shelton, "John Wesley's Approach to Scripture in Historical Perspective," *WTJ* 16:1 (Spring 1981): 32.
3. Wynkoop, "A Historical and Semantic Analysis," file 1237-27, WC, 71.
4. Rob L. Staples, "John Wesley's Doctrine of the Holy Spirit," *WTJ* 21:1 (1986): 97.
5. Wynkoop, "A Historical and Semantic Analysis," file 1237-27, WC, 72.

We then get the sense that Luther's hermeneutical lens in determining Scripture's authority was twofold. On the one hand was Luther's insistence on the literal sense, and on the other hand there was this spiritual sense as well. The spiritual sense, for Luther, was the soteriological focus of the Holy Spirit in both Old and New Testaments. Luther believed that without the ministry of the Holy Spirit the whole of Scripture is law, and with the ministry of the Spirit the whole of Scripture is gospel.[6] For Luther, as Wynkoop understood him, Christ is both the literal and the spiritual sense in Scripture. The reference to the work of the Holy Spirit was, to Luther, referential—that is, to refer us to Christ. The subject matter or inner sense of the biblical text is then illuminated by the Holy Spirit to provide the Christocentric or saving meaning.[7]

Wynkoop's colleague Rob Staples pointed out that this *testimonium Spiritus sancti*, in Luther, is primarily associated with the word of preaching, rather than the written words of Scripture. This means that the *testimonium* was primarily connected to the word in use.[8] In this communication event of the proclamation of God's Word, it is then the operation of the Holy Spirit who makes the connection between the one speaking and the one hearing the living Word.

This duality of two senses in Luther became a connecting point in understanding Wynkoop's use of Scripture in the formulation of her theology of Christian holiness. This will also open the door to assess to what extent Wynkoop kept a balance between Word and Spirit in her use of Scripture. Even though it is not an either-or, Wynkoop came to the conclusion that Luther was more focused on the *purpose* of Scripture than on the question of the *nature* of Scripture. Wynkoop believed that Luther's recognition of this incarnational factor in the doctrine of Scripture was one of the key presuppositions of his hermeneutics, and that provided a basis for her own quest for an existential theology of Christian holiness. Her understanding of Luther's doctrine of Scripture became a guide for Wynkoop's quest to have Scripture be in touch with the real lives of people.

---

6. A. Skevington Wood, "Luther's Principles of Biblical Interpretation" (monograph, originally published London: Tyndale Press, 1946), put online at *Biblical Studies.org.uk*, January 2005, http://biblicalstudies.org.uk/article_luther_s-wood.html, 35.

7. Shelton, "John Wesley's Approach," 32.

8. Staples, "John Wesley's Doctrine," 97.

CALVIN

Wynkoop saw John Calvin as another strong voice of Protestant hermeneutics who shared Luther's hermeneutical principles. As with Luther, so also with Calvin, their doctrine did not make an idol out of Scripture. For Calvin, the purpose of Scripture was to reveal Christ, not to focus on itself. Scripture was not an end in itself but, rather, a vehicle through which the Spirit worked to point the believer to the living Word as the main focus of revelation.[9] Wynkoop quoted from the *Institutes*, where Calvin says, "The Letter therefore is dead, and the law of the Lord slays the readers of it, where it is separated from the grace of Christ, and only sounds in the ears, without affecting the heart. But, if it be efficaciously impressed on our hearts by the Spirit, . . . if it exhibits Christ; it is the word of life."[10]

Here Wynkoop concluded that Calvin's major concern was not with the words *as* words but, rather, with the spiritual message conveyed *in* the words. If the impression of God's Word upon the hearts of readers was to have its full effect, revelation could only come by the Holy Spirit through the Word. The internal witness of the Holy Spirit—the *testimonium Spiritus sancti internum*—was at the heart of Calvin's understanding of what constituted the authority of Scripture. In Wynkoop's view, Calvin's understanding of the inner testimony of the Holy Spirit was essentially the same as Luther's, except that in Calvin "the Word" was not only the instrument but also the object of the Spirit's witness.[11] In Staples's view, this unfortunately opened the door for those following Calvin to put more focus on the Word than on the Spirit's communication to the hearers of the Word.[12] Calvin believed that the revelation to the original writers was not fully comprehensible ("They cared not to announce anything of their own, and obediently followed the Spirit as their guide"[13]), yet Calvin also believed that the writers adjusted their writings to the level of the ordinary person's understanding. Moses, Calvin wrote, "accommodated himself to the ignorance of the common people and adjusted his message to them."[14] This concept of **accommodation** in Calvin was an important fac-

---

9. Wynkoop, "A Historical and Semantic Analysis," file 1237-27, WC, 88.
10. John Calvin, *Institutes of the Christian Religion*, trans. John Allen (Philadelphia: Presbyterian Board of Christian Education, 1932), Vol. I, 9, iii.
11. Staples, "John Wesley's Doctrine," 97.
12. Ibid., 98.
13. Wynkoop, "A Historical and Semantic Analysis," file 1237-27, WC, 84.
14. Ibid., 3.

tor in Wynkoop's use of Scripture. Calvin's principle of interpretation had at its heart the "**analogy of faith.**" Basically, Scripture interpreted itself, and this meant that we were not able to interpret Scripture by ourselves; it all had to come from God. In other words, interpretation was a divinely provided illumination by the Holy Spirit, with the human mind in a passive position.[15] Wynkoop quoted Calvin, "The rule of piety requires that an indulgence in an 'unprofitable degree of speculation' leads the reader away from the simplicity of faith. We should not speak of or desire to know anything 'beyond the information given to us in the Divine word' . . . as soon as the Lord closes his sacred mouth. . . . We should give up our desire of learning."[16]

Wynkoop embraces Calvin's Christocentric view of Scripture and would agree that, for Calvin, it is the Holy Spirit and not reason that becomes the basis for the authority of Scripture. Yet she does show restraint in not fully endorsing Calvin's position. What is unexpected in Calvin's doctrine of Scripture is that the illumination of the Holy Spirit is subjective and "secret," only for the elect.[17] This means that only the elect are given the key to the understanding of Scripture. Calvin did allow for private study of Scripture, but since the Holy Spirit cannot contradict himself, variety of insight was not accepted, and the individual's opinion had to submit to the interpretation of the true church.[18] Considering this, Wynkoop came to the conclusion that Calvin in fact "placed the authority of the Spirit's secret illumination against the authority of the church."[19] In addition, Wynkoop believed that Calvin was not able to escape fully the influence of scholasticism in the formulation of his doctrine of Scripture. She wrote:

> Each argument for the doctrine that Calvin develops, is first rationally developed before it is scripturally grounded. He appeals to common sense and logic and every device of philosophy before he appeals to Scripture to defend the doctrine he has built. The scriptural defense is in the typical Scholastic style—that of the appeal to the proof text. Calvin did not as a rule come to his doctrines by way of true exegesis,

---

15. Wynkoop, "A Critical Analysis of Calvin's Doctrine of Scripture" (article, 1954), file 2227-35, WC, 17.
16. Ibid., 3.
17. Ibid., 17.
18. Ibid.
19. Ibid.

in the modern sense. Rather he first lays out the doctrine as an uncontestable truth, which it would be unthinkable to question. Then he builds his scriptural defense, seldom, if ever, using passages of greater length than three or four verses, and the context is not always carefully consulted.[20]

Given this, the movement of starting with reason, and only afterward moving to revelation, was hardly in keeping in Wynkoop's view with the "analogy of faith" that Calvin so strongly held. However, she did conclude that Luther and Calvin did not worship the word but only the Word. Christ, the Word of God, is the perfect subject for them. From him came the word, and to him the word points. He alone is perfect and infallible.

WARFIELD

B. B. Warfield of Princeton, standing in the tradition of the Westminster Confession, was very influential when Wynkoop was a student. It seems safe to conclude, by the study of the foregoing section, that she concluded that Calvin's major concern was that Christ be exhibited in Scripture and that the Holy Spirit alone could make the Word of God meaningful to the reader. The sacredness of the Bible was in its author and not in the book itself. Calvin's main concern as she interpreted him was with the spiritual message behind the words. The Westminster Confession's[21] articles on Scripture in some ways tried to capture the heart of Calvin's doctrine of Scripture. Article 4 says, "The authority of the Holy Scripture, for which it ought to be believed, and obeyed, depends not upon the testimony of any man, or church; but wholly upon God (who is truth itself) the author thereof: and therefore it is to be received, because it is the Word of God."[22] And in Article 5, "Our full persuasion and assurance of the infallible truth and divine authority thereof, is from the inward work of the Holy Spirit bearing witness by and with the Word in our hearts."[23]

---

20. Wynkoop, "A Historical and Semantic Analysis," file 1237-27, WC, 78.

21. The Westminster Confession (1647) was formulated by a body of British Reformed theologians who, though they had no quarrel with the Church of England on the basis of doctrine, did desire to break with the English church government and ritual. It has become the standard confession for the Reformed position in the Presbyterian tradition, expressing the Calvinist faith.

22. *The Westminster Confession of Faith* AD 1647 (Online: Christian Classics Ethereal Library), 603.

23. Ibid.

The *Westminster Confession* states here that the Bible is the very Word of God and carries its authority in itself. From this wording we can deduce that Scripture was to be interpreted in terms of its own statements. If a passage is obscure, then another passage will give light upon it. In this way it is said that Scripture interprets itself. It does not need an outside source of interpretation. Article 5 of the *Westminster Confession* also indicates that the "witness by and with the Word" was to be understood as making reference to the "living Word" behind the written word. However, by the nineteenth century, it was Wynkoop's view that theologians like B. B. Warfield only honed in on this aspect of the *Westminster Confession*, the fact that it is God's book and it is authoritative in and of itself.[24] The argument is taken even further by Warfield, as Wynkoop understands him, since he believed that it is only the original autographs that were the inspired and authoritative Bible. Even though he stumbled over his own words, Wynkoop thought, in that he understood that there were no original autographs, he still allowed the copies to be reliable in that they carry a "sense" of Scripture.[25]

Wynkoop, however, is quick to show what she believed were the inconsistencies in Warfield's interpretation of the *Westminster Confession*. She wrote:

> Since only the autographs can be equated with the Word of God, then it is only proper to say that the Word of God is not to be equated with what we now possess as Scripture, and we would be forced to say that Scriptures contain the Word of God in order to maintain a distinction between them. If the Word of God lies in the "sense" of the Scripture and not in the letter, then it makes affirmations of infallibility and verbal inspiration illogical and erroneous . . . and to equate Scripture with the Holy Spirit, is unfortunate, in that it either imprisons him within an uninspired document or robs us of any contact with him in the absence of the autographs.[26]

The impact of the *Westminster Confession* and Warfield's interpretation of it would be felt for years to come, as it opened the door to fundamentalism on the American landscape. Wynkoop's assessment of the impact should be noted. First she thought that, since no allowance was

---

24. Wynkoop, "A Historical and Semantic Analysis," file 1237-27, WC, 100.
25. Ibid., 101.
26. Ibid., 103.

made for an outside source of interpretation, the *Confession* closed itself to textual criticism and historical criticism.[27] Second, she thought that what was missing in Warfield's assessment of the *Confession* was the Reformers' emphasis on the living Word. She wrote, "The inspiration ends in the word, according to Warfield, but we don't even have that inspired word."[28] Lastly, there is her sense that the *Confession* isolated the individual from the Word of God. She wrote, "Perhaps the most serious result was the imprisonment of the living Word under bonds of human manipulation. History has shown us that when Scripture was least regarded as a human book, it was most imprisoned by human reason. When it is regarded too much as a supernatural thing, it is least available to human need."[29]

The Role of Modernism in the History of Interpretation

Relevance was at the heart of Wynkoop's passion to bridge the gap between the writer and the hearer. Her quest was to overcome the gap between the abstract ideas in Scripture and the existential concerns of the reader. Her quest was to find a connection between an objective Book and the subjective life of the reader. As we have seen, she saw the Reformation as the casting off of the authority of the Roman Catholic Church to interpret Scripture. With Calvin arose the Confessional period, with a desire to come up with objective principles for biblical interpretation. But in the end, not the church but the Reformation Confessions became the final arbiters to decide what gave the Bible its authority.

As Wynkoop saw it, another period of struggle began in regard to Scripture in which the agent of the challenge was modernism—which she defined in broad terms as anything new in practice or thinking.[30] It arose in the Enlightenment, grew with the scientific spirit, and aligned itself with a type of biblical criticism that questioned the authority and supernatural aspects of the Bible.[31] Modernism was seen to operate on several fronts. New discoveries and thinking on the front lines of science, society, religion, and lifestyle started to make inroads into the schools and churches. This had the effect of labels being put on those who had differ-

---

27. Ibid.
28. Ibid., 105.
29. Ibid., 106.
30. Ibid., 113.
31. Ibid., 114.

ent perspectives than the traditions of the day. In the political arena it was called progressivism, and in its religious form it was called liberalism.[32]

Ronald Kirkemo—the historian of Pasadena College, the Nazarene college near Los Angeles (now Point Loma Nazarene University in San Diego)—captured the mood of this time as he saw it, describing life in California: "Women cut their hair short and hemmed their dresses high. Movies became more exotic and sensual, and materialism flourished as the economy boomed and people wanted to express themselves free from old thought forms and mores."[33] Modernism manifested itself especially in the way Scripture was interpreted. Suddenly, as Kirkemo saw it, the grassroots realism of literal interpretation was being challenged by those German theologians who applied the scientific techniques of history and anthropology to the study of Scripture.[34] The heightened influence of textual criticism, or "higher criticism," questioned Moses's authorship of the Pentateuch, the validity of the virgin birth, the resurrection, and a literal second coming of Christ.[35] All of these "liberal" views left those vested in the status quo to think the Bible had been robbed of its divine inspiration.[36] This tension set the stage for a showdown between the forces of traditionalism and modernism, which in religious circles was structured around a pattern of belief called fundamentalism. George M. Marsden briefly defines fundamentalism in its earlier stages: "Fundamentalists were evangelical Christians, close to the traditions of the dominant American revivalist establishment of the nineteenth century, who in the twentieth century militantly opposed both modernism in theology and the cultural changes that modernism endorsed."[37]

Fundamentalist George W. Dollar's definition of historic fundamentalism, in the two decades from 1920 to 1940, shows that at the heart of this tradition was a fear that the Bible would be replaced as the central, culture-forming force in American life. He said, "Fundamentalism is the literal exposition of all the affirmations and attitudes of the Bible and the militant

---

32. Ronald B. Kirkemo, *For Zion's Sake: A History of Pasadena/Point Loma College* (San Diego: Point Loma Press, 1992), 80.
33. Ibid., 81.
34. Ibid., 82.
35. Wynkoop, "A Historical and Semantic Analysis," file 1237-27, WC, 123.
36. Kirkemo, *For Zion's Sake*, 82.
37. George M. Marsden, *Fundamentalism and American Culture* (New York: Oxford University Press, 2006), 4.

exposure of all non-biblical affirmations and attitudes."[38] Fundamentalists perceived themselves to be in the midst of a religious war over the Bible.[39] A spirit of militancy manifested itself then as one of the leading features of fundamentalism in the early twentieth century. Wynkoop wrote:

> The Modernists assumed an evolutionary hypothesis before they opened the Bible. The fundamentalists assumed an infallible Bible before they had opened the book. Both sides took "ignoble" positions, and held them with an extreme, defiant, and often bitter spirit. Modernism held science to be its authority. Fundamentalism made the Bible its authority, for everything. Both claimed for its authority, infallibility. Science could not be wrong, and the Bible could not be wrong. In this way the split widened and hardened.[40]

The general atmosphere in the 1920s among the fundamentalists became a distrust of the intellect, especially manifesting itself as an anti-scientific attitude.[41] In spite of the distrust in the intellect, fundamentalists did stand in an intellectual tradition of their own, according to George Marsden, fostered by the philosophy of seventeenth-century philosopher Francis Bacon.[42] His focus on careful observation and classification of facts served as a way for the fundamentalists to wed his ideas with their common-sense philosophy. This they did as they took pride in their ability to apprehend facts clearly, especially certain facts as found in Scripture.[43] Theologically, these facts centred around five points—which became the heart of fundamentalism. These points were the infallibility of the Bible, the virgin birth, Christ's substitutionary atonement, the resurrection, and the second coming.[44]

Wynkoop was able to evaluate the unique emphasis of these five points, and what caught her attention was the underlying focus on the supernatural—or, more particularly, the fact of the miracle.[45] This emphasis, to her, defined the core battleground with science. Wynkoop said,

---

38. George M. Marsden, "Fundamentalism and American Evangelicalism," in *The Variety of American Evangelicalism*, ed. Donald W. Dayton and Robert K. Johnston (Knoxville: University of Tennessee Press, 2001), 25.
39. Ibid.
40. Wynkoop, "A Historical and Semantic Analysis," file 1237-27, WC, 129.
41. Marsden, *Fundamentalism and American Culture*, 7.
42. Ibid.
43. Ibid.
44. Wynkoop, "A Historical and Semantic Analysis," file 1237-27, WC, 124.
45. Ibid., 132.

"Science and religion clashed at the level of miracle."[46] It was, however, not the stress on the reality of the supernatural that confused the issues in the controversy but, rather, in her view, an immature view of the whole philosophy of the supernatural. Wynkoop wrote:

> The issue arose something like this. Science denies the miraculous and with it the supernatural. Christianity is supernatural and its faith is proved by the miraculous. Its Bible is supernatural, and therefore must be perfect and infallible. To admit any measure of fallibility and humanity in the Bible would deny its miraculous and supernatural character with the consequent capitulation to naturalism. Its authority would therefore be nullified and the Christian religion would fall apart. Science and biblical criticism attacked that supernatural perfection; therefore fundamentalism rejected science and biblical criticism.[47]

According to Wynkoop, the real error was that fundamentalists equated inerrancy with authority.[48] Words of Scripture became important because doctrines "hung on propositions."[49] Since divergent doctrines depended on the fine analysis of words and tenses, the authority must be verbally inerrant. Thus, the emphasis shifted from divine inspiration alone to verbal inerrancy to protect doctrine. Wynkoop said, "The inerrancy and divine choice of every word of Scripture was made to support the entire structure of revelation up to God himself."[50] Confusing these matters led the fundamentalists to believe that inerrancy is necessary to protect the supernatural nature and authority of the Bible. Wynkoop elaborated, "Inerrancy is an abstract deduction from the presupposition that the supernatural revelation must display its supernatural character to give evidence of its nature and its authority. Since its physical properties are words, words must be the object of its perfection and infallibility. There is nothing else to be perfect but the words."[51]

What this did, according to Wynkoop, was to focus on the medium of revelation and not on the One who is revealed. In so doing, the contact between humanity and the living Word was severed, and Christ no longer

---

46. Ibid.
47. Ibid., 136.
48. Ibid.
49. Ibid., 216.
50. Ibid.
51. Ibid., 137.

was a present, living reality in human lives.⁵² The fundamentalists were unable to see that God's self-disclosure is the first line of defense and not the miraculous in the cause-and-effect relationships of the natural world. Confusing this caused them to bypass the fact of revelation, God's self-disclosure, as *the* miracle.⁵³ Wynkoop wrote, "The one miracle, which is *the* miracle, the place where human reason reels, is Jesus himself. Here, and here only, does final revelation occur because only in this one spot has the supernatural broken into the natural. It could not be accomplished through logic or propositions of truth, but only through Christ."⁵⁴

These issues were crucial for Wynkoop to overcome, since they were at the heart of what she experienced as she and her husband travelled as evangelists in the Church of the Nazarene. Through her own experiences, she encountered the dark world of the legalism that occurs when words become sacred.⁵⁵ This legalism especially manifested itself in the way that women called into ministry were treated. Wynkoop was not a stranger to this pain as she recalled her own calling to preach. She said, "The consciousness of being destined to preach was as clear and urgent as life itself and yet I did not feel free to discuss this with anyone."⁵⁶ As she grew up she remembered women preachers whom she truly admired and who were a great source of encouragement to her. She especially recalled Mrs. Delance Wallace (who was a General Assembly speaker for the Church of the Nazarene) as being "beautiful, gracious, articulate, and enormously effective." On the other hand, she also remembered some rather "loud and brassy women who embarrassed her."⁵⁷

This shift in the mood of the church as a whole was a shift toward fundamentalism. She wrote,"During the '20s and '30s, another strain of preaching was distinctly detected—a strongly flavoured fundamentalism, harsh, judgmental, unyielding, divisive. 'Holiness' began to be mixed with harshness and rigidity. With it came an emphasis on so-called modesty, always directed to women. The danger women were to men began to be preached and I felt strangely alienated and withdrawn."⁵⁸ By then she

---

52. Ibid., 139.
53. Ibid., 137.
54. Ibid., 226.
55. Ibid., 139.
56. Wynkoop, "Birth and Marriage," file 1427-4, WC, 2.
57. Ibid.
58. Ibid.

began to understand that it was not the most popular thing for women to preach.[59] She wrote, "All this infused my mind with tensions, questions, rebellions, which were difficult to tame. Part of the problem was the subtle change in the church. It had begun to lean on a loud fundamentalism. Our 'sanctification' was questioned when we didn't supply the noisy background which was wanted. Some very sincere men and women felt impelled to 'bring the glory down' by 'yelling' in church. I simply curled up inside and almost died of rebellion and shame."[60]

What Wynkoop thought she experienced was the disconnect that happens when the written Word is substituted for the living Word. In the final analysis, Wynkoop considered fundamentalism to be defective in several ways. First, she felt that fundamentalists were not able to stay on the orthodox path because of their tendency to make peripheral truths central. Second, for her, fundamentalists were authoritarian, arrogant, and schismatic in spirit. Third, she considered those adhering to fundamentalism to be reactionary, especially in the way they rejected all science and were unwilling to investigate their own convictions. She also noticed that those endorsing fundamentalism were unable to take responsibility for the culture that surrounded and supported them. Last but not the least, Wynkoop felt that fundamentalism needed enemies to fight to justify its existence. She wrote, "It was so busy defining itself into isolation that it forgot [that] its primary purpose was to give Christ to a hungry world."[61] In the end, all that fundamentalism was able to accomplish was to isolate Christ from the human situation and, in so doing, forget that Jesus was a man and not an idea.

Wiley's Use of Scripture

H. Orton Wiley enters the conversation on biblical interpretation during this volatile period, seeking a middle road between theological liberalism on the one hand and against fundamentalism on the other. Again, as previously noted, Wynkoop was profoundly influenced by Wiley. When his three-volume *Christian Theology* became available in the 1940s, it represented the formal theology of the Holiness Movement. Wiley's views are important to this study because of the way he developed his doctrine of

---

59. Ibid.
60. Ibid., 9–10.
61. Wynkoop, "A Theology of Depth," file 1431-15, WC, 17.

Scripture. His contribution is especially seen in the way he was able to offer an authentic Wesleyan alternative to fundamentalism and theological liberalism by creating a *via media* approach that would place the Church of the Nazarene's Article of Faith on Scripture well within the evangelical tradition. The significance of this intervention in the general mood of the church was to be felt for years to come.

The implications are seen by looking at the development of Article IV in the *Manual*, the official constitution of the Church of the Nazarene. When we track the development of Article IV of the Nazarene *Manual* from 1905 to 1923, the article on the Holy Scriptures remains relatively unchanged. However, when we reach the 1928 *Manual* article, there are significant changes, which reflect a response to fundamentalism.[62] Up to 1923, the Article of Faith (or belief) referring to Scripture read: "By the Holy Scriptures we understand the sixty-six books of the Old and New Testaments, given by divine inspiration, revealing the will of God concerning us in all things necessary for our salvation; so that whatsoever is not contained therein is not to be enjoined as an article of faith."[63] In comparison, the 1928 *Manual* article on the doctrine of Scriptures read: "We believe in the plenary inspiration of the Holy Scriptures by which we understand the sixty-six books of the Old and New Testaments, given by divine inspiration, inerrantly revealing the will of God concerning us in all things necessary for our salvation; so that whatever is not contained therein is not to be enjoined as an article of faith."[64] Obviously the words "plenary inspiration" (meaning the Scriptures are fully inspired) and "inerrancy" are now needed. Everyone thought that the wording in the 1928 Article IV was in line with the fundamentalist sentiment of the day, and it was so adopted by the assembly. This sentiment was echoed in General Superintendent R. T. Williams's bold statement to the delegates of the seventh General Assembly in 1928:

> First, we note with pleasure that there are no differences or divisions among us. We are a perfectly united denomination. In this General Assembly there will be no discussion of modernism or fundamental-

---

62. Michael E. Lodahl, *All Things Necessary to Our Salvation: The Hermeneutical and Theological Implications of the Article on the Holy Scriptures in the Manual of the Church of the Nazarene*, Monograph Series 4 (San Diego: Point Loma Press, 2004), 15.
63. Ibid.
64. Ibid.

ism. We are all fundamentalists, we believe the Bible, we all believe in Christ, that he is truly the Son of God. . . . We must stand for the whole Bible. We do not, as a Movement, believe merely that the Bible contains the Word of God. We believe that the Bible is the Word of God. . . . Every man in this body is a fundamentalist. . . . We believe the Bible and accept it as being the revealed Word of God, immutable, unchangeable, infallible, and sufficient for every human need. A modernist would be very lonesome in this General Assembly.[65]

Given this almost unreserved allegiance to the fundamentalist creed of biblical inerrancy, it is a great irony that Dr. H. Orton Wiley, responsible for the changed wording in the 1928 article on Scripture, singlehandedly steered the Church of the Nazarene away from fundamentalism, even while everyone thought at the same time that they were fully compliant with the fundamentalists' war cry of the day.[66] When Dr. Wiley crafted the wording to say "inerrantly revealing the will of God concerning us in all things necessary to our salvation," he ensured that the denomination's understanding of biblical authority would be rooted in the inerrancy of the message of salvation and not the inerrancy of the text. This is, at the heart, a shift away from fundamentalism and critical data in explaining why fundamentalism did not capture the church. Wiley was able to bring to the forefront the essential and critical role that **prevenient grace** plays, even in regard to the role of Scripture in the life of the seeker.

What is clear is that Wiley's *via media* perspective did not fit the liberals' use of higher criticism, or the fundamentalists' presupposition that Scripture itself is alone the revelation of God. For Wiley, revelation extends beyond the Bible to Christ and into the living organism of the body of Christ, the church herself. It is then Christ as the "living Word" who satisfies a believer's search for truth, and not the Bible on its own terms. Wiley wrote, "Spiritual men and women—those filled with the Holy Spirit, are not unduly concerned with either higher criticism or lower criticism. They do not rest merely in the letter, which must be defended by argument. They have a broader and more substantial basis for their faith.

---

65. Paul M. Bassett, "The Fundamentalist Leavening of the Holiness Movement: 1914—1940," *WTJ* 13:1 (Spring 1978): 15. Bassett here quotes from the seventh General Assembly journal, 1928.

66. Ibid., 20. Bassett confirms Wiley's authorship of the 1928 article, from conversations with Wynkoop and Carl Bangs dated on October 27, 1977, and April 4, 1975, respectively.

It rests in their risen Lord, the glorified Christ. They know that the Bible is true, not primarily through the efforts of the apologists, but because they are acquainted with its Author."[67]

The movement prevalent in the fundamentalism of his day is now reversed in Wiley, as indicated by Bassett: "Instead of a movement from the authority of Scripture to saving faith, the movement is from the believer's saving relationship to Christ to the sufficiency and then to the authority of the Bible."[68] Here we begin to see the significance of Wynkoop's exposure to Wiley's christological view of Scripture. Wiley would become a key mentor to help Wynkoop formulate her position.

John Wesley's Hermeneutics

Wynkoop was not a stranger to John Wesley's theology as she earned her bachelor of theology at Pasadena College. From as early as 1915, ministerial candidates in the Church of the Nazarene were required to read a Wesley biography, a selection of his sermons, and some compilations of his theological work on the doctrine of Christian sanctification.[69] Even though ministerial students had to read a Wesley biography like John Telford's *The Life of John Wesley* and a collection of sermons including "The Scripture Way of Salvation," "Sin in Believers," "Repentance in Believers" and "Perfection," Wesley was respected more for his life and work than for his theology.[70] It was not until after the 1946 publication of Harald Lindström's book, *Wesley and Sanctification: A Study in the Doctrine of Salvation*, and the 1964 release of Leo Cox's book *John Wesley's Concept of Perfection* that Nazarenes began to show interest in placing sanctification under the umbrella of Wesley's process of salvation.[71]

There was yet another crucial step that lay between Wynkoop's older, non-Wesleyan Wesleyanism and the concept of love as the essence of holiness, which Wesley helped her see. She had been preaching holiness as a "second work of grace" exclusively on the evangelistic trails with her

---

67. H. Orton Wiley, *Christian Theology* (Kansas City: Nazarene Publishing House, 1940), 1:143.

68. Paul Merritt Bassett, "The Theological Identity of the North American Holiness Movement: Its Understanding of the Nature and Role of the Bible," in *The Variety of American Evangelicalism*, 93.

69. Floyd Cunningham, ed., *Our Watchword and Song: The Centennial History of the Church of the Nazarene* (Kansas City: Beacon Hill Press of Kansas City, 2009), 295.

70. Ibid.

71. Ibid., 492.

husband. Her true awakening to John Wesley's theology did not begin until a particular Sunday as she preached to a large congregation in San Francisco. She described this crucial event:

> The sermon was flowing along with ease. I was fascinated by my own eloquence. The attention was great. The altar was well filled at the invitation. The people crowded around afterward and said such nice things that I came all too near believing them. Then a little woman with a mission elbowed her way in to me through the crowd. She stood squarely in front of me, not waiting for the nice people around me to give her a chance to talk. "Do you know," she said, "how many times you mentioned Jesus this morning?" I batted my eyes in surprise, wondering whether I had said that word so often that it was offensive. "You said 'Jesus,'" she volunteered, 'two times.'" And then she was gone—mission accomplished. *Well*, I thought, *that really shouldn't bother anyone too much. I was preaching about holiness and the Holy Spirit, surely I could squeeze 'Jesus' in a couple of times without getting out of line.* For several years I ridiculed her publicly for tabulating the number of times a preacher said Jesus, but I never forgot her. Only gradually did I begin to see that one couldn't preach about holiness and the Holy Spirit and leave Jesus out. . . . Only gradually did I begin to see that I had not only found in Jesus the New Testament gospel message, but that I had run straight into the very foundation of Wiley's theology. That is what Wiley was all about and somehow I had not quite understood it. And, amazingly, the contribution John Wesley made came clear. Here was the New Testament, and Wesley and Wiley standing together in proclaiming Christ as the very centre of the gospel. They were saying holiness is "Christocentric." This explosive fact created such a revolution in my thinking that it has never been the same since.[72]

Given Wynkoop's passion to close the credibility gap between creed and life, it is not a surprise to see her drawn to John Wesley. What she experienced in the American Holiness Movement was an emphasis on sanctification that she concluded had become a transaction of human achievement rather than a reliance on Christ. Obtaining sanctification was the end result of an elaborate and rigidly structured, how-to recipe.

---

72. Wynkoop, "Foundations," file 2227-11, WC, 4.

In contrast, Wynkoop saw in Wesley a dynamic, christological, relational, teleological, and socially oriented understanding of sanctification.[73] In the published article "A Hermeneutical Approach to Wesley," Wynkoop focused on Wesley's ability to relate God's grace to human experience, especially the practical way in which sanctification is played out in ordinary people's lives. She wrote:

> Wesley's profound and dynamic religious insight was the power of the Holy Spirit in the life of the Christian. This Power was a real, Spiritual Energy linking the divine reality to human experience. It was the personness of God touching the personness of men. It was an actual moral transformation of human life. It engaged all that the human person is in grace. It put the individual believer into the church, the corporate fellowship. It put the church in the midst of society with a task to do in transforming the world in which men find themselves. The lure of Wesley is not primarily his theology. That was traditional enough. He was not an innovator. The contribution of Wesley is in his ability to put theology into flesh and blood. The goal was theology incarnated in mere man.[74]

In her article "John Wesley: Mentor or Guru?" Wynkoop identifies Wesley as fulfilling the role of a mentor in the articulation of her Wesleyan theology. By this she meant that Wesley was able to give her a dynamic way of doing theology. He was a guide who opened for her new doors of understanding biblical holiness and love.[75]

It was also Wesley's discovery of the existential meaning of redemption in his study of Scripture that drew Wynkoop to him. Wesley understood God's grace as operating in the context of human experience—in history. It was personal,[76] dynamic, and social.[77] This informed his concept of the way the Bible was given and the way it was to be read.[78] Wynkoop wrote, "Wesley's approach to theology pushed past the philosophical supports of Reformation Scholasticism to return to a primitive and direct, but cer-

---

73. Ibid., 9.
74. Mildred Bangs Wynkoop, "A Hermeneutical Approach to Wesley," *WTJ* 6:1 (1971): 14.
75. Mildred Bangs Wynkoop, "John Wesley: Mentor or Guru?" *WTJ* 10:1 (1975): 9.
76. For Wynkoop, "personal" here means anything and everything about man having a bearing on his moral, intellectual, spiritual, responsible self. It is opposed to man considered as an it. (*Theology of Love*, 80.)
77. Wynkoop, *Theology of Love*, 80–86.
78. Wynkoop, "The Whole Wesley in a Broken World" (article, undated), file 1432-5, WC, 8.

tainly not naive appeal to the Bible. The secret of Wesley's method was his biblical orientation. The Bible, reason, and experience kept theology a growing, open-ended, vital, relating process rather than leading into a dogmatic cul-de-sac, which ended relevance."[79]

In the latter part of Wynkoop's life, the so-called Wesleyan Quadrilateral, devised by Albert Outler, was thought to characterize Wesley's hermeneutics. The procedure by which Wesley was thought to have arrived at doctrine was first on the basis of Scripture, then by testing it according to experience, via the test of reason, and finally according to tradition.[80] There was a healthy system of checks and balances built into the way Wesley did his theology. Like the Reformers, Wesley believed the Scriptures to be divinely inspired. In language typical of his time, Wesley believed the Bible to be "infallibly true."[81] It was God-given and free from material error.[82] At first, this looks like a mechanical dictation theory of inspiration, but it would be unwise to count him among those who have sympathies for fundamentalism. Larry Shelton wrote: "Wesley's statements about Scripture must be interpreted from within the context of eighteen[th]-century thought, and efforts to superimpose on various proof texts the framework of twentieth-century fundamentalist **epistemology** must not be considered legitimate examinations of his position on the Bible."[83]

SUFFICIENCY

There is no question that for Wesley, the revelation is Christ. The written Word to him is in essence the revelation of the Revelation. It is from this Revelation that Scripture takes its authority. Reflecting on Wesley's Christology, John Deschner shows that Wesley placed the ministry of Christ speaking under the prophetic work of Christ. He says:

Christ speaking has constituted the church (John 10:27–29). Now Christ also sustains the faith of all believers through his Word (Ephesians 2:20). He stands in the centre of his church, "as the presenter [sic] of the choir," and "sets forth the praises of God . . . by his Word

---

79. Wynkoop, "The Wesleyans" (article, 1980), file 2227-12, WC, 21.
80. Paul Merritt Bassett, "The Holiness Movement and the Protestant Principle," *WTJ* 18:1 (Spring 1983): 11.
81. Ibid.
82. Ibid.
83. Shelton, "John Wesley's Approach," 21.

and Spirit," and he will continue to do so throughout all generations (Hebrews 2:12). . . . Apostles and ministers are the human conveyors of this living Word, but Christ's Spirit is the active power in it, the teacher, the "greater witness" (John 14:26).[84]

Here we can see that Wesley echoes the voices of the Reformation. If we were to leave it at that, we could conclude that there is no difference between the Reformers and Wesley in their agreement that the living Word is the main basis for the authority of Scripture. However, Wesley was able to take the Reformers' understanding of the role of Scripture to a deeper level. To understand the nature and the role of the Bible for Wesley, we have to go back to the Thirty-Nine Articles of Religion of the Church of England, finalized in 1571. According to the sixth article, titled "Of the Sufficiency of the Holy Scriptures for Salvation," "Holy Scripture containeth all things necessary to salvation: so that whatsoever is not read therein, nor may be proved thereby, is not to be required of any man, that it should be believed as an article of the Faith, or be thought requisite or necessary to salvation. In the name of the Holy Scripture we do understand those canonical Books of the Old and New Testament, of whose authority was never any doubt in the Church."[85]

Bassett notes that the article on Scripture's place in the overall confession sends a message about what would have prior importance in one's confession. According to Bassett, the article invites the one confessing to confess faith in Christ first, before a confession is made about Scripture. This signals that the framers of the Thirty-Nine Articles considered a person's relationship with God to have prior significance to a stance on Scripture. When we then get to article six, what one confesses is not the authority of Scripture but its sufficiency for salvation.[86] Bassett shows that the Thirty-Nine Articles were unique in making sufficiency, not authority, the critical concept in describing the nature and role of Scripture.[87] Bassett makes this case by referencing Wesley's sermon "The Means of Grace" in *Wesley's Standard Sermons*.[88] Here Wesley stated that the pur-

---

84. John Deschner, *Wesley's Christology: An Interpretation* (Dallas: Southern Methodist University Press, 1960), 88.

85. "The Thirty-Nine Articles of Religion of the Church of England, AD 1571" (Online: Christian Classics Ethereal Library), 490.

86. Bassett, "The Theological Identity," 77.

87. Ibid.

88. Ibid., 101.

pose of Scripture is found in its ability to accomplish the work of salvation in the hearts of those who heard it. Its authority was based on its sufficiency for salvation. As Wesley saw it, there was a power at work in the written Word, and its redemptive power was the living Word, Christ himself, being revealed to the hearer by the Holy Spirit.[89] This is the point in Wesley's famous preface to the first edition of the *Standard Sermons*:

> I want to know one thing—the way to heaven; how to land safe on that happy shore. God himself had descended to teach the way; for this very end he came from heaven. He had written it down in a book. O give me that book! At any price, give me the book of God! I have it: here is knowledge enough for me. Let me be *homo unius libri*. Here then I am, far from the busy ways of men. I sit down alone: Only God is here. In his presence I open, I read this book; for this end, to find the way to heaven.[90]

When Wesley says, "Only God is here," he is making reference to the work of the Holy Spirit as the sole connecting agent between the reader and the living Word. For Scripture to lead us to salvation, its reading must be accompanied by the internal witness of the Holy Spirit. It is often experience that takes Wesley to Scripture—either his own experience or that of others.[91] Wesley brought experience to Scripture in order to understand experience properly, that is, in the light of salvation (evangelical experience). Wesley could then envision a person coming to evangelical experience without hearing or knowing Scripture. Having said this, Bassett reminds us that "experience" for Wesley served as a confirmation, not only of the truth of the text but also of the believer's relationship with God. He says, "Experience confirms the fact that through the written Word the living Word has done and is doing his redemptive work. If this fact be not at the heart of the 'experience,' that 'experience' is not to be taken as spiritually authoritative. Experience, then, is not an end, nor a goal, but is a result again, a consequence of confirmation."[92]

One can then see that Wesley was primarily interested in the spiritual sense of Scripture, even though he did not ignore the importance of the lit-

---

89. Ibid., 79.
90. John Wesley, "Preface," in *Sermons I*, ed. Albert C. Outler, vol. 1 of *The Bicentennial Edition of the Works of John Wesley* (Nashville: Abingdon Press, 1984—), 105-6 (hereafter cited as *Bicentennial Works*).
91. Bassett, "The Holiness Movement," 11.
92. Ibid., 13.

eral sense in the discipline of biblical interpretation. Historical accuracy and reliability were to Wesley not the main point but, rather, the sufficiency for salvation as Scripture reveals the saving purposes through Christ.[93] According to Randy Maddox, one of Wesley's exegetical principles was that Scripture is to be interpreted according to the "analogy of faith."[94] This term was to Wesley a connecting chain of soteriological truths that served to unify Scripture as a whole. These soteriological truths in particular were, as Maddox noted, "the corruption of sin, **justification by faith**, the new birth, and present inward and outward holiness."[95] Wesley encouraged others to read Scripture with these soteriological filters as a way to show that the primary purpose of Scripture is its sufficiency for salvation.

It is also important to note that Wesley did not want to separate Scripture and worship. As Bassett points out, for Wesley, Scripture gained its deepest relevance when it was "read and sung and practiced along with the great and living history of the church."[96] Searching the Scriptures within the context of the worshiping community took on a sacramental function for Wesley. Along with prayer and the Lord's Supper it became a means of grace.[97]

In summary, the central features of Wynkoop and Bassett's view of Wesley's understanding of the role and nature of Scripture are the following: First, Wesley was able to link the written Word with the living Word in a way that gave priority to Christ. Second, Wesley was able to maintain a proper balance between Word and Spirit in such a way that he did not make the Spirit a prisoner of the Word yet was able to show that the Word is the instrument of the Spirit.[98] Third, the authority of the Word lies in its sufficiency for salvation, and fourth, as Bassett notes, "the witness of the Holy Spirit is first to the Bible's sufficiency and then to its authority and not first to its authority and then to its sufficiency."[99]

---

93. Bassett, "The Theological Identity," 81.
94. Randy L. Maddox, *Responsible Grace: John Wesley's Practical Theology* (Nashville: Kingswood Books, 1994), 38.
95. Ibid.
96. Bassett, "The Holiness Movement," 11.
97. Shelton, "John Wesley's Approach," 22.
98. Staples, "John Wesley's Doctrine," 8.
99. Bassett, "The Theological Identity," 90.

The Role of Scripture in Wynkoop's Theology of Christian Holiness

With this understanding of the way Wynkoop and her colleagues understood Wesley's view of Scripture, we turn to Wynkoop's own view. Her developed position on the issue of biblical authority required a clear distinction between the Reformation-Wesleyan approach and the scholastic Calvinism of Princeton theology and fundamentalism. We see that, for Wesley and Wiley, it was critical to keep the internal testimony of the Holy Spirit and the traditional witness of the church as important checkpoints to assure proper biblical interpretation. Luther particularly, and Calvin in a lesser way, made Christ the interpretative norm. Both demanded a literal and literary interpretation of Scripture but added a further dimension of interpretation that would relate the reader to Christ spiritually. Wynkoop would be fully in line with the Reformers and Wesley, in that she believed Scripture to be the inspired Word of God and that the authority of Scripture points to the living Word and not the text itself. She would echo the words of Wesley and Calvin that the internal testimony of the Holy Spirit is essential for anyone to grasp the revelation from God through the written Word.

Wynkoop did not take the time to defend a specific theory of inspiration, yet one can detect that she had a more spiritual and less verbal view of inspiration. Given her struggles with fundamentalism and her denomination's exaggerated emphasis on experience as a basis for the authority of Scripture, her main goal was to understand in what ways Scripture could be relevant and accessible to the reader. She wrote:

> If we use the Bible as a philosophical escalator upward into the world of absolutes we will have missed the purpose of Scripture and separated it from the real needs of men. If however, on the other hand, we understand the Bible as a communication of God to man in history, not only about his will for man, but also about his predicament and the way he may properly relate himself to the earth, to himself, to mankind and to his Creator we will have found the universal meaning and relevance of the Bible to men of all times and nations and cultures.[100]

For Wynkoop, overcoming the credibility gap between doctrine and life was directly related to the way Scripture is interpreted and pro-

---

100. Wynkoop, "Some Implications," file 1432-7, WC, 5.

claimed. This realization came when she decided to go back to school at the age of forty-five to learn Greek and Hebrew. The main encourager for her to make this decision was her brother, Carl, who at that time started his PhD studies at the University of Chicago. He encouraged her to learn Hebrew and Greek, which, of course, were requirements to enroll in the ThD program at Northern Baptist Theological Seminary in Chicago.[101]

She wrote, "I found I needed a 'new Bible,' the deeper understanding of the old one . . . maybe if I learned the Greek language the Bible would talk to me better."[102] Not long after taking classes in Greek, she decided to put her newly learned Greek to use in re-polishing an old sermon on Romans 12:1–2. She wrote, "I found that 'presentation' to God was an aorist action but that 'transformation' was not aorist at all but a present indicative indicating a very long and arduous process."[103] It began to dawn on her that one of the ways to overcome the credibility gap was to stay with the language of Scripture. By this she meant that it was the recovery of the existential meaning of the scriptural words, not just the theological use of the words.[104]

From her own life experience and through the recognition of her own underlying presuppositions, Wynkoop realized that the Bible, properly used, could become a bridge to life, to involvement, to relevance, and to holiness. In an article written in 1968, Wynkoop brings to focus the importance of the incarnation, "the Word became flesh and made his dwelling among us" (John 1:14). She wrote, "The God that is not dead is the one who manifested himself in 'the Word.' Words are the vehicles of communication, but the only way the full value of words can be preserved is to clothe them with flesh, with full humanity."[105]

THE BIBLE AS DIVINE

This interest in the incarnation drew Wynkoop to Luther, who had made the case that the Bible is both divine and human in the same way that Christ's nature is divine and human. Reconciling the divine and hu-

---

101. Jeremy Bangs, email to author, January 18, 2017.
102. Wynkoop, "My Life," file 1427-2, WC, 4.
103. Wynkoop, "Some Implications," file 1432-7, WC, 4.
104. Ibid., 5.
105. Wynkoop, "Christian Words Incarnated," editorial in *Herald of Holiness*, January 18, 1968, file 1237-28, WC. *Herald of Holiness* (now *Holiness Today*) is a denominational magazine published by the Church of the Nazarene.

man elements without being preoccupied with the metaphysical nature of Scripture was the challenge Wynkoop undertook in defining her theology. As was the case with Luther, Wynkoop did not go down the road of **Nestorianism** (that is, separating the divine and human aspects) but, rather, chose to hold the Bible's supernatural origin and the realm of nature in creative tension without compartmentalization. Even though her heart was caught up with the purpose of Scripture, she undertook the task of reconciling the divine and human elements of Scripture without bypassing the question of the nature of Scripture. She embarked on this journey by showing that both Christ and Scripture are implicated in the self-disclosure of God. She sees both as a revelation of God. For her, each one in its own way partakes of the divine yet is available to the empirical world.

This philosophical wrestling in trying to overcome the gap between the supernatural and the natural elements of Scripture led Wynkoop to the conclusion that it can only be done by God's taking the initiative in communication. If nature is going to comprehend the communication, it will be because God participated in, or accommodated himself to, the limitations that make knowledge possible in nature.[106] For Wynkoop, this accommodation climaxed in the one miracle, which is *the* miracle, the supernatural revelation of the incarnation of Jesus Christ as the Son of God. For revelation to happen and for it to stick, it could then not be accomplished only through propositions of truth or through some abstract comprehension—but only through Christ.[107] However, Wynkoop notes the limitations of the ability of the words of Scripture alone to bring spiritual meaning.[108]

She drives home this point by showing that the disciples' understanding of Jesus was materialistic and unspiritual, in spite of their intimate and prolonged contact with him.[109] She wrote, "If a perfect record could have been effective as revelation, surely the Old Testament and Jesus's own teaching would have produced a radiant church. But it took something more, and the 'something more' is the thing that saves the human record from being merely human."[110] Here, Wynkoop is not saying that the words

---

106. Wynkoop, "A Historical and Semantic Analysis," file 1237-27, WC, 225.
107. Ibid., 226.
108. Ibid.
109. Ibid.
110. Ibid., 244.

are unimportant but, rather, that they are incomplete as revelation. This "something more" that is needed is "spiritual vision." The only way that she was then able to reconcile the divine and human elements of Scripture was to use the lens of "spiritual interpretation."

She wrote, "Intellectual comprehension, meaning the human faculty of understanding as contrasted with what we believe to be sub-human faculties, does not take place in the realm of the sense data, but beyond it. I believe that this realm is a spiritual one—an immaterial, real realm. The spiritual is not a superimposed dimension, but an integral part of nature, therefore subject to human awareness."[111] To be specific, then, for Wynkoop, the final revelation of Scripture and of Christ is mediated in the spiritual realm. Wynkoop believed that the natural categories of interpretation can only tell us *about* Christ, but to be able to *know* Christ and capture the intention of the divine mind, a spiritual category of interpretation is needed.[112] The heart of biblical relevance was the obligation to propose principles of interpretation that will do justice to its spiritual nature.

She wrote, "Spiritual is the deepest realm of understanding, the area where God's revelation of himself is most real and effective. In this view the real word of God is not restricted to the original autographs or to the Hebrew and Greek texts, but extends by divine superintendence from the original inspiration down through every human form of the scripture to English versions, Russian translations and Braille Bibles and hence to the individual."[113]

In a most real way, this vital contact with truth is then made personal through the ministry of the Holy Spirit. Wynkoop noted, "The Spirit's ministry is the essence of relevancy."[114] Scripture is sufficient for salvation only as the Holy Spirit makes it come alive and witness to its truth. Something happened in history when God entered it in the person of Christ and the Holy Spirit. That something did not end in rational concepts but is dynamically made available through the presence of the Holy Spirit.[115] The historical Christ—living, teaching, dying, and rising from the dead—without the interpretative ministry of the Holy Spirit was, to her, not the finished

---

111. Ibid., 228.
112. Ibid., 230.
113. Ibid.
114. Wynkoop, "The Authority of Christian Scriptures" (article, undated), file 2227-3, WC, 23.
115. Ibid.

revelation.[116] Along with Luther, Wesley, and Wiley, we can then say that Wynkoop's interpretation of Scripture was not complete until she had captured the spiritual sense of the text. This life-giving, heart-changing, and mind-enlightening sense underlying the words in Scripture captured her heart. In all these respects, it is then important to note that Wynkoop believed the Bible to be supernatural, from God, and therefore divine.

THE BIBLE AS HUMAN

Wynkoop also pointed out that it is not possible to isolate the divine aspects from the human and natural realms.[117] The influence of Calvin on this aspect of Wynkoop's doctrine of Scripture is especially noted as she also used the concept of accommodation. She wrote, "The Scriptures partake of the human and natural limitations in the sense that they represent a progressive revelation which was accommodated to the capacity of men to receive it."[118] The Scriptures were not just dropped from heaven but came out of the stuff of normal human living.

She noted that the few times the deity wrote on physical objects, the results were quickly destroyed. Both the tablets of stone dropped on Mount Sinai and the words of Jesus, written in the dust, were trampled underfoot.[119] In other words, God used human beings because he was giving special revelation and not just general revelation for which nature would have been adequate. She wrote, "God used men because he had made them capable of grasping spiritual truth. Inspiration—the impulse and revelation—the content of God's self-disclosure, was a spiritual experience. It had to be reduced to human speech and then reduced again to a written language."[120]

This existential understanding helps us to see that, for Wynkoop, Scripture is about communication. It is about a God who is saying something to someone whom he intends shall understand.[121] Rather than seeing the humanness of the record as something less desired or unspiritual, Wynkoop showed that the humanness of the record is for the express purpose of preventing men from giving undue reverence to the medium

---

116. Wynkoop, "A Historical and Semantic Analysis," file 1237-27, WC, 230.
117. Ibid., 242.
118. Ibid., 243.
119. Ibid., 242.
120. Ibid.
121. Wynkoop, "A Theology of Depth," file 1431-15, WC, 36.

of revelation and, in so doing, divert their attention away from Christ himself.[122] She noted:

> If the Bible were simply a textbook of abstract theological statements, our appropriation of them would be on the level of intellectual comprehension only. It would lack the moral element so necessary to biblical understanding. The Bible is a book of experience. Its events occurred in history, among people, in profoundly human involvements. It was not handed down to us on golden plates, but lived out among people. Revelation was not given in a vacuum but concretely, in experience. The language of the Bible is then the language of experience. Because this is so it is timeless and able to bridge the passing cultures without the loss of meaning. There are not many occasions in it where words were given apart from human cooperation.[123]

Therefore, divine revelation, by the inspiration of the Holy Spirit, was given to humanity in a language—that of human experience—that included the heart as well as the mind.[124] This understanding has significance for biblical exegesis. Wynkoop would encourage preachers to take a text and look behind the words to find the human situation to which the words are addressed.[125] In other words, for her, history is important, and the context is as important to the message as are the words.[126] Wynkoop wrote, "The human element in the Bible to which the divine speaks is the common life-blood that keeps the divine meaningful to all who partake of life. The story is the flesh around the idea. It preserves the idea from becoming so detached and irrelevant and intellectualized that it loses all contact with reality. It saves justification and sanctification from abstraction."[127]

Wynkoop was unable to separate the divine from the fallible human element in the Bible. For her, the human element was inspired as well, since the divine speaks through the cultural context and keeps it relevant for all ages. Her use of Scripture brought her once again to a place of moral relevance. Talking about preaching God's Word, she said, "It was made for life, it must remain in life."[128]

---

122. Wynkoop, "A Historical and Semantic Analysis," file 1237-27, WC, 244.
123. Wynkoop, "A Theology of Depth," file 1431-15, WC, 48.
124. Ibid.
125. Ibid., 49.
126. Ibid., 47.
127. Ibid., 51.
128. Ibid., 47.

BALANCE BETWEEN WORD AND SPIRIT

As is already established, Wynkoop recognized that, in order for revelation to take place, God must make himself present in our world and accommodate himself to us to make us experience his presence. With this focus on the human side of revelation also came an increasing emphasis on the role of the Spirit as a medium of revelation beside the Word. Wynkoop's close colleague Rob Staples's use of the concepts *Word* and *Spirit* is relevant here to help us understand this double revelational activity.

For Staples, *Word* stands for the whole communicative nature of the revelational event. This includes both the speaking and the hearing of the Word. *Spirit*, on the other hand, stands for the activity of the Holy Spirit, who opens the ears of the hearer from within and enables the hearer to hear the speaking of God.[129] It is Staples's belief that a balance between Word and Spirit helps us to connect fully with the intended revelation from God to human beings.

To demonstrate this balance, Staples's quotation of Hendrikus Berkhof is relevant. Berkhof wrote, "The Spirit moves through the world in the shape of the Word in its various forms. The Word is the instrument of the Spirit. But the Spirit is not the prisoner of the Word, nor does the Word work automatically. The Word brings the Spirit to the heart, and the Spirit brings the Word within the heart."[130]

The anticipation in this double revelational activity is that God's Spirit communicates and that there is both a message sent and a message received by the hearer. As we have shown, Luther held Word and Spirit together in a creative balance, especially since he associated the testimony of the Holy Spirit with the Word in use, which to him was the Word proclaimed through preaching. Wesley, in turn, also showed a balance between Word and Spirit since he believed that the Spirit's work didn't end with the inspiration of the writers of Scripture but continues to inspire the hearers and readers of God's Word today.

Staples wrote, "John Wesley had a clear understanding of the bi-unity of Word and Spirit. He held the two in proper balance, neither merging Spirit into Word so that the former is imprisoned in the latter, nor separating them to the extent that there are two separate sources of

---

129. Staples, "John Wesley's Doctrine," 7.
130. Ibid., 9. As quoted from Hendrikus Berkhof, *The Doctrine of the Holy Spirit* (Richmond, VA: John Knox Press, 1964), 37.

revelation. Word does not work automatically and Spirit does not work autonomously."¹³¹

Unfortunately, this bi-unity of Word and Spirit was not always held in proper balance in the Holiness Movement. The Holiness Movement tended to overemphasize the subjective and the immediate experience of the Spirit in the individual. In the absence of good exegetical work, experience itself became the source of understanding about experience.¹³² Many times the only validation of the experience was the testimony itself.

Bassett quotes Dunning, who says, "In their enthusiastic proclamation of the creativity of the Spirit, they neglected the fact that the gospel is grounded in specific historical data and in essence relied only upon their own religious feelings or experiences in the Spirit."¹³³

Reflecting on the Holiness Movement, Stephen J. Lennox wrote, "Holiness interpretation, by minimizing reason and tradition, became a bilateral of Scripture and experience and lost its balance. As it tilted, holiness interpretation came to be dominated by experience rather than Scripture."¹³⁴

In this context, Wynkoop shares a special connection with John Wesley. John Wesley, as is already pointed out, thought evangelical experience to be an important focus of theological truth. However, for Wesley, personal experience did not become the source of truth. Instead, he saw the truth of God's Word expressing itself in real life as it is embraced through obedience and love. For Wesley, Scripture took on a confirmatory role when it came to experience. Standing with Wesley, Wynkoop believed the authority of the Word lay in its sufficiency for salvation. Wynkoop wrote, "God acted, not to explain to men secrets of the universe, which they could discover for themselves, not simply to gratify a curiosity about himself, not even to provide a system of laws to be obeyed, but primarily to make a Saviour available to sinful men. Everything meaningful to that end is included in revelation."¹³⁵

---

131. Staples, "John Wesley's Doctrine," 15.
132. H. Ray Dunning, "Christian Perfection: Toward a New Paradigm," *WTJ* 33:1 (1998): 3.
133. Bassett, "The Holiness Movement," 5.
134. Stephen J. Lennox, "Biblical Interpretation in the American Holiness Movement; 1875—1920," *WTJ* 33:1 (1998): 10.
135. Wynkoop, "A Historical and Semantic Analysis," file 1237-27, WC, 241.

For Wynkoop, the preaching or study of God's Word is not just to engage rational concepts designed to stimulate intellectual conversation and thought but also to have a truly moral experience with the living Word. She wrote, "The law of the Spirit is the law of life. It is a life lived with an awareness toward Christ, demanding but one thing—a personal submission to the leading of the Spirit and the lordship of Christ."[136] In her mind, it is only the vital involvement of the whole person, "challenged to the quick by Christ in dynamic spiritual encounter," that can do justice to the truths of Scripture.[137]

This balance between Word and Spirit is best seen in what Wynkoop would consider basic to the biblical preaching of holiness. First, she encouraged preachers to present Christ, writing, "Press the claims of Christ, his love and sacrifice for sin, his absolute lordship which must be made a living reality in the practical life. . . . No biblical preaching can bypass Christ. It is Christ who validates and gives perspective to and sets the bounds around holiness preaching."[138]

Furthermore she said, "2. Press for a personal moral encounter with God, 3. Hold up the cross, 4. Press for decision, 5. Press for continuing commitment, and 6. Exhort to growth in love."[139] The most anticipated fruit of this encounter with spiritual truth is, for Wynkoop, the manifestation of a person's affections and tempers aligning as a life of love.[140]

Wynkoop's use of Scripture stands firmly in the Reformation evangelical tradition, especially as she echoes the voices of Luther and Wesley with her Christocentric view of Christian holiness.

---

136. Ibid., 246.
137. Wynkoop, "A Theology of Depth," file 1431-15, WC, 25.
138. Ibid., 414.
139. Ibid., 415.
140. Wynkoop, "The Authority of Christian Scriptures," file 2227-3, WC, 30.

4
WYNKOOP'S THEOLOGICAL ANTHROPOLOGY

Throughout Wynkoop's existential interpretation of holiness, it is clear that she gave great priority to the study of the doctrine of humanity.[1] She realized that the role she gave to humanity would determine, to a large extent, the nature of the theology she confessed. From early in life, Wynkoop showed interest in the practical matter of understanding how sanctification can be lived out in real life, especially since Wesleyan theology presented sanctification as a "possibility in this life."[2] The importance of her doctrine of humanity to the overall structure of her theology is seen as she made the study of humanity the focus of her master's thesis for Western Evangelical Seminary in 1952. This 180-page thesis is titled "The Biblical Study of Man in His Relationship to the Image of God."[3]

The inductive exegetical approach in her thesis became a watershed mark in her understanding of the moral responsibility that human beings have in their response to grace, and this understanding profoundly influenced every aspect of her doctrine of Christian holiness. She came to understand that a proper conception of the use of the phrase "man created in the image of God" is necessary to a full understanding of every aspect of **soteriology.** She felt that when human nature was viewed as an enemy

---

1. It should be noted that Wynkoop referred continually to humanity as "man," and that term, until after her death, was regarded as an inclusive term and not gender specific. Wherever possible, the term is avoided in this book except in direct quotations.

2. Wynkoop, "Holiness Theology and Moral Development" (article, 1978), file 1425-21, WC, 1.

3. Wynkoop, "The Biblical Study of Man in His Relationship to the Image of God" (master's thesis, Western Evangelical Seminary, 1952), file 1432-3, WC.

to be conquered, this idea had a profound impact on the expectation for existential holiness for everyday life.[4] Wynkoop observed that the Bible says very little *about* the ontology of humanity itself but instead has much to say *to* humanity, especially the nature of human relationships and character.[5] She wrote, "In a word, man made in God's image seems to refer to whatever there is about man that makes it possible to experience any communication with another intelligent being, and particularly to establish a rapport with God—or to reject that fellowship."[6]

Genesis 1:26–27 gives us the main biblical passage upon which many opinions have been formed. "Let us make mankind in our image, in our likeness. . . . So God created mankind in his own image, in the image of God he created them; male and female he created them."[7] Also, the second account of creation in Genesis 2:7 says, "Then the Lord God formed a man from the dust of the ground and breathed into his nostrils the breath of life, and the man became a living being" (paraphr. by Wynkoop of KJV). Our goal is to unpack the significance Wynkoop saw in the difference between "image" and "likeness," as well as the progression she observed in the words "formed," "breathed into," and "becoming."[8]

The fact that humans are made from dust but also in God's image prompted her to use both a soteriological and psychological filter in her theological anthropology. In reference to Adam, she said, "He is a creature of the earth with a 'natural history.' His body is shared with the natural order. He is in history, a part of it. This must never be forgotten."[9] As such, she saw Adam as a dynamic being, who can communicate with God, who, in partnership with Eve, is not to be viewed through Western individualistic lenses but, rather, as a corporate personality. She wrote:

> The Hebrew man found his dynamism, not in static beingness, but in his social relatedness. His "living" self, his totality, stood in relation to a larger unity, the social entity. . . . Hebrew man was in an essential way *one* with "his fathers" and his family, his tribe and his nation. This

---

4. Wynkoop, "Protestant Theology and the *Imago Dei*" (article, undated), file 1432-7, WC, 1.
5. Wynkoop, *A Theology of Love*, 104.
6. Ibid., 105.
7. Wynkoop, "Source Material for the Lectures on the Relation of the Image of God in Man to Sanctification" (article, undated), file 2227-18, WC, 4. Scripture quotations are Wynkoop's partial paraphrases from the KJV.
8. Wynkoop, *A Theology of Love*, 111.
9. Ibid., 114.

was not a crude metaphysical or genetic unity, but a spiritual interconnectedness that penetrates to the core of what mankind is.[10]

Wynkoop was also careful to protect the unity of the person in contrast with Platonist views that uphold a speculative dichotomy, dividing body and soul as separate parts of a person. It was important to Wynkoop to describe a person in terms of what he or she is as a whole. In other words, heart, mind, soul, spirit, conscience, flesh, and body are not distinguishable parts that a person has but, rather, a description of what a person is.[11]

These presuppositions form an important backdrop as we now turn to Wynkoop's perspective on the *imago Dei*. Christian theology has always held that human beings were made in the image of God and that the image was in some measure forfeited in the fall and that in Christ a restoration is effected. However, within the framework of this simple statement lies much difference of opinion. What is obvious is that the roots of this issue affect every major theological problem, and the field of investigation is wide indeed.

Wynkoop's Methodology

The focus of this research is to place the findings of Wynkoop's biblical research on the image of God within the wider spectrum, while at the same time noting John Wesley's position. In doing so, it is important to be aware of the progression of thought that is at work in Wynkoop's research. This begins with Hebrew and Greek word studies but then broadens to include a biblical study of Jesus's and Paul's perspectives on human nature and finally concludes with the theological implications of the *imago Dei* being the *imago Christi*.

The use of word studies in the 1950s was an acceptable method of doing biblical theology. However, since the 1961 publication of James Barr's work *The Semantics of Biblical Language*, the word-study method is no longer seen as an entirely valid method. Primarily, Barr calls for the recognition that linguistics, context, and sentences are more reliable than just the words themselves. He wrote, "The linguistic bearer of the theological

---

10. Ibid., 123.
11. Ibid., 122.

statement is usually the sentence and the still larger literary complex and not the word or the morphological and syntactical mechanisms."[12]

In light of Barr's assertion, it would be easy to dismiss Wynkoop's findings based on word studies, but it would be good to keep in mind that she did not rely on word studies as the only foundation for her theological conclusions. Laying a foundation of her understanding of the *imago Dei* will hopefully serve as an important springboard to filter her theological leanings, especially the ideas of moral freedom and moral responsibility.

Her leanings toward the Eastern tradition is one of the surprising outcomes of her research, especially given that she was writing as an evangelist within the context of the American Holiness Movement of the mid-twentieth century.

A comparison of early Wynkoop with later Wynkoop, as reflected in her book *A Theology of Love* (1972), shows no significant change in her position on the present subject matter. What is interesting is that she did not feel comfortable publishing the conclusions she reached in her thesis. In the chapters on the *imago Dei* in *A Theology of Love*, the conclusions of her thesis are conspicuously absent.

The argument is ordered into three stages: The first is the original perfections of the *imago Dei* in Adam and Eve. Here, the intent is to explore in what does the image and/or likeness of God in human beings consist. Are these terms used synonymously, or is there a theologically significant distinction between them? Second, the fall and defacement of that image; what effect did the fall of human beings and the entrance of sin have upon them? Are human beings totally depraved? Is their humanity or essential nature altered? Third, to ponder on the mystery of grace and the promise of the image's renewal, how fully will this recovery be effected and when and in what manner?

The Meaning of the Terms "Image" and "Likeness"

One of the main problems Wynkoop sought to address is the scriptural basis of the phrase, loss, and restoration of the image of God.[13] Undertaking a word study of *eikōn* in the Greek New Testament raised serious questions for her as to the accuracy of the expression in so far as the im-

---

12. James Barr, *The Semantics of Biblical Language* (London: Oxford University Press, 1961), 269.
13. Wynkoop, "The Biblical Study of Man," file 1432-3, WC, 13.

mediate work of redemption was concerned.[14] This led Wynkoop to an investigation of the Genesis account of humanity's creation and a Hebrew word study of the two terms *tselem* (image) and *demuth* (likeness). Her word study involved a process of looking at every occurrence of these two words in every state and stem, against its *context*, throughout the Old Testament, to determine the possibly significant difference between them. Each term was then compared with the Greek equivalent in the **Septuagint** translation. The terms "image" and "likeness" were then carried into the New Testament to see if they were used in essentially the same way as the corresponding Hebrew words in the Old Testament.[15]

Using Gesenius's *Hebrew and English Lexicon*, Wynkoop found that the word *tselem* (image) is a cognate of the verb *tsalam*, which literally means "to be shady or dark." From this concept of shade, the idea of shadow developed. A shadow, then, being the dark portion cast in the outline of the original object, was an image.[16] As she tracked *tselem* throughout the Old Testament, she found that the word was mainly used as a representation for persons or things in some concrete form, the only exception being Genesis 9:6 and Genesis 5:3, where the image relates to human beings. She concluded that everywhere in the Old Testament, "image" carried the idea of a concrete substance representing some idea or prototype. The image was a definite conformity to a pattern or mould.[17]

In contrast to "image," she found that "likeness" resembled more of a progression in meaning. Using A. B. Davidson's *Analytical Hebrew and Chaldea Lexicon*, she discovered that in the **Niphil**, "likeness" meant "to be or become like" and in the **Piel**, "to resemble."[18] Her excursion through the Old Testament brought these initial observations: "Image has within it the idea of conformity to a pattern, objectively. It is the recipient of an action. It is the result of something. There is form and substance to it. It is passive. Likeness, on the other hand, implies activity on the part of the object. It is changed or changes itself from one quality or condition to another or resembles another object in some particular."[19]

---

14. Ibid.
15. Ibid., 11.
16. Ibid., 16.
17. Ibid., 17.
18. Ibid., 18.
19. Ibid., 19.

Moving on to the Septuagint, her exploration further confirmed that the Greek scholars were consistent in the distinctions made between image and likeness and consistently translated *eikōn* for *tselem* and *homoiōsis* for *demuth* throughout the entire Old Testament.[20] This trend continued in the Greek New Testament. Wynkoop found that the word *eikōn* showed the same consistency in use as in the Old Testament. All of the usages suggest quite definite, concrete, objective entities of either the mould or that which is moulded.[21] Wynkoop further observed that the distinctions between image and likeness were sustained even in the New Testament. Likewise, *homoiōsis* (likeness) and its cognates, meaning, "like, similar, correspondence to, to be or become like," had the same usage in the Greek as in the Hebrew. This distinction came into even sharper focus as Wynkoop observed that the church found it necessary to make a strong distinction between image and likeness as it took a stand against Arianism: "*Eikōn* always assumes a prototype from which it has been derived and drawn; while *homoiotēs*, *homoiōsis*, and words of this family express a similarity or resemblance, which implies no **ontological** kinship. Only the term image could be applied to Christ in his relationship to God, never merely a likeness. The first is a family tie, a solid filial relationship; the second is a comparison of some detail, an approximation."[22]

From the foregoing analysis, Wynkoop reached a number of conclusions. First, she believed that a sufficient case could be made from a biblical standpoint to distinguish between "image" and "likeness" in reference to man's relationship to God. She believed she had demonstrated that the Hebrew terms are distinct and almost never confused in usage throughout the Old Testament. The Septuagint consistently translates *eikōn* for *tselem* and *homoiōsis* for *demuth*. Second, she concluded that it is not accurate, or even scriptural, to speak of an image lost or defaced as a result of the fall. Nor is there any warrant for speaking of the image being restored. The New Testament language rather points to the use of language like "renewed," always in the progressive tense.[23] Third, "image" includes all that is essential to human beings as such, in a very concrete way, including moral qualities that God was said to have found very good. In other

---

20. Ibid., 20.
21. Ibid., 21.
22. Ibid., 24.
23. Ibid., 25.

words, whatever God is, a human being is his outlined shadow in such a way that he or she is able to shadow forth the essential features of the prototype.[24] Fourth, "likeness" throughout the Hebrew and Greek usage suggests a comparison of qualities of personality, a potential in moral and spiritual matters that hangs in the balance of human probation.[25]

Having said all this, Wynkoop realized that very little is said in the Old and New Testaments concerning the exact meaning of the *imago Dei*. The clearest implications come from the New Testament, where the spiritual aspect of a person is recognized as the essence of his or her being and, with that, a person as a responsible being, possessing faculties of intelligence, volition, and affection.[26] Looking at verses like Ephesians 1:4, "We were chosen before the foundation of the world to be holy and without blame in love" (paraphr. by Wynkoop), and Ephesians 1:12, "that we should be to the praise of his glory" (paraphr. by Wynkoop), Wynkoop concluded that humanity's moral capacity is clearly implied as being a constituent element of its created being.[27]

This came into clearer focus as she looked at the role human beings were given to have dominion over God's creation. Even though Wynkoop did not consider dominion in and of itself to be the image, she did see dominion as a demonstration of the image, especially in the way that dominion required an intelligent personality capable of understanding, choosing, and having fellowship.[28] Since dominion was not the image but the demonstration of the powers resident in the image, so the withdrawal of the delegation to rule was not of itself loss of the image but a demonstration of God's estimate of the moral unfitness of man to rule.[29] Wynkoop wrote, "Having usurped the place of God he lost his vice-royalty. He was a deposed prince, compelled to serve that which he had been made the master. He retained the faculties of lordship but lost his 'portfolio.'"[30] Pulling all her biblical studies into a concise statement, Wynkoop summarized her findings thus: "Man, as an image of God, was spirit as well as body,

---

24. Ibid.
25. Ibid., 26.
26. Ibid., 39.
27. Ibid., 40.
28. Ibid., 41.
29. Ibid., 48.
30. Ibid.

intelligent, moral, wholly related to God in the context of truth."[31] One can then conclude with the assessment that Wynkoop was more comfortable with a relational understanding of the image, seeing Adam as an "imager" (as in, being a mirror) rather than a view that locates the image as a substance in humans.

Finding Wynkoop's place within the wider interpretations of the terms "image" and "likeness" is an important aspect of this research. This will help us to see in what ways she related to Wesley and opened the door for her own unique contribution to advance a deeper understanding of sanctification. Representing the West, we now turn to a brief survey of the *imago Dei* as seen through the eyes of Augustine, Luther, and John Wesley.

The Western View of the *Imago Dei*

Wynkoop was aware that her view of the difference between "image" and "likeness" differed from the Western tradition, including Wesley. Representing the West, Augustine believed that Adam and Eve were created in a complete and perfect state. In his work *On Nature and Grace*, Augustine said, "Man's nature, indeed, was created at first faultless and without any sin; but that nature of man in which every one is born from Adam, now wants the Physician, because it is not sound."[32] In his work *On the Trinity*, Augustine tries to make sense of the Trinity and postulates that the Trinity is reflected in the very structure of the mind itself. Humanity was made in the image of the Trinity, and the image of the Trinity in the mind then consisted of the three faculties of memory, intellect, and will.[33] Considered in and of itself apart from God, the mind is the image, yet the relational aspect only becomes relevant as Augustine speaks of the renewal and "forming again" of the mind after the image of God: "This trinity, then, of the mind is not therefore the image of God because the mind remembers itself, and understands and loves itself; but because it can also remember, understand, and love him by whom it was made. And in so doing it is made wise itself. But if it does not do so, even when it remembers, understands, and loves itself, then it is foolish.

---

31. Ibid., 41.
32. Saint Augustine of Hippo, *A Treatise on Nature and Grace* (London: Aeterna Press, 2014), 16.
33. Saint Augustine of Hippo, *On the Trinity*, 10:12 (London: Aeterna Press, 2014), 454.

Let it then remember its God, after whose image it is made, and let it understand and love him."[34]

Love (*amor*) is a key integrating factor in Augustine's understanding of the *imago Dei*.[35] According to Dr. T. A. Noble, for Augustine, wisdom and foolishness are directly related to the way a person directs his or her love. Love is either directed to oneself or to the Creator. When love is directed to oneself, this motivational pattern is described as *concupiscentia*, but when the same faculty is redirected toward love of God and love of neighbour, it is *caritas*.[36] For Augustine, love was an essential part of what it means to be human. One can already see much commonality between Wynkoop and Augustine, in that they both have a "theology of love."

For Augustine, the renewal of the image of God was directly connected with the work of the Spirit in the renewing of the mind.[37] Augustine did sometimes speak of the "forming again" of the mind as a renewal of man's "likeness" with God. This distinction between "image" and "likeness" Wynkoop claimed Catholicism later picked up and emphasized.[38]

LUTHER AND CALVIN

Wynkoop was aware that the Reformers, for the most part, denied the probability of a difference in the meaning of "image" and "likeness."[39] They viewed these two concepts as synonyms, a Hebrew parallelism pointing to the same thing.[40] They merged these two concepts into one concept, namely "image," yet divided this single concept into two aspects, namely the necessary and accidental—or, the natural and moral. This was primarily because they believed in a unified personality and did not deal with man on the basis of certain faculties that are part of his nature.[41] It is significant to note that Wynkoop believed this distinction was based purely on philosophical

---

34. Saint Augustine of Hippo, *On the Trinity*, 14:12, ed. Paul A. Boer, Sr. (Online: Veritatis Splendor Publications, 2012), 646.
35. T. A. Noble, *Holy Trinity, Holy People: The Theology of Christian Perfecting* (Eugene, OR: Cascade Books, 2013), 110. [In Erich Przywara, *An Augustine Synthesis* (New York: Sheed and Ward, 1936), 33–44; Augustine, *Psalmus contra partem Donati* CXXII, 1 (*Nicene and Post-Nicene Fathers*, 1st ser., ed. Philip Schaff [1888; repr., Peabody, MA: Hendrickson Publishers, 1994], 8:593).]
36. Noble, *Holy Trinity*, 59. [Augustine, *Enarrationes in Psalmos* XXXI, ii.5 (*Corpus Christianorum, Series Latina*, 38.228).]
37. Augustine, *On the Trinity*, 14:16, ed. Paul A. Boer, Sr., 659.
38. Wynkoop, "The Biblical Study of Man," file 1432-3, WC, 8.
39. Ibid., 10.
40. Paul Ramsey, *Basic Christian Ethics* (Chicago: University of Chicago Press, 1980), 261.
41. Wynkoop, "The Biblical Study of Man," file 1432-3, WC, 10.

grounds without scriptural precedence.⁴² Both Luther and Calvin felt that as a result of the fall the image of God—and, with it, all goodness—was so far lost and gone that no possible human act or desire could be anything but evil. In his *Lectures on Genesis*, Luther said that since humans have lost the image, they could never know what it really was. So completely is this image lost, he thought, that even to speak of it is to speak of a thing unknown, inexperienced.⁴³ He does, however, speculate on what the image might have been. For Luther the image is this:

> "That Adam had it in his being and that he not only knew God and believed that he was good, but that he also lived a life that was wholly godly; that is, he was without the fear of death or of any other danger, and was content with God's favor." All of that was lost and would be fully restored only after Judgment Day. In its place had come death and the fear of death, blasphemy, hatred toward God, and lust. "These and similar evils are the image of the devil, who stamped them on us."⁴⁴

Here, Luther's picture of humanity is so dark that his perspective on the image of God leaves humanity in a totally passive state. Wynkoop realized that Calvin's position veered slightly from Luther, in that he made a distinction between the natural and moral images. He saw all the natural endowments in the natural image and spiritual qualities in the moral image. The whole image was defaced by sin, but only the spiritual qualities were entirely lost in the fall. But, so altered was fallen humanity in both of these views that actual righteousness could never be acquired in his human existence.⁴⁵ In Wynkoop's view, the implications of these views were far reaching. The slightest movement toward God had to be of God's own initiative with no possible cooperation from humans. This position, as far as Wynkoop was concerned, "led to an **imputation theory** of restoration, making actual righteousness impossible."⁴⁶

---

42. Ibid., 14.

43. Jaroslav Jan Pelikan, *The Christian Tradition: Reformation of Church and Dogma (1300—1700)*, vol. 4 of *The Christian Tradition: A History of the Development of Doctrine* (Chicago: University of Chicago Press, 1984), 142.

44. Ibid. [Luther, *Lectures on Genesis* 1:26, *D. Martin Luthers Werke* (Weimar, 1883), 42:47-48].

45. Wynkoop, "The Biblical Study of Man," file 1432-3, WC, 43. See also T. F. Torrance, *Calvin's Doctrine of Man* (Eugene, OR: Wipf and Stock, 1997).

46. Wynkoop, "The Biblical Study of Man," file 1432-3, WC, 32.

JOHN WESLEY ON THE IMAGE OF GOD

Wynkoop also differed on this from John Wesley, who reflected the Reformers when he related the impact of the fall on humanity. Reflecting on Genesis 1:26–27, Wesley explored the spiritual nature of Adam and Eve and affirmed that they were beings created in the image of God. The "image" was not primarily viewed as an inherent possession but, rather, humanity's capacity to stand before God in a living relationship called forth by divine grace.[47]

The image as a mirror, reflecting God, would be a good descriptive metaphor to describe Wesley's understanding of man's posture before God.[48] Wesley observes, "'God is love.' Accordingly, man at his creation was full of love; which was the sole principle of all his tempers, thoughts, words, and actions. God is full of justice, mercy, and truth; so was man as he came from the hands of his Creator. God is spotless purity; and so man was in the beginning pure from every sinful blot; otherwise God could not have pronounced him, as well as all the other work of his hands, 'very good' (Gen. 1:31)."[49]

Here Wesley took on a perspective reflected in the West in that he viewed man as being created perfect. Man was able to reflect God perfectly, yet Wesley observed that man "was not made **immutable**," but "created able to stand, and yet liable to fall."[50] Maddox affirms this position, giving us a comprehensive assessment of Wesley's position after looking at Wesley's sermons "The Image of God" and "The General Deliverance" as well as Wesley's *OT Notes* on Genesis 1:26–28. He concludes: "Wesley undeniably assumed (like the Western tradition) that humanity was created in an original state of complete perfection."[51]

When Wesley explored the image of God in greater detail, he did so along three major lines. He spoke of the natural image, the political image, and the moral image. In his sermon "The New Birth" on John 3:7, Wesley wrote, "Not barely in his *natural image*, a picture of his own immortality; a spiritual being, endued with understanding, freedom of will, and

---

47. Theodore Runyon, *The New Creation: John Wesley's Theology Today* (Nashville: Abingdon Press, 1998), 13.
48. Ibid.
49. John Wesley, Sermon 45, "The New Birth," in *Sermons II*, vol. 2 of *Bicentennial Works*, 188.
50. Ibid., 189.
51. Maddox, *Responsible Grace*, 67.

various affections; nor merely in his *political image*, the governor of this lower world, having 'dominion over the fishes of the sea, and over all the earth;' but chiefly in his *moral image;* which, according to the apostle, is 'righteousness and true holiness' (Eph. 4:24). In this image of God was man made."[52]

The natural image consisted of those endowments that made humans "capable of God." Since God is a Spirit, so, too, the image of God is spirit. Man's spiritual nature, as his natural image, is then endowed with understanding (reason), will, and freedom.[53] For Wesley, these capacities were not just capacities humanity possessed but capacities given as gifts from God, to enable human beings to carry out their calling to image and reflect their Creator.[54] According to Wynkoop, Wesley had more of a soteriological, rather than an anthropological, interest in the nature of man. She stated her view, "Wesley did not speculate about the 'image.' He was content to see man in terms of religion. His statements relative to the image usually were in reference to some factor in the saving procedure. We probably never find Wesley speaking of what man might be ontologically. That which is involved, then, in any discussion of the *imago Dei* in Wesley will be found to be a spiritual quality. The 'image' is a religious matter, not a substance matter."[55]

In terms of *understanding*, the first endowment of the natural image, Wesley viewed this as a human being's capacity to distinguish between right and wrong.[56] This capacity to understand was originally as perfect as it could be, in that a human being was able to apprehend all things clearly according to truth.[57] With the endowment of the *will*, Wesley had in mind those aspects of a person's spiritual nature that expressed his tempers and affections in harmony with his Creator.[58] Maddox indicates that Wesley did not speak of the will under the general categories of rational self-determination but, rather, equated the will with the affections. This, to Wesley, was the motivating disposition of a human being, which—at

---

52. Wesley, "The New Birth," *Works*, 2:189.
53. Kenneth J. Collins, *The Theology of John Wesley: Holy Love and the Shape of Grace* (Nashville: Abingdon Press, 2007), 52.
54. Runyon, *The New Creation*, 14.
55. Wynkoop, *A Theology of Love*, 106.
56. Collins, *Theology of John Wesley*, 52.
57. Ibid.
58. Ibid.

its deepest level—was expressed as a desire to love God with all of his heart.[59] The last endowment of *liberty* was added to the gifts of understanding and will so that humans can exercise their affections as habitual dispositions without rendering such actions as totally determined. Wesley was, therefore, aware that God created humans as responsible agents and took them seriously as genuine partners in which covenant relations can be established.[60] Love for God could then only arise and thrive in freedom, without which humans would merely be robots.[61]

The second aspect of the *imago Dei*, according to Wesley, the political image, reveals that humans are not only related to God and to one another but also to nature and to other creatures.[62] Here the idea of humans as stewards and caretakers of God's creation is at the heart of what Wesley meant.[63] It is primarily humans' role as partners, through which the blessings of God are reflected in human actions toward the rest of creation, that constitutes this aspect of the image.[64]

The third characteristic of the image of God is the moral image. Wesley spoke of man as being created in the natural and political image "but chiefly in the moral image." This is the chief mark of the human relationship to God but also the one most easily distorted.[65] The relational aspect of the image comes into sharp focus here as humans reflect the holy love of God. In his sermon "The End of Christ's Coming," Wesley spoke eschatologically of the purpose of Christ's coming, especially as manifested in the moral image of God: "As a free agent, he steadily chose whatever was good, according to the direction of his understanding. In so doing, he was unspeakably happy; dwelling in God, and God in him; having an uninterrupted fellowship with the Father and the Son, through the eternal Spirit; and the continual testimony of his conscience, that all his ways were good and acceptable to God."[66]

Wesley here gives us a picture of the human being who is created with the ability to orient his or her understanding and will (affections) around

---

59. Maddox, *Responsible Grace*, 69.
60. Collins, *Theology of John Wesley*, 53.
61. Ibid.
62. Ibid., 54.
63. Runyon, *The New Creation*, 17.
64. Ibid.
65. Ibid., 18.
66. John Wesley, Sermon 62, "The End of Christ's Coming," *Works*, 2:475.

the holy love of God. When the first humans use the powers of freedom, inherent in the natural image, to reflect the righteousness and love of God unassisted, we get a picture of what Wesley meant by the moral image. This is at the heart of what separated human beings from the beasts in the field: humans were capable of God.

Theodore Runyon postulates that the moral image could not have been a capacity within humanity or a function that can be employed independently of the Creator but, rather, a "relationship in which the creature receives continuously from the Creator and mediates further what is received."[67] This mutual receiving and reflecting between God and humans was a relationship of openness, welcoming the life of God and cooperating with God through obedience.[68] For Runyon, the moral image is then more descriptive of a relationship than a capacity *per se*. Collins, on the other hand, does not describe the moral image only as a relationship but also speaks of "*the seat* of holiness and love," as a basic predisposition in the constitution of human beings.[69]

Both scholars affirm Wesley's position that God created human beings in a dynamic relationship, endowing them with the power to choose and use their freedom either to orient their affections around God or around themselves. This meant that freedom and moral responsibility went hand in hand. Collins believes that Wesley connected the moral image with the moral law.[70] For Collins this means that original humanity was placed in a "valuational context," where there was structure that underlined the righteousness that God required as a basis for his relationship with humans.[71] The moral image is then to be seen as the "consequence of" or "the result of" the proper use of the powers of human beings' will and understanding, making possible a transparent reflection of God's holiness and righteousness. The natural image then becomes the base where moral responsibility is anchored and where either sinful or holy outcomes are made possible, all based on how human beings use their freedom.

According to Wesley, this perfect world and possibility for "spiritual respiration" all came crashing down when Adam and Eve chose to orient

---

67. Runyon, *The New Creation*, 18.
68. Ibid.
69. Collins, *Theology of John Wesley*, 63.
70. Ibid., 56.
71. Ibid., 57.

their affections around themselves and not around God. He describes the fall of humanity: "Accordingly, in that day he did die: He died to God, the most dreadful of all deaths. He lost the life of God. . . . He lost both the knowledge and the love of God, without which the image of God could not subsist. Of this, therefore, he was deprived at the same time, and became unholy as well as unhappy. In the room of this, he had sunk into pride and self-will, the very image of the devil."[72]

The extent to which the fall affected the Adamic *imago Dei* is so extensive that Wesley concluded that the moral image was completely lost. This loss to Wesley was not only a loss in relationship but also a dispositional change. The natural image, on the other hand, is not lost but is so corrupted that there is not much left for God to deal with. Wesley follows the Reformers in describing this condition: "The eyes of thine understanding are darkened . . . the affections are alienated from God, all thy passions, both thy desires and aversions, thy joys and sorrows, thy hopes and fears are out of frame."[73] This depravity encapsulates the whole man as he concludes: "from the crown of the head to the sole of the foot, there are only wounds and bruises and putrefying sores."[74] The final outcome of human beings' condition is, then, such that if human beings are to be redeemed it can only be as a result of the grace of God.

Wesley's distinctive understanding of God's restoring grace comes into sharpest focus in his doctrine of prevenient grace. It is the grace that "goes before," bringing attention to God's very first activity in fallen human lives. Wesley identified both pardon and power as benefits that come with prevenient grace.[75] The benefit of pardon is seen in the forgiveness of inherited guilt, which was part of Wesley's belief of inherited guilt from original sin.[76] The benefits of power are seen in the partial restoration of human beings' sin-corrupted faculties, just enough that they might sense the overtures of God's saving grace and respond to that offer.[77] This partial restoration is then once again targeted to human beings' under-

---

72. Wesley, "The New Birth," *Works*, 2:189.
73. John Wesley, Sermon 7, "The Way to the Kingdom," in *Sermons I*, vol. 1 of *Bicentennial Works*, 225–26.
74. Ibid., 226.
75. Maddox, *Responsible Grace*, 87.
76. Ibid.
77. Ibid.

standing, their liberty, and their will.[78] The partial restoration of faculties will become an important issue of disagreement between Wynkoop and Wesley's theologies.

Why Wynkoop Begged to Differ

Our evaluation of these historical positions in tandem with Wynkoop's points to fundamental differences between her and Wesley. The impression from Wesley's analysis of the *imago Dei* is that it was all or nothing. Wesley's portrayal of the movement from perfection to corruption is very Western in its outlook. Adam in his state of perfection before the fall either reflects perfectly, or he does not. There is no middle ground or room for growth or development. Wynkoop observed that Wesleyan theology followed the Reformers in their denial that there is a significant difference between "image" and "likeness." She wrote, "While denying the probability of a difference in the meaning of these two terms, they uniformly affirm that image must be conceived under two aspects, namely *essential* and *incidental* or *natural* and *moral*."[79]

To Wynkoop this denial cannot be sustained, since she clearly saw a progression in thought in the biblical Hebrew and Greek use of these terms. H. Orton Wiley also followed the Reformers in their understanding of the image of God. For him the natural or essential image was comprised of spirituality, knowledge, and immortality. The moral or incidental image "has to do with the rightness or wrongness in the use of" the powers represented in the natural image. The moral image was lost in the fall.[80] Wynkoop parts ways with Wiley since she believes that Wesleyan theology tried to maintain a distinction between the essential image and the accidental image, the natural and the moral, while at the same time denying the difference between them.[81] She wrote, "They have said that the image was lost and marred by sin, and restored in Christ but at the same time affirming that the image is **ineffaceable**. To preserve the dignity of man and his moral freedom on the one hand, and the total dependence on God for his salvation on the other, they have taken a position rather

---

78. Ibid., 88.
79. Wynkoop, "The Biblical Study of Man," file 1432-3, WC, 14.
80. Wiley, *Christian Theology*, 2:31–38.
81. Wynkoop, "The Biblical Study of Man," file 1432-3, WC, 44.

difficult to defend, namely, that part of an image was lost, another part retained, thereby separating constituent parts of man."[82]

Given these historical interpretations and her scriptural analysis, it is clear that Wynkoop wants to maintain a distinction between image and likeness, but she is also careful to note that image and likeness are not separate entities or faculties but, rather, two aspects of a single creation.[83] Wynkoop would be more comfortable to make a distinction between *actual* and *potential* rather than *essential* and *incidental*. The *actual* would include everything from self-consciousness to primitive righteousness with the *potential* referring to the adjustment and development required to maintain an integrated image.[84] She wrote, "It would be inaccurate to say either or both were lost in a primary sense. Can image describe a truly moral quality? Does not the very connotation of moral require a probationary choice, which the term image, as used in the Old and New Testaments, cannot sustain? Following the same reasoning, is not likeness more conformable to all that probation implies? Is it not fulfilment of God's original expectancy when he made man to be conformed to the image of his Son?"[85]

Wynkoop was convinced that the clear teaching of Scripture, from Genesis to Revelation, positions fallen humanity in a morally responsible relationship to God. She set out to argue from a basic premise that God's grace is universal, affording lost human beings the power to choose or reject God's provisions of salvation and healing. She wrote, "It is difficult to see how the New Testament can be intelligible apart from some measure of belief in real human freedom, extending beyond the change effected by the fall."[86] Giving weight to her statement, she called the biblical appeal to human conscience and the obedience required of the law as witnesses to the responsible nature of human beings.[87] She wrote:

> The function of conscience in those outside the province of special revelation and law is clearly stated in the first three chapters of Romans. It precedes law. It is as binding as law. Violation of it carries the same penalty as broken law. It, apparently, represents the moral

---
82. Ibid.
83. Ibid., 45.
84. Ibid.
85. Ibid.
86. Ibid., 49.
87. Ibid.

structure of righteousness, once active in Adam's inner nature. It remained in fallen man to approve or disapprove conduct in the light of objective standards of law. It must once have been the subjective "law written in the heart" which, because of the progressive degrading of human intelligence, volition and affection, was rendered less and less dependable as a guide to truth. Paul's frequent reference to a "good conscience" would strengthen this position. It is a factor of primal moral importance.[88]

The law also becomes a measure by which she is able to determine the capacity and potential of fallen humanity to reflect moral responsibility once again. Wynkoop confirms that the law was the structure of righteousness that was originally implicit in humanity's proper relationship to God.[89] Sin broke that fellowship by violating the law, the structure of righteousness. However, Wynkoop did not believe that the law, in and of itself, brought the separation between God and humanity.[90] In her view, human beings retained their capacity for fellowship but "marred the moral union essential to communication."[91] It was then human beings' moral nature set against the law of God that describes the nature of the position that they find themselves in after the fall. The law is the form of truth that fallen humans can understand, and therefore, personal responsibility through the law remains as a form of the truth they once sustained to God.[92]

Wynkoop called Paul's reflections in the early chapters of Romans a witness to the moral responsibility required of human beings:

Paul's solemn charge against both Jews and Gentiles as recorded in the first three chapters of Romans was on the basis of man's ability to understand and keep God's law. Even the heathen "held truth," and the indictment was that they held it in unrighteousness. He specifically said that they knew God but that they refuse to glorify him as such. They also knew the ordinance of God and the punitive sanctions involved and deliberately repudiated that which they knew, and delighted in their disobedience. No clearer statement can be made

---

88. Ibid., 50. Wynkoop here references Romans 1:18ff.; 2:12; 14—16; 1 Timothy 1:5, 19; and 2 Timothy 1:3 as support for her findings.
89. Wynkoop, "The Biblical Study of Man," file 1432-3, WC, 51.
90. Ibid.
91. Ibid.
92. Ibid., 52.

than the one in this passage, to the effect that Paul considered man a morally and emotionally responsible person, intellectually qualified to discharge that responsibility. If this were not true, God's wrath would be not only absurd but also immoral.[93]

Wynkoop's biblical research here helped her to understand that fallen humanity remains intellectually, volitionally, and morally responsible. There is not a law for the sinner and another for the Christian but only one law for all, with divine approval for those who keep it and divine condemnation for those who do not. Wynkoop concluded that the whole human person, which has in any way to do with him as a morally responsible agent, is preserved even in fallen humanity.[94] In all of her research in this field, Wynkoop did not find a single passage of Scripture that gave any hint that humanity was absolved from responsibility for sin because of the loss of any facet of personhood or moral sensitivity.[95] Wynkoop said, "If the image is lost so that man is totally depraved, then redemption must be in principle only, not in experience."[96]

Wynkoop clearly departed from Wesley, whose description of humanity's fallen position was more in line with the Reformers. Wesley's position does leave a puzzle, bringing with it tensions caused by contradictions in his position of the state of fallen humanity. Wynkoop was surprised to discover that Wesley believed fallen humans to be responsible, in spite of his description of humans being spiritually dead as they come into the world. She references Wesley's sermon "The Almost Christian," in which he describes the pre-Christian faith of a servant. "What is implied in being almost (a Christian)? First, heathen honesty . . . By the rules of this they were taught that they ought not to be unjust, etc. Again, the common heathens allowed, that some regard was to be paid to the truth as well as to justice. . . . Yet, again, there was a sort of love and assistance, which they expected one from another."[97]

And in referencing John Fletcher's *Third Check to Antinomianism*, Wynkoop shows Wesley making a difference between death and the different stages of spiritual life as the person ascends toward becoming an

---

93. Ibid., 53. Wynkoop here references Romans 1:18–20 and 32.
94. Wynkoop, "The Biblical Study of Man," file 1432-3, WC, 56.
95. Ibid.
96. Wynkoop, *A Theology of Love*, 147.
97. Wynkoop, "The Biblical Study of Man," file 1432-3, WC, 60.

adult in Christlikeness. Wynkoop believed that moral responsibility forms the backdrop behind these different degrees of growth:

> If you read the Scriptures without prejudice, you will see that there are several degrees of spiritual life, or quickening power. 1) The living "light which shines in the darkness" of every man during the day of his visitation. 2) The life of the returning sinner . . . 3) The life of the heathen, who like Cornelius, "fears God and works righteousness" according to his light . . . 4) The life of the pious Jew, who like Samuel, fears God from his youth . . . 5) The life of the feeble Christian . . . who is "baptized with water unto repentance" . . . 6) the still more abundant life of the adult or the perfect Christian.[98]

It seems that for Wesley the natural image continues to serve as the center for responsibility, even though it is severely distorted in the fall. The other possibility would be that Wesley is holding on to a partially restored moral image.

In summary, we can see that, for Wynkoop, "image" seems to refer to the experience of standing before God in responsible personhood. "Likeness" makes sense when the focus is on what humanity does with the experience of moral freedom. This brings us to a place where we ponder the mystery of grace and the promise of the image's renewal. It raises the question: How fully will this recovery be effected and when and in what manner?

The Redemption of Humanity

As we have seen, Augustine, influencing the West, believed that Adam and Eve were created in a complete and perfect state. As we now turn to Eastern thinkers to consider their contribution to this conversation, we find Wynkoop leaning toward the East, especially as she related the concept "likeness" with the ideas of "becoming" and "development." The theological implications of Wynkoop's thoughts on image and likeness show strong similarity with the **Greek fathers**. Reflecting on the nature of the *imago Dei*, she said, "The basic insight of the Patristic Fathers regarding the *imago Dei* is worthy of serious consideration."[99] To that she added, "The great Greek theologians taught that the image was something common to all men, continuing even after the fall. They said that the like-

---

98. Ibid.
99. Ibid., 6.

ness was something 'toward which man was created, that he might strive after it and attain it.'"[100] Wynkoop specifically referenced Irenaeus as a significant voice for the Eastern tradition, writing:

> Irenaeus's theology is the first really true Christian theology. His method as well as his content was Christian and a sound pattern for Christian theology today. . . . Especially important is his theory of "**recapitulation**" and the way he portrayed Jesus as living out the whole history of humanity. . . . Irenaeus attached fundamental importance to the incarnation and interpreted Christ's work as giving saving value to all parts of life as no one else did. Of particular importance is the way that he supplied a doctrinal basis for belief in the resurrection of the flesh.[101]

To illuminate Wynkoop's theological anthropology, we now consider a brief survey of Irenaeus's thought on the *imago Dei* as representative of one aspect of the Eastern views regarding fallenness.

IRENAEUS OF LYONS (CA. AD 140-202)

Irenaeus developed four concepts that underpinned his first comprehensive Christian theology. These concepts were the good mind of God (divine intellect), God's plan of salvation (divine economy), the summing up of all things in Christ (recapitulation), and the sharing of the believer in God's salvation (participation).[102] In the face of those Gnostics who divided the divine fullness into a multitude of **aeons**, Irenaeus insisted that God is one and three: one Father, one Son, and Holy Spirit.[103] Irenaeus put forth the idea of movement and progression over time as God creates humans and brings them to perfection.

In the middle of this historical motion stands Christ as the central vision for humanity.[104] Matthew C. Steenberg wrote, "The human race, which pre-dates the historical events of the birth, passion and resurrection of Christ, does not pre-date the one thus born, crucified and risen, but from the first to the last takes its reality from the one there seen and

---

100. Ibid., 24.
101. Wynkoop, "Irenaeus" (lecture, NTS, May 10, 1976), file 222-2, WC.
102. Eric Osborn, "Irenaeus of Lyons," in *The First Christian Theologians*, ed. G. R. Evans (Oxford: Blackwell Publishing Ltd., 2004), 122.
103. Ibid.
104. Matthew C. Steenberg, *Of God and Man: Theology as Anthropology from Irenaeus to Athanasius* (London: T&T Clark, 2009), 1.

touched, yet from all ages known."[105] Steenberg here helps us to see that Irenaeus had a particularly Christocentric reading of human creation. As he tried to assert himself against the heresies, Irenaeus was more inclined to exegete the creation of humanity from the Gospels, using Genesis as support rather than a foundation. It is then John 1:3, rather than Genesis 1:1, that became his key text.[106] The confession "that all things were made through him, and without him nothing was made" and "the Word who was with Father in the beginning" became the primary lens through which Irenaeus viewed earlier scriptures.[107]

In contrast to the Gnostics, who viewed matter as evil, Irenaeus emphasized the goodness of creation. This he did by showing that God forms humans (body and soul) out of mud with his two hands, which to Irenaeus represent the Son and the Spirit.[108] He said, "And therefore throughout all time, man, having been moulded at the beginning by the hands of God, that is, of the Son and of the Spirit, is made after the image and likeness of God."[109] The phrase "two hands of God" not only speaks of God's direct involvement in the creation of humanity but also gives us a beautiful picture of his divine embrace. The reason Irenaeus believed that we are created in the image of God is that humanity was fashioned out of mud after the pattern of the body of the incarnate Christ.[110] When the Spirit eventually glorifies our bodies with the same radiance of the glorified Christ, then we will come to be in the likeness of God as well.[111] Irenaeus directly connected one hand with image and the other with likeness.

Irenaeus also took the position that Adam was not created perfect but, rather, created as an infant in the image of God with the intent to come to be in the likeness of God at the end of a process of development.[112] The point is not physical, but moral, childhood. Adam is described as "a little one," "a child" who had "his discretion still undeveloped."[113] So, even

---

105. Ibid.
106. Ibid., 27.
107. Ibid.
108. Eric Osborn, *Irenaeus of Lyons* (Cambridge: Cambridge University Press, 2001), 91.
109. Philip Schaff, *Ante-Nicene Fathers* (Online: Christian Classics Ethereal Library), I:28, 557.
110. Denis Minns, *Irenaeus: An Introduction* (London: Geoffrey Chapman, 1994), 60.
111. Ibid.
112. Ibid., 61.
113. Mary Ann Donovan, *One Right Reading? A Guide to Irenaeus* (Collegeville, MN: Liturgical Press, 1997), 132.

though Adam was created in the beginning in the image of God, Irenaeus anticipated Adam to grow toward the likeness of God.[114]

When Irenaeus quoted Genesis 1:26–27, he had in mind, not just the modelling of humans from mud but a creative act that would embrace the whole of salvation history.[115] Once again, even a close reading of Genesis 2:7 is read from the perspective of the incarnation. Steenberg says, "It is the same Jesus who spat into the dust and by the mud healed the man born blind (cf. John 9:1–12) who at the dawn of creation took up the dust to fashion humanity."[116]

The key concept is the continuity between Christ and Adam. This continuity is again connected with the incarnation. Denis Minns says that, for Irenaeus, "Christ's flesh must be Adam's flesh, for only so can Christ be the 'head' of those who have their 'head' in Adam. That Christ's flesh is Adam's flesh, is guaranteed for Irenaeus, by the virgin birth. Adam was formed from earth before it had been tilled; Christ was formed from the flesh of Mary without any male intervention. Moreover, because she was herself a descendant of Adam, the flesh from which Christ was formed, was one with Adam's flesh."[117] The idea here is that God became what we are so that we can become what God is.[118] God is, in Christ, reconciling the world to himself with special emphasis on the cross. He is our redeemer who, with true flesh and blood, summed up in himself the ancient formation of Adam.[119]

It is also important to note that Irenaeus identified freedom of choice with the first sense of human likeness to God. Mary Donovan points out that, for Irenaeus, "human beings are free to do good or evil, to believe or not, and even 'to accept or to refuse that gift of the Spirit which is the likeness (*homoiōsis*), which alone is able to make [the human person] pursue conduct pleasing to God.'"[120] With freedom also comes moral responsibility. This is the case Irenaeus made. Adam was weak, incomplete, a moral infant, possessing by the Spirit a likeness to God that he lost through disobedience. Yet Adam stayed in the hands of God as the Spirit

---

114. Minns, *Irenaeus*, 61.
115. Ibid.
116. Steenberg, *Of God and Man*, 27.
117. Minns, *Irenaeus*, 88.
118. Osborn, *Irenaeus*, 103.
119. Ibid.
120. Donovan, *One Right Reading?*, 134.

communicated the life of Christ to bring about renewal and liberation. Osborn says, "The likeness in Adam is extended rather than replaced, including his freedom of choice. Within the divine economy, there is no separation between creation and salvation. Christ comes to complete that perfection to which creation was called."[121] For Irenaeus, participation was the defining factor of the life that will grow into eternity.

WYNKOOP

Even though Wynkoop arrived at her theological conclusions through her own biblical exegetical work, it is interesting to see how Irenaeus's ideas on the *imago Dei* are reflected in her theological anthropology. When Wynkoop sought New Testament passages to substantiate the theory that humanity is restored to the image of God, she could not find any.[122] What she did find were particular references to Christ: Christ is "the image of God" (2 Cor. 4:4, KJV); Christ is "the image of the invisible God, the firstborn over [all creation]" (Col. 1:15, KJV); human beings are to be "conformed to the image of [God's] Son" (Rom. 8:29, KJV) and "renewed in knowledge after the image of him who created them" (Col. 3:10, KJV). Those who behold "the glory of the Lord . . . are changed into the same image from glory to glory" (2 Cor. 3:18, KJV).[123] Wynkoop concluded that the New Testament seemed to point to Christ as God's image, as the prototype for the "new man" that redemption proposes. She referenced the "new man" created in Christ Jesus (Eph. 4:24, KJV), who is to partake of "the divine nature" (2 Pet. 1:4, KJV), and then concluded, "It is in this realm of likeness, representing as it has been shown to do, the moral capacity of men that grace operates. The entire New Testament message stresses a moral likeness to Christ as the purpose implicit in creation, as the goal of redemption, and as the test of Christian experience."[124]

Wynkoop was particularly interested to bring to light the correlation between the ideas of "sonship" and "likeness" as a process for redemption.

Interrelationship of Father and Son to the Human Race

Wynkoop invited us to go back to the Genesis record, where God purposed to make humans in his image and likeness, and brought our atten-

---

121. Osborn, *Irenaeus*, 216.
122. Wynkoop, "The Biblical Study of Man," file 1432-3, WC, 110.
123. Ibid.
124. Ibid., 111.

tion to the fact that, in the accomplishment of his purpose, only the image was created. It appeared to Wynkoop that "likeness" was left in question. Rather than seeking to resolve the "likeness omission question" within the Old Testament context, Wynkoop looked to the New Testament for clues to unpack this theological puzzle, leading her to the following proposition:

> Because of the fact that in the creation account the likeness of God in men was left an open question, and because Adam was never called the son of God, and because Paul, in Romans, said that the original purpose of God was that men were to be conformed to the image of his Son, and in the Ephesian letter said that they were predestined to the adoption of sons through Jesus Christ, the writer is of the opinion that Adam's probation should have culminated in sonship. This would have consummated the creation purposes of God. Adam's failure robbed him of all probationary rights and possibilities. It cut him off from the life of God. The purpose and function of grace is then to restore men to the level of probation and hence to the possibility of sonship as originally intended.[125]

Wynkoop referenced John 1:12–13, where John says that those who had received the "light" and who had been born of God were not thereby made sons but were given the "power to become the sons of God" (v. 12, KJV).[126] Wynkoop also found confirmation in the distinction Paul makes between servants and sons in Romans 8:15 and Galatians 4:1–7.[127] She continued to unfold her case: "If men were predestined to the adoption of sons and to be conformed to the image of God's Son, it is evident that there is some vital relationship between Christ as Son of God and the race of men, and that that relationship is involved in the redemptive process."[128]   Wynkoop here wanted to establish that redemption centres foremost in Christ as the image of God and that it is to the image of Christ, and not a lost and restored image of God, that believers are to be conformed.[129]

The Father-Son relationship within the Godhead, then, has a direct bearing upon the matter under consideration. Wynkoop said:

---

125. Ibid., 112. Wynkoop here quotes Ephesians 1:5 and Romans 8:29.
126. Ibid., 113.
127. Ibid., 114.
128. Ibid., 115.
129. Ibid., 116.

God, as Father, who proposed sonship in men, could only be revealed by the Son. To be eternally Father, Christ must be eternally Son. This relationship is unique. No other person is Son as the second person of the Godhead is to the Father. . . . In creating man in the image of God and later revealing that the second person of the Godhead was the Son, in an eternal relationship, it is clearly seen that something of the capacity for sonship must be in the constituent nature of man.[130]

Using Robert B. Girdlestone's *Synonyms of the Old Testament*, Wynkoop discovered that the word "likeness," not "image," described the manner in which Christ took the form of man.[131] Affirming Girdlestone's work, Wynkoop quoted Romans 8:3, where Paul talks about God "sending his own Son in the likeness of sinful flesh," and Philippians 2:7, where Paul describes Christ as taking on the form of a servant who was "made in human likeness." These texts revealed to Wynkoop that "the Son *is* the image of God, and that he is not *made* in the image, and is, therefore, the firstborn of all creation."[132] The implications are that Christ's participation with the human race is under terms of *likeness*, and this is also to be the relationship of the race to him.[133] Using Richard Trench's *Synonyms of the New Testament*, Wynkoop further realized that this likeness is "the likeness of *schema*, or outward appearance, rather than *morphe*, which indicates the more fundamental character which was to be man's relationship to him."[134] The reason Paul said that men and women were to be conformed to the image of God's Son now becomes evident. Wynkoop said, "Having been made in his image, metaphysically, men are obligated to become like him ethically, in his moral lineaments as revealed in his perfect sonship."[135]

The Moral Basis of Sonship

The heart of Wynkoop's argument was that there has to be a moral basis for sonship. It cannot be on the basis of nationality, as in being part of the Jewish race:

---

130. Ibid., 117.
131. Ibid.
132. Ibid.
133. Ibid., 118.
134. Ibid.
135. Ibid.

If the relationship of Father and Son is intrinsic to the Trinity, whose image man bears, something of that same capacity must be a part of the moral capacity of man. The Son, in this eternal relationship, must be, then, the moral prototype toward which moral probation was designed and toward which men were to be conformed by the filial obedience of free love. . . . As the Son is to the Father, so men have been given the capacity of becoming, and to this end moral probation exists.[136]

Wynkoop described the terms of sonship as Christ "coming to his own," to those whose prototype he was. He came under the terms of human probation by tasting death for every man, being tempted in all points like as we are and thereby providing within himself a way back to God.[137] Jesus then shows us the moral basis for sonship. Wynkoop saw the process of ascending to the adoption as sons strikingly set forth in Hebrews 2:10: "For it became him, for whom are all things, and by whom are all things, in bringing many sons unto glory, to make the captain of their salvation perfect through sufferings" (KJV).[138] It is at this point that the full significance of Wynkoop's distinction between image and likeness appears. There is an important difference between image as constituent equipment, which identifies human beings as human, and the disposition human beings make of their powers.[139] The "new human being," the human being "created in Christ Jesus," is not a human new in any metaphysical sense. The human being did not lose anything of his metaphysical image in the fall. He is to have no new image, in that sense, in redemption.[140] It was important for Wynkoop to stress the ethical nature of this union with Christ. Human beings can "possess the mind of Christ," be moulded into the image of Christ, but this union is not to be thought of in a metaphysical way, as in a "blending" in which both parties lose their unique identities.

The basis for Wynkoop's proposition now comes to its climax. Wynkoop believed that Adam was placed under probation for the purpose of moral testing to validate his character. But Adam failed. God's response to this failure is a response of grace that not only provides redemption

---

136. Ibid., 120.
137. Ibid., 122.
138. Ibid.
139. Ibid., 123.
140. Ibid.

but also extends the term of probation to cover the possibilities originally intended by God for human beings. Wynkoop brought three scriptures together to illustrate the purpose of God's redemption: "God chose you from the beginning unto salvation in sanctification of the Spirit and belief of the truth. (II Thessalonians 2:13) God chose us in him before the foundation of the world, that we should be holy and without blemish before him in love; having foreordained us unto adoption as sons . . . (Ephesians 1:4–5) whom he foreknew, he also foreordained to be conformed to the image of his Son. (Romans 8:29)"[141]

As Wynkoop saw it, these passages reflect the three eternal goals for humanity—namely sanctification, sonship by adoption, and conformation to the image of the Son.[142] The first of these goals is what Adam had in his grasp but forfeited by believing the lie. Wynkoop postulated that the whole redemptive scheme is centred on the task of raising humans to this level again in order that the original purpose could be realized.[143]

Wynkoop would then view humanity as being created in the image of God. We are to be conformed to the image of God's Son, and within these two statements lie the distinction and difference between image and likeness and the basic moral purpose of humanity's creation. She wrote, "God's minimal line for man must not be forgotten, namely that we should be holy and without blemish before him in love. From that line man fell and to that line again all redemption is directed. But this moral relationship is but the beginning, not the end of man's existence. From this line upward to the measure of the fullness of the stature of Christ, is the purpose for which man was made" (see Eph. 4:13; 5:27, KJV).[144]

Placing Irenaeus and Wynkoop side by side brings illumination to Wynkoop's position. It is clear that she related more to the East than to the West on this point. We can see that the themes of the economy of salvation, recapitulation, and participation were present in both theologians. What stands out in reading Irenaeus and Wynkoop is their Christocentric reading of human creation. Both use the New Testament as their primary resource in describing the *imago Dei*. Both make a distinction between

---

141. Ibid., 147. Scripture quotations are Wynkoop's partial paraphrases from the KJV and, for Rom. 8:29, from the RSV.
142. Ibid.
143. Ibid.
144. Ibid., 156.

the "image of God" and the "likeness of God." Whereas the "image" denotes the human potential for life in God, the "likeness" opens the door for the progressive realization of that potentiality. Initially, it would appear that Irenaeus placed more emphasis on the work of the Holy Spirit in the historical appropriation of the two hands of God. However, as will be shown later, Wynkoop showed her hand (the focus on the Holy Spirit) very strongly.

Irenaeus and Wynkoop also based their anthropology more on creation, since in their view humans did not lose their ability to cooperate with God after the fall. Since humanity continues in the hands of God, "human freedom" as a characteristic of "likeness" thus remains, even after the fall. For both Wynkoop and Irenaeus, "human freedom" is not to be seen through the lens of humanism but, rather, as God's grace assisting the human will through his embrace, all the way from the beginning of creation, through the time of probation, and continuing after the fall toward the goal of Christ*likeness*. The potential for the human will to be freed to cooperate with the Holy Spirit is thus always present. However, as was shown by both Irenaeus and Wynkoop, human beings continue to use this freedom to rebel, or attempt to remove themselves from the hands of God.

Wynkoop and Irenaeus also showed similarity when it came to the use of the idea of "participation." We will later encounter Wynkoop describing "entire sanctification" in relational language as a journey of "full participation" with the Holy Spirit in his work of re-creation.

Wynkoop's position was that moral probation existed before the fall and moral probation continues to exist after the fall. Since "likeness" is found in the realm of human personhood where moral probation operates, the potentiality for "likeness" remains, even in fallen humanity. Grace, then, does not have to re-create or restore the moral disposition of humanity but, rather, operates to renew or redirect the disposition that remained intact. Given the availability of grace, the verdict is not that humanity *could* not believe but that humanity *would* not believe.

Back to Wesley

Wesley's trajectory of growth in the movement from a child to an adolescent and eventually to an adult shows similar patterns of development and growth as is seen in the theological anthropology of Wynkoop.

This is so in spite of the fact that there is strong disagreement between Wesley and Wynkoop on the content of the "image," and the condition of humanity after the fall. For Wynkoop, probation starts before the fall; for Wesley, probation begins after the fall as humanity encounters God's free enabling grace as stages in the way. Wesley's concept of the renewal of the image of God expands beyond the initial offerings of what the image consisted of in humanity's original condition before the fall. Postulating the renewal of the image with its end goal as Christlikeness, Wesley now speaks of the image of God as love and righteousness.

Wynkoop brings our attention to Wesley's sermon, "Upon our Lord's Sermon on the Mount." Here Wesley says, "Righteousness, as was observed before, is the image of God, the mind which was in Christ Jesus. It is every holy and heavenly temper in one; springing from, as well as terminating in, the love of God, as our Father and Redeemer, and the love of all men for his sake."[145] In Wesley's sermon "The New Birth," Wesley speaks of the renewal of the image not as humanity trying to go back to where Adam was before the fall but as a renewal pointing forward to Christ, who is the image. Wesley says, "Gospel holiness is no less than the image of God stamped upon the heart; it is no other than the whole mind which was in Christ Jesus; it consists of all heavenly affections and tempers mingled together in one."[146] In a word, holiness was to Wesley the renewal of the image of God. That image was love characterized by Christlikeness.

The influence of Wesley on Wynkoop can be seen more in the bigger themes of Wesley's "open-ended thinking," his foresight, and his teleological approach to the economy of salvation.[147] Wynkoop references Wesley's sermon "The Single Eye," which serves as an example of the teleology implicit in Wesley's dynamic concepts of man and salvation. Here humans are postulated as beings who "aim," either toward God or away from God.[148] Wynkoop quotes Wesley saying, "And, walking in this light, he cannot but 'grow in grace, and in the knowledge of our Lord Jesus Christ.' He will continually advance in all holiness, and in the whole image of God."[149] Given the trajectory of the Greek fathers, who saw "likeness" as

---

145. Wynkoop, *A Theology of Love*, 108.
146. Wesley, "The New Birth," *Works*, 2:194.
147. Wynkoop, *A Theology of Love*, 65–70.
148. Ibid., 70.
149. Ibid.

something "toward which man was created," one can conclude that Wynkoop and Wesley are in agreement, especially on humanity after the fall. The following themes were highlighted by Wynkoop to show the basis for her common position with Wesley: "(1) That God made man unfinished;[150] (2) that man is involved in the finishing process; (3) that the finishing is a process; (4) that God has furnished the material for the task; (5) that finishing is not something implanted in man apart from his activity in respect of it; (6) that holiness is dynamic and is the way and the goal of the restoration of and development in the whole image of God."[151]

---

150. Here I am uncertain about what Wynkoop means, since she believed Wesley took the position that Adam was created perfect.
151. Wynkoop, *A Theology of Love*, 70.

Wynkoop at age sixteen.

Seated, Carl and Mary; *on the back row, from right to left*, Mildred followed by Bernice, Thelma, Florence, and, *in the center*, Olive and Carl Jr.

Ralph and Mildred on the occasion of Mildred's graduation.

Tying the knot, December 27, 1928.

Sign speaks for itself.

Mildred in her late forties.

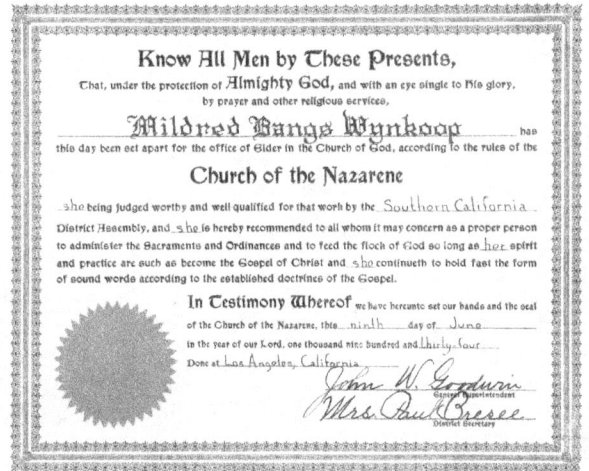

Mildred's ordination certificate.

Ralph and Mildred, travelling evangelists.

Mildred teaching theology in Taiwan.

Mildred in her study, Trevecca Nazarene University.

First published monograph, 1967.

Mildred in Japan.

Mildred teaching through an interpreter.

Mildred with the camera the students gave her as a gift before she left for Japan.

Mildred in her early seventies.

Mildred speaking at Trevecca Nazarene University.

Ralph, full-time evangelist.

Mildred with her brother, Carl, who was, at that time, considered the leading scholar on Arminius.

5
THE DIVINE-HUMAN INTERACTION

• • •

Christ as the "living Word" and Christ as the "image" became important building blocks in the way Wynkoop constructed her existential theology. The practical significance of the "living Word" becoming flesh and living among us, calling for humanity's renewal in the image of Christ, was at the heart of Wynkoop's exploration. These key theological concepts set the table for us to take a deeper look into the presuppositions of Wynkoop's anthropology. As we have seen, Wynkoop based her anthropology more on creation and believes that humanity did not lose its ability to respond to God after the fall.

Wynkoop inherited significant shifts that were taking place in the early twentieth century. At the time that Wynkoop was a student at Pasadena College in the late 1920s, several theological shifts were underway in the American Holiness Movement and American Methodism as a whole. Robert E. Chiles describes these shifts coming in three waves: (1) from revelation to reason; (2) from sinful man to moral man; and (3) from **free grace** to free will.[1] The question that we then have to ask is, to what extent did these streams influence Wynkoop? We have already addressed the first shift and have shown that, for Wynkoop, the movement was from revelation to reason. The remaining two shifts now need our evaluation to see how the scales tilted in Wynkoop's theology. Does the fact that Wynkoop believed that humanity did not lose its ability to cooperate with God after the fall tilt the scales toward an emphasis on free will? In order for us to understand the religious environment in which Wynkoop formulated

---

1. Robert E. Chiles, *Theological Transition in American Methodism: 1790–1935* (New York: Abingdon, 1965), 175.

the philosophical underpinnings of her theology, we will look at the early-twentieth-century American Holiness Movement's understanding of the divine-human interaction. What influence did Wesley's understanding of free grace have on the religious environment of revivals and the way people were encouraged to appropriate the grace of God?

"Free Grace" or "Free Will" in the American Holiness Movement

According to Wynkoop, in Western Christianity the relationship between God and humanity in soteriology has been generally understood in terms of one of two sharply differing positions first formulated by Augustine (AD 354—430) and Pelagius (AD 409) in their famous fifth-century controversy.[2] The key question, as Wynkoop formulated it, is the age-old question raised between Augustine and Pelagius over the priority of God's sovereign will versus humanity's free will. The solution that gives the priority to God's action in the salvation drama is generally categorized as Augustinian, and the solution that posits freedom of response in humans is usually termed Pelagian.[3] In opposition to Augustine, Pelagius took the position that humanity does not inherit a sinful condition but basically acquires sin from the bad examples of the human race. Human beings are therefore born free, as Adam was free, and can choose either good or evil.[4] This freedom is absolute, meaning that the human will does not need assistance to respond in a responsible manner. Bassett says, "Practically what [Pelagius] was committed to was a confidence that the human will was created capable of choosing good or evil and that while the Fall had corrupted the functioning of that will and the world in which it functions, it had not corrupted the basic character of the will itself. . . . Pelagius believed that the human being lives in a world that is morally fallen but that the individual's participation in that fallenness is up to the individual."[5]

This sounds very similar to Wynkoop's position, yet closer investigation shows that there are major differences between Pelagius and Wynkoop. Wynkoop would agree with Pelagius that human beings did not lose their disposition after the fall to stand in a responsible relationship

---

2. Wynkoop, *Foundations of Wesleyan-Arminian Theology*, 25–27.
3. Wynkoop, *A Theology of Love*, 209.
4. Wynkoop, *Foundations of Wesleyan-Arminian Theology*, 25.
5. Bassett, *Exploring Christian Holiness*, 2:101 [Augustine, *De gratia Christi (On the Grace of Christ)*, 1.17].

with God, but she parted ways with Pelagius because she would anchor the possibility of an obedient response to God not in humanity's natural ability but in the enabling power of God's grace. For Pelagius, grace as a cause is unnecessary to move the will toward God, yet we see Pelagius not hesitating to reference the grace of God, even insisting that without it no one can win eternal life.[6] Closer scrutiny led Wynkoop to conclude that Pelagius understood grace to operate in a completely different way than was seen in the theology of Augustine. For Pelagius grace is manifested in God's endowing humanity with free will, reason, and conscience. Wynkoop said, "Pelagius meant by divine grace, not some indwelling divine power or substance, but instruction and enlightenment."[7] According to Bassett, for Augustine it was not so much that the individual participates *in* the fallenness of the world, but the individual *is* the fallenness of the world.[8] Bassett continues, "Augustine believed that experience shows us that humankind, having rebelled against God, is a mass or heap of sin. It cannot bring itself to goodness, it cannot return to God on its own strength . . . so, if human beings are to be saved, the process of salvation must begin outside of them."[9] Grace, for Augustine, is the primary cause to move the will toward God.

In this controversy, some scholars in the Holiness Movement thought Augustine made too much of God's sovereignty and Pelagius made too much of the natural ability of humanity. Wynkoop wrote:

> It should be noted that Pelagius and Augustine were each attempting to preserve valid truths. Pelagius was concerned about preserving human dignity and moral responsibility, which was necessary and proper to do. Augustine wanted to preserve the absolute sovereignty of God and the absolute need for his grace in relation to salvation, which was also right. But in the tension of controversy a false antithesis was forced between these two points of view. Each man, in overemphasizing his truth, tended to lose the opposite correcting or complementary truth. Pelagius lost the need for God's grace and Augustine lost the concept of true moral responsibility.[10]

---

6. Wynkoop, *A Theology of Love*, 26.
7. Wynkoop, *Foundations of Wesleyan-Arminian Theology*, 26.
8. Bassett, *Exploring Christian Holiness*, 102.
9. Ibid.
10. Wynkoop, "Protestant Theology and the *Imago Dei*," file 1432-7, WC, 2.

In the midst of these two opposite poles represented by Augustine and Pelagius, she placed Wesley with a position that has been called the *via media*. In Wynkoop's view, Wesley held these two doctrines together (human inability and personal responsibility) without falling into either the Augustinian or Pelagian camp. Wesley insists that human beings cannot move themselves to God, being entirely dependent on God's enabling grace; but he also argues that they are responsible before God for their own salvation, being free to receive or reject Christ. Wynkoop thought Wesley understood that, for Arminius, Christ is the elect man first, before individuals, and saw Arminius's view as a major corrective of Calvinism's errors.[11] Wynkoop wrote, "Arminius's view of predestination understood God's grace as strengthening moral life rather than weakening it. Grace was not an arbitrary imposition of the will of God on passive people. Grace is not an arbitrary divine cause, but the free gift of God's enablement."[12]

For Wesley, salvation is the "entire work of God." As Chiles observes, this means it is the whole work of God, grace "reaching back into man's life prior to salvation and forward to bring salvation to fulfilment."[13] Chiles brings our attention to Wesley's sermon on "Free Grace," wherein Wesley makes reference to the grace of God being "free in all" and "free for all."[14] In this sermon Wesley says, "Whatsoever good is in man, or is done by man, God is the author and doer of it."[15] It also means that every human being receives God's gift of prevenient grace, which "waiteth not for the call" of any man, but is universally given.[16] As Collins sees it, as an initial gift, prevenient grace is irresistible; especially when it is connected to the graciously restored faculties, it cannot be refused.[17] As we have seen, Wynkoop took the position that humanity's disposition to stand responsibly before God after the fall remained intact, which indicates an irresistible manifestation of prevenient grace.

Chiles refers to Wesley's sermon "On Working Out Our Own Salvation," where Wesley writes, "First. We are to observe that great and im-

---

11. Ibid., 6.
12. Ibid., 5.
13. Chiles, *Theological Transition in American Methodism*, 30.
14. Ibid., 148.
15. Ibid., 149.
16. Ibid.
17. Kenneth J. Collins, *The Scripture Way of Salvation: The Heart of John Wesley's Theology* (Nashville: Abingdon Press, 1997), 44.

portant truth which ought never to be out of our remembrance: 'It is God that worketh in us both to will and to do of his good pleasure.' The meaning of these words may be made more plain by a small transposition of them: 'It is God that of his good pleasure worketh in you both to will and to do.'"[18] The sermon actually has two points: "First, God works, therefore, you *can* work. Second, God works, therefore you *must* work."[19] Here we get the picture that humans share responsibility in their own salvation, not by nature, but by grace. Wesley avoids Pelagianism because the initiative in the process of salvation is from God, who invites response.[20] It is in this way that theologians arrive at a synergistic interpretation of Wesley.

Having established this foundation, we are now left with the task of discerning how well Wesley's understanding of free grace held together as this doctrine crossed the Atlantic and landed on American soil. And more particularly, how is Wesley's understanding of free grace interpreted in the Holiness Movement and specifically in Wynkoop's theology?

Daniel Berg, in his article "The Theological Context of American Wesleyanism," gets to the heart of the question of this divine-human interaction. He asks, "Given that grace does not coerce nevertheless enables, how does an 'uncoerced will' differ from a 'free will?'"[21] It is Berg's suspicion that the Wesleyan version of "free grace instead of free will," as expressed in the American context, has taken on a synergistic flavour with emphasis on the native ability of human beings.[22] When we follow some of the main influencers of Methodist theology in America, there seems to be a slippery slope away from Wesley's position on free grace. By the time we move from Richard Watson (1781—1833) to John Miley (1813—1895) and then to Albert Knudson (1873—1953),[23] the American frontier is singing songs of free will with gusto around the campgrounds of Methodism.

---

18. Chiles, *Theological Transition in American Methodism*, 150.
19. Ibid.
20. Collins, *The Scripture Way of Salvation*, 44.
21. Daniel Berg, "The Theological Context of American Wesleyanism," *WTJ* 20:1 (1985): 5.
22. Ibid.
23. Richard Watson is the first important systematic theologian among Wesley's heirs. His most important writing is his opus, *Theological Institutes*, which was the standard text for the course of study from 1825 until 1876. John Miley is the second representative American Methodist theologian. As a professor of theology at Drew Theological Seminary from 1873 until his death, his two-volume *Systematic Theology* was his most noted work. Albert Knudson is the theological representative for the first third of the twentieth century, during which time American Methodism started to emphasize personal idealism. The decisive figure in this

Chiles argues that, for Richard Watson, prevenient grace does not override man's freedom. For Watson grace works by persuasion, not by coercion, and good desires produced by the Holy Spirit may be resisted.[24] Watson insists that we cannot repent without the grace of God, yet he also affirms that repentance cannot be willed for human beings without their consent.[25] Chiles argues that with John Miley, the conversation shifts from God's grace as the primary actor in the process of salvation to an emphasis on the rational character of choice.[26] Prevenient grace is given a very limited place in his overall *ordo salutis* as he makes free agency the governing doctrine. Grace is set in the context of freedom, and thus we see a complete reversal of the classical Wesleyan and Reformation principle of *sola gratia*.[27] This quotation from Miley says it all, "For the question of moral freedom, it is indifferent whether this capacity be native or gracious."[28]

The sobering reality is that these transitions in Methodist circles also created a ripple effect in the theology of the Holiness Movement. The shift from free grace to free will can be seen in microcosm on the campus of Pasadena Nazarene College through the work of theologians like H. Orton Wiley and A. M. Hills. It is important to note that Wynkoop was a reader for both of these theologians and helped proofread their work while she was a student at Pasadena College.[29] These theologians are representative of two streams already detectable in the early twentieth century in the Church of the Nazarene. As early as 1919, a formal request by the General Department of Education was made to H. Orton Wiley to write a full-range systematic theology. It would take Wiley twenty years to deliver on this commitment. In the meantime, A. M. Hills wrote his own systematic theology while a member of the faculty at Pasadena College and published it in 1931 under the title *Fundamental Christian Theology*, nine years earlier than Wiley's three-volume *Christian Theolo-*

---

development was Borden Parker Bowne, but Knudson drew the implications of personalist philosophy into a theological system. Knudson taught at Boston, and some of his works appear on the study list from 1916 until 1948. His treatment of systematic theology in *The Doctrine of God* and *The Doctrine of Redemption* is his most important work (Chiles, *Theological Transition in American Methodism*, 33–35).

24. Chiles, *Theological Transition in American Methodism*, 160.
25. Ibid., 163.
26. Ibid., 170.
27. Paul M. Bassett, "A Study in the Theology of the Early Holiness Movement," *Methodist History* (April 1975): 64.
28. Chiles, *Theological Transition in American Methodism*, 171.
29. Wynkoop, "My Life—1961" (article, 1992), file 2223-24, WC.

gy.³⁰ Because Wiley's work was not finished and a systematic theology was needed, Hills's books were listed in the course of study during the years 1932—1940.³¹ Hills and Wiley took opposite sides in their whole approach to theology and their interpretation of holiness. Hills was a well-known preacher throughout the Holiness Movement, who was first to the press with a systematic theology, even though his theology did not end up as the official theology of the church.³² During those eight years from 1932 to 1940, because Hills's book had been in the course of study, a position on holiness was propagated that eventually would prove to have been against the Nazarene position. Wynkoop found herself caught in this riptide between Wiley and Hills, not only on campus but also as she travelled with her husband as an evangelist in the Church of the Nazarene.³³ The important question confronts us: What made the theologies of Hills and Wiley different?

Placing these theologies side by side helps us to detect the shifts as indicated by Chiles. This shift from revelation to reason is especially evident in the work of Hills, who unknowingly contributed to the infiltration of fundamentalism into the Church of the Nazarene. Hills came into the Church of the Nazarene from the Congregationalists. He had studied under Finney and Fairchild at Oberlin and in the Divinity School at Yale under Timothy Dwight.³⁴ By his own admission, his primary focus was on combatting the errors of Calvinism, by which he meant the predestinarian views of such men as Charles Hodge and the declarations of the Synod of Dort.³⁵ In Hills's efforts to reject the doctrinal rigidities of Dortian Calvinism, according to Paul M. Bassett, he at the same time unknowingly used the methodological presuppositions of that same orthodoxy, as propagated by the inerrancy movement from Princeton.³⁶ Bassett says, "Hills carried his non-Calvinistic emphasis on human freedom on vehicles supplied by a very Calvinistic understanding of the role of reason in theologizing, and a Calvinistic understanding of the authority and role

---

30. Bassett, "A Study," 64.
31. Wynkoop, "Foundations," file 2227-11, WC, 6.
32. Ibid.
33. Ibid.
34. Bassett, "A Study," 65.
35. Ibid.
36. Ibid.

of Scripture in the same process."[37] The great irony is that Hills's identification with Finney's Pelagian focus on free will placed him at odds with the fundamental Wesleyan doctrines of prevenient grace. In his efforts to show the truth of the doctrine of free moral agency, as over and against predestination, "he was blind to the fact that he had in large part been converted to Princetonian Calvinism at the point of its confidence in the theological potency of reason."[38]

Wynkoop presented a paper, "The Foundations of *A Theology of Love*," on June 3, 1975, to the pastors of the Nazarene Florida district. What speaks volumes is her handwritten note in the margins of this paper. As she reflected on the theology of free grace in Wesley and Wiley, she wrote: "This is my position."[39] Wynkoop also wrote, "Hills was Anti-Calvinist, Wiley was pro-Christian."[40] When it came to the will, Hills glorified the human will as being completely free from any and all outside influences. In order to refute Calvinistic election, Hills took an extreme view on freedom. Wynkoop wrote, "Hills, in order to combat the errors of the personal predestination view of Charles Hodge especially, lumped all Calvinism together under that error and fought Calvinism as such, denying even Biblical predestination. In contrast to this he affirmed absolute free will. To defend free will he reached back into history to Arminius and made him the authority for anti-Calvinism, forgetting that Arminius lived and died a Calvinist and taught, not free will but, prevenient grace and a predestination that made Christ the elect man."[41]

Hills's argument was the classical one—that if there is no freedom of the will, there is no moral responsibility; if there is no moral responsibility, there is no sin; if there is no sin, there is no need for redemption.[42] Wiley, on the other hand, took the Wesleyan position, which rejects free will and affirms free grace. By this, Wiley meant that God's prevenient love preserves all people for salvation.[43]

When it came to faith, Hills saw it as a human achievement, a virtue. Wiley, on the other hand, saw faith as a personal relationship with God.

---

37. Ibid.
38. Ibid., 67.
39. Wynkoop, "Foundations," file 2227-11, WC, 9.
40. Ibid., 7.
41. Ibid.
42. Bassett, "A Study," 67.
43. Wynkoop, "Foundations," file 2227-11, WC, 7.

Rather than faith having merit, for Wiley it was precisely that which ends all merit. Wesley, Watson, and Wiley spoke of faith within the context of saving grace. Hills spoke of faith within the context of his ongoing insistence on the free moral agency of human beings. For Wiley the emphasis was on what grace can do to give us faith; for Hills the emphasis was on what faith can do to obtain grace.[44] The domino effect caused by Hills's position on the free will of human beings affected every aspect of his theology. Wynkoop wrote, "Because Hills had given away prevenient grace, he could not find a way to adequately account for sin. He said the same things Wesleyanism said about sanctification, but meant very different things. By robbing the process of sanctification of grace, so much was laid on the human will as to make the transaction a human achievement rather than a reliance on Christ."[45]

In Hills's anthropology, the human will was seen to play such a decisive role in both justification and sanctification that grace was seen as an aid, not the cause.[46]

Given this absolute contrast between Hills and Wiley, we can now understand why Wynkoop found herself in such a theological crunch. The challenge for Wynkoop was that the rigid methodology of A. M. Hills, so easy to make sermons from, became the adopted culture that lay under the preaching of most Nazarene evangelists of that day. Sanctification was limited to a crisis experience, standardized by means of certain specific conditions that were to be met.[47] Wynkoop showed how the altar instructions ended up becoming a rigid how-to recipe with the following pattern: "1. Conviction of want, 2. Repentance for not seeking earlier, 3. *Feel* the importance, 4. Believe it is for *you*, 5. Hunger and thirst for it, 6. Obedience to code of dress and behavior, 7. Consecration, 8. Faith."[48]

Wynkoop saw this extreme emphasis on clock-time "crisis" as a departure from Wesley's position. He was more interested in the content of holiness, rather than the structure or time it took to attain a certain level. Those eight years of exposure to the theology of A. M. Hills made Wynkoop aware of holiness theology that had more affiliation with hu-

---

44. Ibid.
45. Ibid.
46. Bassett, "A Study," 71.
47. Wynkoop, "Foundations," file 2227-11, WC, 9.
48. Ibid., 8.

manism than it did with orthodox Wesleyan theology. What rippled through the Church of the Nazarene was a neat set of propositions that were proclaimed clearly and fervently. It was intellectually easy and logically respectable, but it was not able to deal with moral problems.[49] In the process, behaviour became standardized, and sanctification was measured by the keeping of church rules.[50] Wynkoop said, "God got away from us while our faith and obedience was [sic] under trial. How often we hurried back to the public altar not sure whether we should be saved and sanctified all over again, or just sanctified, or, maybe, saved again with sanctification still intact."[51]

"The sad irony of this," wrote Wynkoop, "is that Wiley has been 'read' through Hills's Greek eyes. It was Hills's position that Wiley refuted, but in a positive, gracious way, never directly in opposition to Hills. I had to face very consciously the sectarianism of Hills and choose deliberately the 'church theology' based soundly on Scripture (not philosophy) of H. Orton Wiley."[52] Given this exploration, this writer concludes that Wynkoop's theology did not tilt toward the emphasis on free will but stands rather comfortably with Wesley and Wiley's emphasis on free grace.

Wynkoop and the Boston Personalist Tradition

Having considered the shift from free grace to free will, the question still remains whether Wynkoop participated in the theological transition from sinful man to moral man, as outlined by Chiles. Not only was there pressure in her own denomination to lean toward free will, but a similar challenge also came from the field of religious philosophy—namely Boston personalism—to endorse human native ability as a basis for divine-human interaction. In order to answer this challenge, Wynkoop undertook the writing of "An Existential Interpretation of the Doctrine of Holiness," in which she defined her theology as a relational theology of love. Wynkoop was aware that relational theology lies at the watershed between two very different ways of thinking and, therefore, of doing theology. For her the challenge was not with the use of the term "relational theology" but, rather, with the way in which human nature was defined and how

---

49. Ibid., 10.
50. Ibid.
51. Ibid.
52. Ibid.

grace interacted with it.⁵³ She saw a difference between a philosophical approach and a religious-existential approach. We need to clarify whether Wynkoop defined this relationship on a metaphysical or moral basis. Wynkoop related the scope of the challenge:

> The simplest way to get into the issue of relationalism is to remind ourselves that Wesleyanism, or holiness theology, relates God's grace and human nature. That is, something existential happens at the point of meeting and in the ongoing life from that meeting. All of us agree to that. It is what happens that is the difficulty. Those who feel that some sub-rational, sub-responsible, basically sub-personal, hyper-supernatural change is effected in the soul by God which gives rise to the new relationship, understand God and humans and sin in a very different way than those who understand the salvation event to be a climax of the process of prevenient grace bringing the whole person to the grand meeting place where the awakened sinner, in the full light of his moral responsibility, and with his whole heart, cements his commitment to the welcoming Saviour.⁵⁴

Wynkoop did not believe that salvation occurs "deeper down and farther back" in some non-personal part of the human self, while some of the rest of the self waits outside.⁵⁵ However, clarity is still needed because of her use of language and concepts that could be associated with **philosophical idealism** and personalism. This brings us to the place where we can ask questions about other influences on Wynkoop's theology. Given her interest in a personal connection between God and humans, what exactly did she mean by "personal"? When Wynkoop described the Holy Spirit as a "real spiritual energy linking the divine reality to human experience . . . the 'personness' of God touching the 'personness' of man," did she want to show a metaphysical similarity between humans and God?⁵⁶ She wrote, "'Personal' means anything, and everything, about man having a bearing on his moral, intellectual, spiritual, responsible self. . . . It cannot include any merely physical, as distinguished from human, aspect of man—nothing below the rational."⁵⁷

---

53. Wynkoop, "Recent Developments in Holiness Theology" (article, undated), file 1304, WC, 5.
54. Ibid., 1.
55. Ibid., 5.
56. Wynkoop, *A Theology of Love*, 78.
57. Ibid., 80-81.

Was she hereby fulfilling the personalist's desire to discriminate spiritual being from natural being and thereby nullifying her own position on the Hebraic unity of the person? These questions show how important it is for us to determine under which label Wynkoop operated. It would be easy to confuse her quest for the whole person to be engaged in moral responsibility as an expression of the free moral agency of the personalist. To address this, we will need a brief account of the world of personal idealism, specifically the development of Boston personalism. We will also need to consider the extent to which personalism was able to make a contribution to traditional Wesleyan theology and finally close this discussion with Wynkoop's own perspectives on personalism.

BOSTON PERSONALISM

Boston personalism's contribution to faith and learning is significant when one considers the intellectual climate in American philosophy and religion in the late nineteenth century. This was a very difficult and desperate time for intellectuals in the church. Not only did they have to deal with the popularization of evolutionary thought, by such as Herbert Spencer, but also revivals became less and less anchored in thoughtful reflection.[58] With the onslaught of modernism and liberalism, many in the religious community retreated into scriptural literalness and a profound resistance to learning of all types.[59] In the field of philosophy, materialism and naturalism became the popular positions of the time. In this environment, it became increasingly evident that a proper philosophical alliance for Christian theology was badly needed. Borden Parker Bowne (1847—1910), a Methodist and philosophy professor at Boston University, proposed a "solution" to this dilemma. Bowne's thinking and life were part of a growing urban university, whose theological school was a dominant force in America's theological climate as it battled with the tension between faith and reason. His contribution to the thought world came to be known as "personal idealism" and, later, "personalism."[60]

Through the philosophy of personalism, the thoughtful religious person was given a choice, given the extremes of subjectivism (Schleier-

---

58. F. Thomas Trotter, "Boston Personalism's Contributions to Faith and Learning," in *The Boston Personalist Tradition in Philosophy, Social Ethics, and Theology*, ed. Paul Deats and Carol Robb (Macon, GA: Mercer University Press, 1986), 16.
59. Ibid., 17.
60. Ibid.

macher) and naturalism in both its materialist and positivistic forms.[61] Personalism in Bowne and his followers emphasized the basic rationality of the world. This knowable and understandable world makes possible the structures of intellectual life. This was in contrast to a philosophical world where there was no moral purpose, no causality, but only randomness.[62] Personalism was a way of thinking about the whole of reality and experience. It was, in essence, a worldview that helped students to see how all things hang together, especially when it comes to thinking about humanity, God, nature, evil, suffering, freedom, and ethics.[63]

With the publication of his major work *The Philosophy of Personalism* in 1927, Albert Knudson (1873—1953), a later philosophy professor at Boston University, saw personalism as the philosophy best qualified to provide an intellectual foundation for Christian theology.[64]

As a religious philosophy, personalism is of very recent origin. The term "personalism" was first used philosophically by Goethe and Schleiermacher (1799) and was only introduced in the United States by Walt Whitman in 1868.[65] Even though Boston personalism is one of the first comprehensive systems of philosophy developed in America, it had very ancient intellectual roots.[66]

One key influencer for modern personalism is Gottfried Leibniz (1646—1716), whose *The **Monadology*** represented the universe as consisting of simple psychic monads who are always active ("to be is to act") under a pre-established harmony.[67] Essentially, these monads are windowless. Knudson says, "The monads have no windows through which anything could come in or go out."[68] It is important to note that substance as realized both in the infinite and in finite monads was not seen as passive but active. So what distinguishes one individual from another is the way

---

61. Ibid.
62. Ibid., 18.
63. Rufus Burrow, Jr., *Personalism: A Critical Introduction* (St. Louis: Chalice Press, 1999), 1.
64. Albert C. Knudson, *The Philosophy of Personalism: A Study in the Metaphysics of Religion* (New York: Abingdon, 1927), 14.
65. Edgar Sheffield Brightman, "Personalism," in *A History of Philosophical Systems*, ed. Vergilius Ferm (New York: Philsophical Library, 1950), 340.
66. Deats, "Introduction to Boston Personalism," in *The Boston Personalist Tradition*, 3.
67. Brightman, "Personalism," 342.
68. Knudson, *Philosophy of Personalism*, 185.

it acts rather than any substance it contains.⁶⁹ Leibniz's contribution laid a foundation for the immaterialism and activism of modern personalism.

Equally influential and original was George Berkeley (1685—1753), who taught that reality consists of active spirits and their passive ideas. For him, "nature exists only in spirits, primarily in the divine spirit (person), and then communicated as 'a divine language' to human spirits."⁷⁰ Berkeley's immaterialism had a direct influence on the personal idealism of Bowne. It is also important to mention Rudolph Hermann Lotze (1817–81). In both the preface of Bowne's *Studies in Theism* (1879) and in *Metaphysics* (1882), he acknowledges his general obligation to his friend and Professor Hermann Lotze of Göttingen. According to Burrow, even though Lotze was Bowne's teacher, Bowne went beyond Lotze by making both person and freedom central to his philosophy.⁷¹ He wrote, "Lotze stopped just short of applying the category of person to God, thereby leaving 'the fundamental reality only less vague than Hegel's absolute.' Bowne, on the other hand, 'presses on to the assertion of personality in the World-Ground with all that such an assertion implies.'"⁷² In other words, both Bowne and Lotze saw the impossibility of assuming the absentee God of absolute idealism. Whereas Lotze spoke of the "Supreme Good," Bowne went on to speak of a "Supreme Personality" that can act and be acted upon. "And," says Ralph Tyler Flewelling, "herein is the chief point of difference between Lotze and Bowne."⁷³

Bowne, who taught at Boston University from 1876 until his death in 1910, was a formative influence in modern Methodist thinking and a theistic, idealistic personalist. According to Knudson, the Bowne-type personalism is the most typical, or "normative," understanding of personalism.⁷⁴ Bowne built his theistic personalism philosophy upon person as a metaphysical concept. Person was, for Bowne, the fundamental principle of explanation, the master principle capable of explaining all other principles.⁷⁵ Even though there was an element of mystery surrounding person, Bowne

---

69. Ibid., 186.
70. Brightman, "Personalism," 342.
71. Burrow, *Personalism*, 30.
72. Ibid.
73. Ralph Tyler Flewelling, *Personalism and the Problems of Philosophy: An Appreciation of the Work of Borden Parker Bowne* (New York: Methodist Book Concern, 1915), 106–8.
74. Knudson, *Philosophy of Personalism*, 87.
75. Burrow, *Personalism*, 11.

would rather choose the mystery of person than the mystery of some form of impersonal mechanism to reference ultimate reality. In his work *Personalism*, Bowne says, "We affirm that impersonalism is a failure whether in the low form of materialistic mechanism or in the abstract form of idealistic notions, and that personality is the real and only principle of philosophy which will enable us to take any rational step whatsoever."[76]

All personalists agree that in person we find the best clue to the nature of reality. Their famous phrase was "personality is the key to reality." Burrow says, "This phrase does not point to any individual human person, but to the objective structure of reality itself. That is, the phrase 'personality is the key to reality' is a metaphysical statement. It points to the idea that the real is personal or some self or selves. Reality is personal. As a metaphysical principle, person is not identical to the human person, 'however true it may be that the personalistic principle is exemplified in human personality.'"[77]

Idealistic personalists do not see the body to be part of the human person but, rather, see the body as itself a personal activity (either of God or of systems of "monads") that interacts with the human person.[78] Personalism also distinguishes between self and person. It acknowledges the existence of many levels of selves and persons, ranging from the lowest forms of self to the highest supreme cosmic self or person—God.[79]

Following Leibniz and Berkeley, personalism contends that being is thoroughly causal and active. It is in fact not being that actually exists; rather, what exists are agents. Reality is not just mind or thought, then, but also will or agent.[80]

In order to do any explaining, one must assume that there is a mind, intelligence, or person that is able to bring coherence to reason and experience.[81] In *Studies in Theism*, Bowne says, "Just think about this: Can an impersonal, unthinking substance explain anything at all? Mind, intelligence, or person may not be able to fully explain itself and precisely how

---

76. Borden Parker Bowne, *Personalism* (Boston: Houghton, Mifflin, and Company, 1908), 263.
77. Burrow, *Personalism*, 94.
78. Brightman, "Personalism," 340.
79. Burrow, *Personalism*, 97.
80. Ibid., 93.
81. Ibid., 86.

it came to be, but it goes a long way toward explaining all other things."[82] Brightman says, "For personalists, everything is mental. Everything that exists is, for them, in, of, or for a mind on some level."[83]

In addition to viewing all reality as personal, personalism emphasizes freedom. Burrow says, "All being is both personal and free. To be is to be free and to act or have the potential to do so. To be free is what it means to be a person; to be a person is to be free."[84] The nature of reality itself is freedom. This aspect of personalism is critical, since the implications are that God does not create persons and then *give* them freedom. Persons are actually created *in* freedom.[85] The discovery and value of the self lies in the context of self-determination. In this context the self has the freedom to create its own spiritual environment and realizes itself in so doing.[86] Everything then begins with the experience of the self. One can see the far-ranging implications of this postulate for Wynkoop's theology, especially as it comes to the question of moral responsibility and the person's native ability to respond.

PERSONALISM AND RELIGIOUS BELIEF

Bowne builds his doctrine of God on a postulate that the mind has a right to advance since it has a "right to itself." In other words, one's relationship with God starts with oneself. In this regard Bowne sees the mind as a living organism with many interests that give it its driving power. Since we are rational, Bowne assumes that the universe is rational. Since we are moral, Bowne assumes that the universe is righteous at its roots. The working mechanism for all of this is the constant invention of hypotheses under the stress of experience.[87] Bowne seems to follow Kant in his method of grounding the moral sense. The idea of moral obligation arises within the mind itself. Wynkoop said, "For Bowne, man began as potentiality rather than an actuality. Being a candidate for humanity rationally and morally, his true self is not given, but is something to be attained. The

---

82. Borden Parker Bowne, *Studies in Theism* (New York: Phillips & Hunt, 1879), 284.
83. Brightman, "Personalism," 346.
84. Burrow, *Personalism*, 87.
85. Ibid.
86. Wynkoop, "The Philosophy of Idealism and Its Influence on Religion in America" (monograph, 1953), file 2227-35, WC, 14.
87. Ibid., 22.

'free spirit' or autonomy of the mind, in imposing duty upon itself, gives the only meaning to moral obligation."[88]

The religious implications of Bowne's philosophy can best be presented from a collection that Bowne's wife put together from some of the sermons he preached. In the introduction to this collection called *The Essence of Religion*, his wife gives the heart of Bowne's religious philosophy: "The great end of religion is a developed soul, a soul with a deep sense of God, a soul in which faith, courage, and resolution are at their highest."[89]

In his sermon "The Supremacy of Christ," he makes several related assertions. Christ, though supreme, in a sense is but one of many religious teachers.[90] In another sermon, "Religion and Life," he declares that life is not irreligious, but it does need to be subordinated to the Christian spirit in order for man to realize himself and glorify God. The Christian spirit, rather than moving away from life, moves into it and possesses it. In this way the kingdom of God and the "kingdom of man" will come.[91] The atonement and forgiveness of sin are "important doctrines of theology," but only so if they are rightly conceived. These doctrines are a "statement of God's great love and become great inspirations and are full of comfort."[92] "Salvation," Bowne says in his sermon "Partnership with God," "is not God's deepest thought concerning men, but the training and development of souls as the children of God. Salvation is but an incident of this greater purpose."[93] He wrote, "The filial spirit working itself out in loving submission and active obedience, this only is salvation. God above looking down in condescending grace and loving invitation, and man below looking up in filial surrender and aspiration, and then the soul's Godward flight forever and ever—there is no other salvation."[94]

BOSTON PERSONALISM AND ITS INFLUENCE ON WILEY

It did not take long for Boston personalism to become influential, especially around Methodist/Wesleyan circles. Part of the attraction was that it was not just a theory taught in the classroom, but it was also seen

---

88. Ibid., 25.
89. Borden Parker Bowne, *The Essence of Religion* (Boston: Houghton Mifflin Company, 1910), vi.
90. Ibid., 5.
91. Ibid., 41.
92. Bowne, *Studies in Theism*, 87.
93. Ibid., 243.
94. Ibid., 250.

as a way of life—a way of living in the world.[95] It is fair to say that Bowne's influence was especially felt among Wesleyan-oriented scholars in America. One reason that Bowne's personalism had such a powerful impact in America comes down to sheer numbers. Ministerial students flocked to Boston University, and numerous students left the graduate school to serve as college presidents, professors, and church leaders.[96]

Partly because of these graduating masses, personalism was the dominating philosophical position in scores of colleges and churches across the land, including those of the Church of the Nazarene. A number of Nazarenes enrolled in the doctoral programs at Boston University (such as Russell V. DeLong, the first philosophy professor at Nazarene Theological Seminary who studied under Edgar S. Brightman and Peter Bertocci, who became Brightman's successor).[97] Ralph Tyler Flewelling at the University of Southern California and John Wright Buckham at the Pacific School of Religion, among others, brought personalism to the West Coast. The movement of Boston personalism from east to west is especially relevant for the purpose of this research, since H. Orton Wiley did graduate studies under Buckham.

A Congregationalist minister, Buckham arrived at Pacific Theological Seminary in 1903 as a professor of Christian theology.[98] Matt Price, in his research on Wiley, indicates that Buckham became Wiley's mentor during his seminary days. This relationship began in 1910. For three years, both in the classroom and at Buckham's home around the fireplace, Wiley was introduced to Buckham's philosophy of personalism.[99] In 1959, Wiley presented a series of graduate lectures at Nazarene Theological Seminary in Kansas City, Missouri. This series of lectures was titled "A Study of the Philosophy of John Wright Buckham in Its Application to the Problems of Modern Theology." Matt Price's handwritten notes, taken from these lectures, help us to get a deeper understanding of the impact Buckham had on Wiley. Price shares Wiley's admission of Buckham's impact on his

---

95. Burrow, *Personalism*, 2.
96. Trotter, "Boston Personalism's Contributions," 20.
97. Rob Staples, "Re: Personalism" (email to Matt Price, February 16, 2000).
98. J. Matthew Price, *We Teach Holiness: The Life and Work of H. Orton Wiley (1877—1961)* (doctoral dissertation, University of Kansas, 2006; Holiness Data Ministry Digital Edition), 12.
99. Ibid., 14.

life, "I invite you to consider Dr. Buckham's personalism, with the hope that it will prove of value to you, as it has across the years to me."[100]

While endorsing all of the main tenets of theistic personalism,[101] Buckham's type of theistic personalism can be described as progressive/dialectical personalism because he placed special emphasis on the developmental process of the "individual or self becoming a person."[102] Buckham endorsed one of the main tenets of theistic personalism, which makes a distinction between self and person.[103] He builds on this principle as he anticipates movement from the realm of nature to the realm of the spirit, from self to person, from person to community, and from community to the great community—the kingdom of God.[104] By a series of free, selective, self-determining acts of the self, it enters the moral and spiritual realm and becomes a person.[105] The significance of the individual then increases as the conception of God becomes more personal, and the personal obligation becomes more direct.[106]

Our quest is to see how much of Buckham's philosophy was reproduced in Wiley and, in turn, how much it influenced Wynkoop. The influence of Buckham's philosophy can be seen in Wiley's three volumes of *Christian Theology*. In the title for chapter 13 of *Christian Theology*, volume 1, Wiley describes God as "Perfect Personality." In addition, Wiley wrote, "Personality has proven to be the ultimate reality through which alone the Absolute can be understood."[107] What are we to make of this statement? Since Wiley would see himself more as a theologian than a philosopher, the question arises as to the relation between his philosophy and his theology. Did his philosophical stance tilt his theology so that the latter became simply the development of a metaphysical system using the language of Christian doctrine? Or were his perspectives imported from

---

100. H. Orton Wiley, "A Study of the Philosophy of John Wright Buckham in Its Application to the Problems of Modern Theology" (lecture, Nazarene Theological Seminary, October 1959), 1.
101. John Wright Buckham, "An Outline of a Philosophy of Personalism," *The Personalist* 3:4 (October 1922), 244–53.
102. Price, *We Teach Holiness*, 13.
103. Burrow, *Personalism*, 97.
104. Price, *We Teach Holiness*, 13.
105. Ibid., 14.
106. Ibid.
107. Wiley, *Christian Theology*, 1:292.

secular thought to support and validate Christian teaching previously accepted? The latter seems more persuasive.

At first glance, it looks as if Wiley had settled on an impersonal ontology to describe the Trinity and to accommodate both its unity and diversity. Wiley chose the Greek patristic perspective to describe the Trinity as "three **hypostases** in one *ousia*." This was Wiley's foundational statement in order to describe the Trinity as personal in the sense of the Trinitarian distinctions.[108] It would have been good if Wiley had taken the next step to describe the Trinity as tri-personal, but instead he wrote, "The failure to apply the term 'person' to the whole being of God gave rise to the modern controversies between philosophy and theology concerning the nature of personality."[109]

At this juncture, the influence of personalism seems to get the upper hand. However, when we compare his chapter "God as Perfect Personality" with his chapter "The Trinity," we get a more complete picture. It is important for Wiley to describe the Trinity as a unity of essence and a distinction of persons. Wiley wants to avoid all the classical Trinitarian heresies of **Sabellianism, Monarchianism,** and **Tri-theism** by staying with the Nicene Creed. He quotes John 10:30, "I and my Father are one" (KJV), and then adds his own interpretation, "that is, one being, not one person."[110] By translating *hypostases* or the Latin *subsistence* as "persons" and then anchoring this diversity in the *essence*, Wiley does end up with a tri-personal perspective. In order to describe the manner in which the essence and the persons interact, he uses the classical idea of *circumcessio* or **perichoresis**: Wiley says, "The term signifies an intercoherence of the persons of the Trinity, or that property, which by reason of identity of essence, they can communicate with each other without confusion of persons. It guards the unity of the Godhead, by affirming that the three persons do not exist alongside of each other as separate individuals, but that they permeate and penetrate one another, and so exist not alongside but in and through one another."[111]

By using the concept of *perichoresis*, Wiley was able to stress the social aspect of the Trinity. He does not leave this discussion in the abstract but continues to show that the Holy Spirit reveals that the relationality

---

108. Ibid., 291.
109. Ibid.
110. Ibid., 407.
111. Ibid., 435.

of the Trinity is anchored in love. Wiley continued, "It is the work of the Spirit proceeding from the Father and the Son, to glorify this necessary relation into one of freedom and love."[112] This love is then seen in the economy of God's dealings with humanity: "We may confidently believe that the triune God exists eternally in the sphere of love; that this love gave Jesus Christ our Lord as a propitiation for sin; and that it is into this holy fellowship of divine love that his finite creatures are to be received through the gift of the Holy Spirit."[113] Wiley here gives us a picture of a Trinitarian community that is dynamic and responsive, not absolute and unaffected or **impassible**. The point here is that Wiley's position on the Trinity, even though influenced by the personalism of Buckham, remains in the boundaries of solid Christian orthodoxy. Noble indicates that it is not a threat to Christian orthodoxy (or Nazarene orthodoxy) to speak of Christian holiness in terms of love, personhood, and relationships, since these terms have their origin in the Trinity.[114] The conclusion at this point is that Wiley wrote some of his theology in light of personalism, rather than being dominated by it. But further light is needed. We now turn to Wynkoop's perspectives.

WYNKOOP ON BOSTON PERSONALISM

Wynkoop's position on personalism comes to light as we look at correspondence between Wynkoop and Rev. Gideon Tredoux, in which the issue of personalism is specifically addressed. This letter, dated January 11, 1982, not only sheds light on the place of personalism in Wiley's theology but also gives us keen insight into Wynkoop's own perspectives on Boston personalism.[115] Wynkoop makes key observations about Wiley and her own position on personalism. Wynkoop wrote:

---

112. Ibid., 429.
113. Ibid., 379.
114. Noble, *Holy Trinity*, 217.
115. The background of this letter between Rev. Gideon Tredoux and Wynkoop will help to frame this conversation. Rev. Tredoux, born and raised in South Africa, became one of the pioneer pastors for the work of the Church of the Nazarene in the Republic of South Africa. After twenty years of pastoral ministry among the Dutch-speaking Afrikaners, he came to the USA to study at the Nazarene Theological Seminary during the years 1975 to 1977. During this time, Wynkoop served as theologian-in-residence at NTS. Wynkoop presented a Wesleyan understanding of Christian holiness, which stretched him, since he had only been exposed to the American Holiness Movement's understanding of holiness. Subsequently, upon graduating with an MDiv, Gideon returned to South Africa to teach systematic theology at the Nazarene Theological College in Johannesburg and introduced Dr. Wynkoop's book *A Theology of Love* as one of the required textbooks. This decision created controversy, and Gideon ended up having

The key to an understanding of Wiley and Wesley (and us) is "personal relationship" in contrast to "philosophical relationalism"—that is, religion vs. philosophy. This keeps our religion personal, real, vital rather than impersonal, mechanical, legal, merely psychological.

"Relationalism" is a label which "Boston University" theologians have given to Nazarene Wesleyan theologians. We have never called ourselves "relationalists" until recently. We do not mean by "relation" what the Boston Personalists mean. Labels need to be defined. The philosophical personalists mean by relationalism that "person" is not real. We do not call Wesleyanism "personalism." Others call us that. Wesleyans teach that every step in salvation, from the decisive "crisis" times to our daily walk with God, is living in a close personal relationship to God. We have a close relationship with him that involves our whole life. This is not philosophical, but religious.

In order to understand Wiley it is necessary to know that he was not a personalist. He very carefully helped us to see the very real difference between Wesley's view (and the biblical views) of man and the philosophical personalist's view. In the classroom Wiley often warned us against confusing metaphysical statements and moral statements. I presume nothing Wiley said had any greater influence on us (at least, me) than this truth.

Biblical writers were not philosophizing, that is, trying to tell us what human nature is, in itself, but how human beings are to relate themselves to God, to each other and to God's earth. This never meant that human nature was not real, but that the real issue was what we, as responsible persons, do with Jesus Christ and his demands on us. Wiley was anxious that we students would not expect God to change our

---

to defend Wynkoop's theology at a special meeting of the District Advisory Board (it was almost a heresy trial). The conclusion of this theological stir was that Professor Gideon Tredoux had to resign as the theology teacher at the Bible college purely because he presented Dr. Wynkoop's concepts of relational theology in the classroom. During this time, several theological letters were sent back and forth between Dr. Wynkoop and Professor Tredoux. Some of the controversy that ensued was Dr. John E. Riley (previous president of Northwest Nazarene University)'s response paper to Professor Gideon Tredoux's position paper about what he was teaching at the Nazarene Bible College in South Africa. Professor Tredoux's position paper is titled "A Dialogue on the Doctrine of Holiness," a paper submitted to the pastors of the South African European district in defense of his teaching at the Nazarene college. Dr. Wynkoop's evaluation of Dr. Riley's response to Professor Gideon Tredoux's paper gives us more insight into what Dr. Wynkoop's position on personalism is.

physical human nature (a sort of mutation of something in us) but that our whole human person would be given back to God for him to use.

Paul's "altar call" (Rom. 12:1) is to this point— "Present your bodies, a living sacrifice . . ." We are to be engaged in being "transformed" (which is explained in 12:3—15:13). "Transformation" is in the present indicative, meaning it is a process and not a sudden personality change. Wiley would stress the fundamental requirement to "present our bodies" to God, which is what Wesleyans teach is a right relationship to God.

In Wiley's day, the term "relationalism" was not used, but "being in right relationship to God" was used. Unless we make the clear distinction between a "right relationship" (a religious meaning) and "relationalism" (a whole philosophical system) we cannot understand Wesleyanism. The term "relationalism" is a philosophical foreigner (to biblical and theological fields), which can distort Wiley and Wesley (and, alas, Wynkoop, Greathouse, Staples, Reed, Carver, etc.).

Wiley, learning from Wesley and the Bible, used the kind of language that can be interpreted as substance (metaphysical). This is the reason we need to understand "presuppositions." The New Testament was written in Greek because those who were to read it were using the Greek language. But what was said by the NT writers was said from the dynamic, flexible, moral, spiritual—Hebraic—presuppositions. The philosophy of Greek thought is simply smashed by the profoundly religious meaning of the Christian gospel. Because of this, we must be careful to avoid metaphysical interpretations.

Now, we must distinguish carefully between the narrow, definitive theological way of speaking and the descriptive source of theological language. In reading Wiley, you will notice that one of the most important parts of each section is the biblical background. His theological sections are foundationed [sic] in the biblical study. The biblical studies are profoundly relational in the biblical, experiential, life situation sense. He carries this foundation over into the theological teaching. If we do not do this with him, we miss his point all together.[116]

In addition, a very important research paper presented to the department of philosophy at Northern Baptist Theological Seminary in 1953,

---

116. Wynkoop to Professor Gideon Tredoux (correspondence, January 11, 1982), file 1427-17, WC.

titled "The Philosophy of Idealism and Its Influence on Religion in America," shows Wynkoop sinking her teeth into Boston personalism. Her reaction to the personalism of Borden Parker Bowne is broken down into the things that seemed favorable to her, as well as those things that seem to cut across her biblical faith. In light of all the projections upon Wynkoop, even some among her own peers, labelling her as a Boston personalist, it is appropriate to state her response verbatim. She wrote:

> Personalism seemed right in affirming the essential dignity of mankind and the individual, and maintaining a belief in his moral nature by its faith in a certain measure of freedom, and self-determination. Man is not of nature and the material world but a spiritual being, primarily a self, a knowing self, capable of receiving dependable knowledge.
>
> Personalism appeals to me as it affirms God as Creator and Sustainer of the cosmos. It seems right in its faith in a resulting intelligible world, dependable and predictable, because of its Maker. Personalism believes in a real communication between God and man. It recognizes truth as a norm outside of finite selves. It respects the laws of reason.
>
> I like personalism's view of the dynamic relationship of God to his world, in contrast to the static idea of his relationship, a fixed God and a fixed world. Personality in God seems to demand a more flexible conception than the rigid Absolute of older thought.[117]

But there were aspects of personalistic idealism that seemed less attractive to her, especially as she viewed it against her biblical faith. She wrote:

> Metaphysically, it tends to lose the clear distinction between God and man, and in some cases, God and nature, both of which must be kept in clear definition if biblical teaching is to retain any meaningfulness. Man, though of a like nature as God, stands over and against God. His value is not absolute in the universe, but derived from God and subject to forfeiture under the terms set up by God himself. He is not capable of moral autonomy, or any other autonomy, but a creature exercising his created faculties under an imposed moral order, to which he is personally responsible. Personalism tends to lose sight of the "high and lofty One that inhabiteth eternity, whose name is Holy" (Is. 57:15 [KJV]).

---

117. Wynkoop, "The Philosophy of Idealism," file 2227-35, WC, 33.

Personalism tends to place God and man on an equal level. This homo-centricity is a total repudiation of biblical faith.

Another aspect of personalism that is unbiblical is the tendency to lose the grip of the biblical doctrine of sin. Men trapped in an unfavourable social environment cannot be expected to demonstrate perfect deportment in the world. They have two counts against them. A few more million years ought to display a race of men more nearly equated with what the image of God was meant to mean. But this is not biblical teaching. In it, sin is a personal affront to God's authority and person. Sin is a moral issue, not a bout with immaturity. I must vote for the biblical view of sin.

The biblical doctrine of salvation looks crude and ignorant against Bowne's anthropology, and is an insult to his theism. It has not been demonstrated that man can dispense with supernatural help in regard to his moral adjustment to his God. In this respect, also, man is a dependent creature and shows his highest nobility in an attitude of humility and obedience and love. The philosophy of personalism is in error to the point that it attempts to make unnecessary the provision of salvation that is biblically recorded.

Idealism's epistemology, which makes revelation unnecessary and therefore the Bible a relic of an ancient day with no authority for to-day, I believe, is in error.

It is undoubtedly possible to subscribe to a proper Christology in personalistic philosophy, but I believe it is difficult to do so.

Christian theology is in shambles without the central structure of a triune God. No part of it can be rescued from meaninglessness so far as the nature of man, sin, or redemption is concerned, outside of the concept and implications of the Trinity. That truth is the keystone in the Christian arch. Personalism tends to lose that doctrine. It is lost in the idea of God, in the idea of man and its rejection of special revelation. To the point that this basic conflict with traditional Christianity fails of resolution, I feel that I cannot endorse it.[118]

Her final analysis of personalism is that it is egocentric and not theocentric. We see her being very comfortable under the label of Christian

---

118. Ibid., 34–35.

existentialism. She is very concerned about the moral relationship between God and humanity, not necessarily the metaphysical.

Following Wynkoop's response to Riley in defense of Tredoux and reading her response to Bowne-type personalism, it is clear that Wynkoop and those adhering to the philosophy of personalism have many concepts in common yet are miles apart in their presuppositions. This applies especially in the way that concepts like self, person, personhood, moral agent, personality, and freedom are used. It is incumbent upon us to discriminate carefully between these categories of thinking and place them in their proper context. Person under the umbrella of personalism is different than person filtered through a Hebraic, biblical lens. Wynkoop saw the need to define these terms and put them through her Christian-existentialist filter. This task is undertaken in her main work *A Theology of Love* in the chapters called "The Meaning of Moral" and "The Psychology of Holiness."

A Problem of Language

It is important to understand the presuppositions underlying the common use of terms, as is seen in the philosophical world of Boston personalism and the Christian-existentialist world of Wynkoop. The following terms have already been defined as some of the key tenets of personalism were articulated. However, it is important to briefly revisit these terms, in order to make a direct comparison between Wynkoop and those in the field of personalism.

In personalism "moral agent" finds its moorings in the reality of the soul or self. As we have seen in Leibniz's *Monadology*, without real selves there is no personalism. In personalism's "hall of fame," great debt is owed to Plato, who thought of the soul as an immaterial substance that is invisible, immortal, and yet active. Plato is credited for his belief that the soul has the power of self-motion, but Berkeley and Leibniz gave greater significance to the activity of the soul by interpreting it largely in causal terms. They thought of the soul as an agent rather than as a merely existing entity. "To be is to act" became a key tenet of personalism. What is significant, given the issue under discussion, is to note that in personalism, the soul or self (however defined, substantialistic or activistic) is distinguished from the body. Idealistic personalists do not take the body to be part of human personality, but regard it as itself a personal activity (either of God or of systems of monads) that interacts with the human person.

That is to say, the soul, self, or person is metaphysical in the world of Boston personalism.

For Wynkoop, on the other hand, moral agency is not anchored in the Greek philosophical perspectives of the self-movement of the soul. In personalism, the soul is understood as a separate aspect of a person, somehow distinct from the body. The soul is the creative source of the body and continues to exist after the body dies. Wynkoop, on the other hand, found herself more at home in the Hebraic scriptural teachings that a soul exists not as a separate aspect from the body but only as a body. Reflecting on the dynamic view of the Old and New Testament writers, Wynkoop wrote, "The soul of man as a totality finds its expression in many ways in the central organs of the body, such as the heart, the liver, the kidneys and the bowels. Any of these may at any given moment express the 'soul' . . . the unity of personality is everywhere assumed. Heart, mind, soul, spirit, conscience, flesh, body are not distinguishable parts of man put together as something man *has*. These are what a man *is*."[119]

In Wynkoop's world, the trichotomous view of a human being as body, soul, and spirit has to give way to the more biblical view of a human being as a unified personality. She wrote, "Any multiple view of personality makes the Christian life a source of conflict, not of peace. It makes salvation destructive of wholeness and integrity in that grace sets the soul against the body. It impugns the grace of God. A disturbed personality becomes the badge of Christianity, and death a saviour."[120]

When it comes to the "movement of the soul," or the "agency" aspect as used in personalism, Wynkoop did not engage in ontological speculation. When a human being acts, he or she acts as a unity. It is the whole person who acts. She took her cues from the biblical teaching, where the heart and feet are used as metaphors characterizing the action and attitudes of the whole person.[121] Echoing her response to Dr. John Riley, Wynkoop explained herself in an unpublished article, "Recent Developments in Holiness Theology": "Evangelical relationalism does not defend its concept of man on philosophical grounds but on religious grounds. It takes seriously the observation that no biblical writer defines human nature but only describes what man is. This description is never abstract

---

119. Wynkoop, *A Theology of Love*, 122.
120. Ibid., 200.
121. Ibid.

but always existential. The sub-structure of man is not the interest of any writer, but what man does and why he does it and what he ought to do is the consuming interest."[122]

When Wynkoop then chose "moral" and combined this concept with "agency," it was anchored in a totally different world than the world of personalism. In fact, her whole project, called "An Existential Understanding of the Doctrine of Holiness," which later became "The Theology of Depth," was to show an alternative perspective to the metaphysics of personalism. Her interest in "moral" was soteriological, not philosophical. She used "moral" out of a conviction that the Bible speaks primarily to the moral condition of humanity and holds humanity responsible. Over and against personalism's dualism, Wynkoop used "moral" to emphasize the unitary principles of personhood. Moral does not mean that the human always knows what is right or does what is right, but it does mean that he or she acts in relation to right and wrong. In other words, for Wynkoop, integrity was a base requirement for nature to be moral.[123] She stayed consistently with her position reflected earlier in our study on the state of humanity after the fall. She wrote:

> Holiness theology stands or falls at this point. Theology that does not take human integrity into consideration cannot take biblical holiness seriously. Any theology, even "holiness theology," that supposes that God bypasses the deepest moral integrity of man is not biblical. . . . No man is ever given any comfort by the suggestion that since he is "in sin" and under the bondage of sin, and his mind is darkened and his will perverted, he is absolved from responsibility regarding it. Never can it be found in Scripture that a man sins because he cannot help it, and therefore can excuse himself.[124]

In simple terms one can say that by the word *moral*, Wynkoop meant that the whole person is committed. Wynkoop believed that moral is personal and that personal is moral. This is to be seen in contrast to operating in universal categories where people are treated with preconceived notions as an "it" versus a "you."[125]

---

122. Wynkoop, "Recent Developments," file 1304, WC, 6.
123. Wynkoop, *A Theology of Love*, 171.
124. Ibid.
125. Ibid., 173.

While studying in Chicago in the mid-1950s, Mildred and her brother, Carl, met fairly frequently, discussing, among other things, **process theology**. At that time Carl was studying under Loomer, Hartshorne, and Meland. These conversations influenced Wynkoop toward an interest in understanding reality as characterized by "being in relation."[126] These conversations also exposed her to engage the thoughts of Martin Buber. She found Buber's ideas in his book *I and Thou* to be very helpful. Her write-ups in the margins of her own copy of Buber's classic reveal clearly that she liked Buber's emphasis that *existence* is primarily relational. Buber's emphasis on the primacy of the immediate encounter between a human person and another being caught her attention. She recognized the need for an "other" as essential to wholesome development and therefore believed that "moral" can only find its fullest realization in the context of fellowship.[127] She said:

> Personal relationship becomes a reality when two selves—two "I's"—open themselves to each other, respect the moral autonomy of each other, honor the personal integrity of each other, esteem each other as they esteem themselves, share themselves with each other without demanding mindless capitulation from each other, and then respond to each other in the profound awareness of mutual intercommunication. In this encounter which defines fellowship, the integrity of each is maintained and enhanced without the surrender of anything essential to selfhood.[128]

We can then say that for an act to be moral in Wynkoop's existential world, it has to involve the whole person in responsible decision. God does not bypass the integrity of human beings whom he made for love and fellowship.

In personalism, all being is both personal and free. To be is to be free and to act or have the potential to do so. To be free is what it means to be a person; to be a person is to be free. Freedom is first a metaphysical category, however true it may also be that this principle is exemplified in human personality. This means that freedom is intrinsic to the self and does not result from choice. The value of the self lies in the context of self-determination. In this context the self has the freedom to create its own

---

126. Jeremy Bangs (email to author, January 18, 2017).
127. Wynkoop, *A Theology of Love*, 86.
128. Ibid., 169.

spiritual environment and realizes itself in so doing. Personalism does not spend a lot of time talking about external grace being needed for a human being to engage in moral decisions. At best, grace is seen to meet humanity's native ability halfway. But this is a far cry from Wesley, Wiley, and Wynkoop, whose emphasis is on free grace, not free will.

For Wynkoop, to be a self means moral freedom. This freedom is not metaphysical, as in personalism, but real. This freedom may not be great (since human beings are not free not to sin), but in order to maintain personal and moral integrity, this freedom has to be real, not fictional.[129] Wynkoop believed that part of the makeup of human beings is their ability to make decisions and to initiate one course of action rather than another. She wrote, "Men are not free to choose the consequences of an act, but they are free to decide in which consequences they prefer to become enmeshed so far as a relationship to God is concerned."[130] It is not that human beings have free will so much as that the self freely and responsibly wills. For her, to be personal is to be responsible. This means that in Wynkoop's understanding, persons are not free *not* to be responsible.[131] Here she found support from Wesley, who wrote:

> You know how God wrought in your own soul, when he first enabled you to say, "The life I now live, I live by faith in the Son of God, who loved me, and gave himself for me." He did not take away your understanding; but enlightened and strengthened it. He did not destroy any of your affections; rather they were more vigorous than before. Least of all did he take away your liberty; your power of choosing good or evil: He did not force you; but, being assisted by his grace, you, like Mary, chose the better part. Just so has he assisted five in one house to make that happy choice; fifty or five hundred in one city; and many thousands in a nation; —without depriving any of them of that liberty which is essential to a moral agent.[132]

Wesley showed that the grace of God enabled and empowered human beings but did not coerce a response to God's overtures of grace. It was important to Wynkoop to protect the integrity of the person and to make

---

129. Ibid., 202.
130. Ibid.
131. Wynkoop, "A Theology of Depth," file 1431-15, WC, 86.
132. Quoted by Wynkoop in *A Theology of Love*, 170.

sure that the human will, though assisted and enabled by the Holy Spirit, responded to the overtures of God's grace uncoerced.

Furthermore, this life of freedom is not lived as an unattached individual but always in relation to God and others. Moral freedom can only be understood in the context of the self sustaining a responsible relationship to other selves.[133] And herein lies the rub. Human beings on their own, even with all that remained intact after the fall, can only exercise their freedom with divine assistance. Wynkoop did not believe that the self has the freedom to create its own spiritual environment.

Previously, we have concluded that humanity continues in the hands of God and that human freedom, as a characteristic of likeness, remains, even after the fall. We have also concluded that human freedom is not to be seen through the lens of humanism but, rather, as God's grace assisting the human will through his embrace, all the way from the beginning of creation, through the time of probation, and continuing after the fall toward the goal of Christlikeness. The potential for the human will to be freed to cooperate with the Holy Spirit is, thus, always present. However, as was shown, human beings continue to use this freedom to rebel or to remove themselves from the hands of God.

And now, Wynkoop shows her other hand. She said, "It is only through the Holy Spirit that human beings can understand moral freedom in the relationships of persons."[134] The only normal person, then, is the one in whom the Holy Spirit dwells. No one can know himself or herself apart from this indwelling. Her succinct description of the state of human beings after the fall says it all: "The apparatus is intact in fallen man, but the light is out." In other words, the moral mould is cast, but only through the prevenient ministry of the Holy Spirit can humans reach their God-given potential. Only in fellowship with the Holy Spirit can human beings experience true self-realization and assurance. Self-awareness and personal identification, then, are all wrapped in the ministry of the Holy Spirit. Only through the Holy Spirit are human beings truly brought face-to-face with their real selves.[135] Wynkoop wrote:

> The Spirit's activity is the most deeply personal relationship possible to men. He preserves the objective atonement from abstraction, artifi-

---

133. Wynkoop, *A Theology of Love*, 202.
134. Wynkoop, "A Theology of Depth," file 1431-15, WC, 142.
135. Wynkoop, *A Theology of Love*, 203.

ciality and antinomianism. In the ministry of the Holy Spirit all intermediaries, ritualistic, legal, **sacerdotal** and creedal are pushed aside. In his presence men are immediately confronted by God. This is not metaphysical—or mystical, but moral in the ultimate sense. The Holy Spirit applies truth morally, not simply intellectually as thought or empirically as experience or moralistically as law. It is whole person-to-person confrontation and communication.[136]

In personalism, "person" is the key to ultimate reality. Only in active intelligence or person do we find the fundamental explanation of the world and what happens in it. As a metaphysical principle, person is not identical to the human person, however true it may be that the personalistic principles are exemplified in human personality. In personalism the universe is seen as a society of selves or persons who interact and are united by the will of God. The union between persons and God is through the divine will. Even so, selves never act in isolation and are not mere modes of God, but uniquely individual. In personalism social categories are fundamental and ultimate.[137] Also, in personalism, the soul becomes the base camp for communication between the human person and the supreme Person. Bowne says, "The soul, in interacting with its body, is in fact interacting with the cosmic Person."[138]

Wynkoop, on the other hand, true to her Hebraic roots, saw person or self not as a metaphysical entity separate from the body but, rather, as a unity, fully grounded in real life. She said, "The Hebrew man knew nothing of an **Aristotelian bifurcation** between matter and form, essence and substance, numina and phenomena. Hebrew man was a materialist in the best sense. He lived in a real world, a good world. He profoundly respected himself because he believed God had made him. He was not concerned with metaphysics but with personal relationships. What he experienced was the real, not a shadow."[139]

Whereas personalism made a distinction between self and person and anchored development and maturity in the movement from the self to the person, Wynkoop did not make a distinction between self and person.

---

136. Wynkoop, "A Theology of Depth," file 1431-15, WC, 142.
137. Burrow, *Personalism*, 89.
138. Quoted by Peter A. Bertocci, "Borden Parker Bowne and His Personalistic Theistic Idealism," in *The Boston Personalist Tradition*, ed. Paul Deats and Carol Robb (Macon, GA: Mercer University Press, 1986), 66.
139. Wynkoop, *A Theology of Love*, 201.

She said, "The personality is the self. Remove the self and no personality remains."[140] It is this whole self that "is always in movement, outgoing, expanding, reaching for completion, restless, seeking, driving." She said, "One who has not become a true self will never be able to take his place in a society of selves."[141] In fact, she saw a person only reaching full potential through other persons. This corporate personality was, to Wynkoop, at the heart of what it means to be a person. She said, "The Hebrew man found his dynamism, not in static beingness, but in his social relatedness. His 'living' self, his totality, stood in relation to a larger unity, the social entity. . . . Hebrew man was in an essential way one with 'his fathers' and his family, his tribe and his nation. This was not a crude metaphysical or genetic unity, but a spiritual interconnectedness that penetrates to the core of what mankind is."[142]

It was, however, the divine community that became, to her, the main anchor point to bring understanding of what the true nature of person is. For Wynkoop, human beings were never intended to exist apart from the fellowship of the Godhead.[143] For her this was not a solitary experience but, in essence, an invitation to reflect (as part of a community) the very essence of the Trinity, which to her is a divine society of love. This communal understanding of the nature of personhood would become a key factor in the way Wynkoop went about describing the *essential* nature of the Trinity. This will come as a surprise to many, since Trinitarian language is conspicuously absent in her main work, *A Theology of Love*.

What is a curious phenomenon is that Wynkoop has two chapters on the Holy Spirit in her unpublished, 430-page manuscript "A Theology of Depth," yet these two chapters are left out in her 1972 publication *A Theology of Love*. One chapter is titled "The Holy Spirit" and the other chapter "The Communion of the Holy Spirit."[144] The chapter on "The Communion of the Holy Spirit" is especially relevant to understand her position on the Trinity. Some of the mystery is cleared up in correspondence between Charles Carter and Wynkoop.

---

140. Wynkoop, *Foundations of Wesleyan-Arminian Theology*, 114.
141. Wynkoop, *A Theology of Love*, 203.
142. Ibid., 123.
143. Wynkoop, "A Theology of Depth," file 1431-15, WC, 140.
144. Ibid.

Carter wrote to Wynkoop to give her feedback on her newly published *A Theology of Love*. Part of his critique was the lack of emphasis on the Holy Spirit. In response, Wynkoop shared with Carter the reason the chapter on the Holy Spirit was not included in *A Theology of Love*. She wrote, "Dr. Carter, I left out a chapter on the Holy Spirit (from the book) largely because I need a little more time to criticize my own observations. I do have the chapter written but feel it needs maturing before exposing it."[145] This is very unfortunate, since this chapter completes her views on the role of the Holy Spirit in her existential exploration of Christian holiness. When we now revisit the metaphor of "the two hands of God" as used in the theology of Irenaeus, Wynkoop has shown the one hand to be Christ (who is the Image), but what is needed is the other hand, the work of the Holy Spirit, to complete the divine embrace. To address this part of her existential theology we now turn to her focus on the communion of the Holy Spirit.

The Communion of the Holy Spirit

Wynkoop would agree with Bowne that personality is the key to understanding ultimate reality. However, as we have already discussed, her understanding of personhood is grounded not in the metaphysics of idealism but in the biblical-existential manifestation of the Godhead incarnated in real life. Her interest in the **immanent Trinity** is not speculative or philosophical but soteriological. Therefore, it is not a surprise to see Wynkoop using the existential experience of the Godhead in the economy of salvation as a gateway into her reflections on the immanent Trinity. The person and work of the Holy Spirit becomes, for her, the key to gaining understanding into the inner workings and being of the Trinity. She wrote, "To the early church the Holy Spirit was a matter of practical experience, not theoretical speculation. In the course of progressive revelation, any possible speculative idea about God became existential in the incarnation."[146] In addition to the Holy Spirit, Wynkoop also believed that a biblical understanding of personality goes a long way to bringing understanding of the Trinity. She used both a psychological and social analogy of personhood to reflect on the ontological nature of the Trinity.

---

145. Wynkoop to Charles Carter (correspondence, August 25, 1973), file 2223-4, WC.
146. Wynkoop, *A Theology of Love*, 140.

Wynkoop found the Trinity easier to explain by means of what she was discovering about personality than by philosophical expressions, which, in her mind, were hard to conceptualize. Because of the personal nature of the Holy Spirit, Wynkoop was not willing to settle on an impersonal ontology to describe the Trinity. She wrote, "Our Western individualism tends to create a problem relative to the Trinity that is not necessarily in the fact of the *tri-personal* nature of God. Rather than try to understand the philosophical formulae, 'three subsistences in one substance, or essence,' on the basis of our knowledge of personality it is better to let the revelation of the nature of God tell us something about personality."[147]

As we have already seen, for Wynkoop, personality cannot be separated from community and, in a sense, personality was to her essentially community. In other words, to be a person is to be in relationship. She underscored her position by going back to the Hebraic understanding of corporate personality. She quoted Alan Richardson as he reflects on the unique, biblical understanding of personality. He wrote, "The biblical idea is never confused by our modern concept 'of distinct personalities, hard and impermeable, each sharply distinguished from the others.' Rather, persons 'flow into one another.' This never means a loss of identity but an overlapping of mutual concerns so that a man lives in his sons, or he may receive the spirit of another and in some sense be that other man."[148]

This inner and external involvement in a social context helped Wynkoop understand what revelation told her about the ontological nature of the Godhead. For her, the social nature of the Trinity was the first step away from mechanistic determinism into moral freedom.[149] In this moral freedom, Wynkoop found the personal nature of the Trinity. She wrote, "In Genesis the God of creation meets us after a council session in which the decision, 'Let us make . . .' is the verdict . . . that later declaration that 'God is love,' is simply an elaboration and characterization of the nature of God as a social being. There is one God, says the Bible, but God is a divine society."[150]

We should especially pay attention to the wording "God is love." This, to Wynkoop, meant that love is not only experienced but also completed

---

147. Wynkoop, "A Theology of Depth," file 1431-15, WC, 136.
148. Ibid.
149. Ibid., 137.
150. Ibid.

within the being of God.[151] According to Wynkoop, community is essential to love. Love in this context is the pouring forth of the self into the selves of others.[152] Wynkoop's use of the terms "mutuality" and "togetherness" brought her very close to the ancient idea of *perichoresis* as she described both the unity and diversity of the Trinity.[153] In summary, we can affirm that, for Wynkoop, the ontology of the Godhead is tri-personal, whose very being is communal. Wynkoop's position sounds similar to the position taken by Zizioulas in his book *Being as Communion*. T. A. Noble summarizes Zizioulas's concept:

> The key point about the Christian doctrine of the Trinity was the assertion that three persons are one . . . what unites them is their koinonia, their communion. However, that is to be seen as an *ontological* statement. The communion *is* their being (*ousia*). One cannot separate their being from their interpersonal relations. They do not first exist and *then* relate to each other. They exist (or better, "subsist") in their relationship to each other. The words "begotten" or "proceed" are not to be understood impersonally, materially, or semi-physically. Rather they are to be understood as meaning that the three persons have their very being as they are from, to, and in each other in a fully *personal* way. They do not exist independently as separate monads or "individuals" for whom personal relationships are optional or added characteristics. They have their very being in mutual indwelling (*perichoresis*), for as the One God they are indivisible.[154]

Wynkoop is convinced that we cannot know the Trinity apart from the activity of the Holy Spirit. It is precisely the Holy Spirit that makes all Christian doctrine practical and relevant to life. Not only does the Holy Spirit personalize Christian truth, but the Holy Spirit also reveals the Trinity and personalizes Christ.[155]

In conclusion, we can say with confidence that Wynkoop did not endorse the philosophy of Boston personalism. Even though she used similar language, we have shown that she operated from the living, existential experience of the Christian, understood biblically. There are a few fac-

---

151. Ibid.
152. Ibid., 139.
153. Ibid.
154. Noble, *Holy Trinity*, 218.
155. Wynkoop, "A Theology of Depth," file 1431-15, WC, 134.

tors in personalism that she found helpful, especially the *dynamic* aspect of God's relation to his world. As far as labels go, to label Wynkoop as a personalist would be unfounded. It is best to locate Wynkoop in the biblical world of true relationships as opposed to the philosophical world of relationalism. We can then affirm that Wynkoop did not participate in the shift from "sinful man to moral man," as described by Chiles.

6
WYNKOOP'S SOTERIOLOGY

In this final chapter, we will attempt a critical overview of Wynkoop's theological emphases, trying to see particularly how far her theology of the Christian life was an authentic, twentieth-century development of the theology of John Wesley. It is good to remind ourselves again that Wynkoop was not doing theology from below (or from an anthropological perspective); she was merely interested in discussing the human side of redemption. She said, "God's grace is on one side, man's integrity is on the other side. Salvation is offered—to sinners who are morally responsible. To keep the integrity of both these truths is the heart of the gospel message."[1]

As we travel on foot with Wynkoop, we have already established that there is teleology at work in her theology. The trajectory of growth and development is also evident in Wesley as he viewed salvation as a teleological process comprised of a series of stages and degrees within the life of grace.[2] Collins helps us to see that these stages are expressed in various forms as stages of faith, of assurance and degrees of love.[3] Wynkoop, in turn, showed that the image of God remained intact and placed more emphasis on "likeness" as a key element of growth and development in her teleological trajectory. Whereas Wesley's teleology starts in the fall, Wynkoop's teleology originates in creation. Yet, in spite of these differences, it is remarkable to see that they both have Sonship as their goal. If we begin with the end in mind, we can see that, for Wesley, Christian perfection

---

1. Wynkoop, "A Theology of Depth," file 1431-15, WC, 165.
2. Maddox, *Responsible Grace*, 159.
3. Collins, *Theology of John Wesley*, 293–95.

serves as a controlling principle. The teleological structure of his theology gives meaning to perfection. In other words, every step in redemption is a means to an end, a progress toward a goal, which we will come to find is, for Wesley, perfection in love. Wynkoop arrived at the same conclusion. Our methodology will be to investigate the key teleological anchor points in Wynkoop that support her doctrine of Christian perfection while referencing the influence of Wesley. These existential anchor points will provide the structure through which we can deepen our understanding of Wynkoop's theology.

From the outset, one realizes that there is an interrelatedness in Wynkoop's use of terms that makes it impossible to lift one out for study apart from reference to the others. Four terms seem to cling together and support each other: faith, sanctification, sin, and love. Careful attention to these terms will reveal their essential relatedness at a level below the surface, and by their light, we hope to gain a deeper understanding of the underlying principles that shaped Wynkoop's theology. Since we are not just dealing with ideas but with human beings, human nature will always be an underlying current as we look into the teleological and existential nature of faith, sanctification, sin, and love. The object of our investigation so far has been to track Wynkoop's quest for a true moral response to God's overtures of grace. We set out to research her claim that sanctification proceeds along the lines of moral integrity. The particular relevance of this conviction is now expanded, as we look at the element of faith in Wynkoop's theology. For her, no word better tied in to the whole concept of the moral than "faith."[4]

On Faith

Wynkoop's chapter on faith in *A Theology of Love* has as its title "The Function of Faith." This is significant, since Wynkoop wanted to show that faith is a "living, dynamic exercise."[5] It serves an ongoing function in the Christian life. Faith is not to be seen as an end in itself but as a means to an end. This is evident in Wynkoop's assessment that "grace [is] actualized by faith," "we walk by faith," and "Christ dwells in the heart by faith."[6] Her trajectory for faith begins as "repentance for sin," continues

---

4. Wynkoop, "A Theology of Depth," file 1431-15, WC, 164.
5. Wynkoop, *A Theology of Love*, 222.
6. Ibid., 236.

"in love and obedience," includes crisis experiences along the way, and in the end serves as a "permanent, settled principle of life."[7] Wynkoop made a distinction between "faith *as* obedience" and "faith *and* obedience" as a way to describe the characteristics of faith. By the aforementioned category, Wynkoop meant that faith should be seen as a "walk in the light." She said, "The light of the Holy Spirit leads us to Christ where we find forgiveness. This is justification. God treats us as if we had never sinned. We are God's children. But 'conversion' is more than a change in our relationship to God; it is also the infusion of new life—called in theology, regeneration or the new birth. Justification is not separate in time, but does represent distinctly different functions in the life of the person. . . . The 'walk' refers to the ethical aspect of salvation, which is precisely the area of sanctification."[8]

Wynkoop did not want to project faith as an abstract category standing outside the life a believer lives. For her, growth, or the process of obedience, is implicit in faith. By differentiating between faith *and* obedience, Wynkoop wanted to show that obedience proceeds by decision.[9] Wynkoop here brought attention to the crisis aspect of the journey of faith. She said, "As we walk in the light we are brought face to face with anything in our hearts or lives which may prevent the full measure of love from being given to God. The process is the deepening of love by obedience. At every point where light reveals a barrier to full love, obedience makes a definite choice and decision. It involves a crisis."[10]

We can see that faith, for Wynkoop, is not a substitute for obedience. It *is* obedience. Wynkoop believed that obedience must have the ingredient of faith in it to *appropriate* righteousness, and conversely, faith must include obedience to make it saving faith.[11] Faith is not exhausted or completed in any crisis decision but must become a way of life.[12] This way of life is a walk in the light of the Holy Spirit. Wynkoop said, "The growth in faith is an experience of self-discovery with the Holy Spirit as guide. This process is teleological. The depth of self-will and pride, which dictate the policies

---

7. Wynkoop, "The Relation of Justification and Sanctification" (article, undated), file 1437-22, WC, 3.
8. Ibid., 4.
9. Ibid.
10. Ibid.
11. Wynkoop, *A Theology of Love*, 242.
12. Wynkoop, "Relation of Justification," file 1437-22, WC, 5.

of life, must be plumbed and uprooted so that the love which has come into our lives may take its place and become the ruling power."[13]

We can then say that, for Wynkoop, legitimate faith experiences were seen to be teleological. The idea of growth and development was more important than just a specific episode. It was to be caught up in the kingdom of God (the reign of Christ) as a partner with Christ in the re-creation and renewal of this broken world. At this level, we see a very close connection between Wynkoop and Wesley. The way Wynkoop relates to Wesley is especially evident in Wesley's covenant theology as he focuses on the economy of salvation as a movement "from faith to faith." Stanley J. Rodes, in *From Faith to Faith*, indicates that the servant/son metaphor is a key component in Wesley's teleology.[14] There is a parallelism at work in Wesley's soteriology as he looks at the history of God's dealings with humankind and then postulates the same pattern in the individual's journey of faith.[15] Rodes describes this trajectory as a movement from the "faith of a servant," who is under "a spirit of bondage and fear," to the "faith of a son," who now comes under "the spirit of adoption."[16] The point of arrival at sonship is when "Christ is revealed in your heart."[17]

Here we come full circle back to the fact that Wesley and Wynkoop shared a similar passion for sonship, where "likeness" is fulfilled in Christ. It is "faith working through love" (Gal. 5:6, NRSV) that expresses the essence of Wynkoop's understanding of faith. Wynkoop said, "As important as 'faith' is to salvation, faith never is said to satisfy the law of holiness. Love is the fulfilment of the whole law."[18] She did not mean that there is a contradiction but that the saving relationship to God has two sides, and neither is complete without the other.[19] Wynkoop was convinced that faith that is absorbed with itself (as in those who propose a "perfection of faith") has no relationship to life, but the faith that re-establishes love cap-

---

13. Ibid.
14. Stanley J. Rodes, *From Faith to Faith: John Wesley's Covenant Theology and the Way of Salvation* (Eugene, OR: Pickwick Publications, 2013), 181.
15. Ibid.
16. Ibid., 186.
17. Ibid., 184. It is important to note here that Rodes did not interpret Wesley's understanding of God's acceptance of the faith of a servant as meeting the qualifications for justifying faith. Acceptance was relative to the dispensation one was under. Justifying faith only belongs to the one who has arrived at the faith of a son or daughter.
18. Wynkoop, "A Theology of Depth," file 1431-15, WC, 183.
19. Wynkoop, *A Theology of Love*, 242.

tures the heart of her teleological understanding of salvation.[20] She said, "Love is the goal of faith and is the substance of sanctification. But love by its very nature is not a passive thing. It is as a rushing, tumbling river."[21] Therefore, there is no place in her soteriology for a solitary expression of the work of God. Faith and love have to go together.[22] Wynkoop said, "The feeling we need is that intense, consuming, warm, compassionate love that sparks action and involvement, that flows away from itself endlessly into the lives of others. The best of feelings that merely bubble up and eddy back into the self will not only poison the spring but also mock the thirsty world around."[23]

We see this connection between faith and love as a prominent aspect in Wesley's theology as well. Wynkoop quoted excerpts from Wesley's sermons to show that she stood in solidarity with Wesley in this aspect of his theology. In "An Earnest Appeal," Wesley says, "We acknowledge no faith but that which worketh by love." In "Nature of Enthusiasm," he says, "Being a Christian means having a faith which is active in love."[24] In "The Law Established through Faith," Wesley says:

> Faith itself, even Christian faith, the faith of God's elect, the faith of the operation of God, is still only the handmaid of love. . . . Love is the end of all the commandments of God. Love is the end, the sole end, of every dispensation of God, from the beginning of the world to the consummation of all things. . . . Let those who magnify faith beyond all proportions so as to swallow up all things else, and who so totally misapprehend the nature of it as to imagine it stands in the place of love, consider further that as love will exist after faith, so it did long before.[25]

Wynkoop believed that Wesley's emphasis on love served as a "footnote" to the Reformation emphasis on "faith alone."[26] For Wynkoop, Wesley's emphasis on love introduced a new dimension to faith that was as far reaching as the "faith versus works" emphasis of Luther. She said, "In Reformation thought, saving faith encourages the Christian to trust the

---

20. Wynkoop, "Relation of Justification," file 1437-22, WC, 2.
21. Ibid.
22. Runyon, *The New Creation*, 162.
23. Wynkoop, "The Holy Spirit and Pentecostalism" (article, 1974), file 1437-22, WC, 8.
24. Wynkoop, "John Wesley's Doctrine of Perfection in the Light of His Whole Theology" (article, 1963), file 1432-3, WC, 13.
25. Wynkoop, *A Theology of Love*, 222-23
26. Ibid., 223.

one who saves him, and in this confidence love is fostered and developed. Love is a byproduct of faith. In Wesley, faith is itself an element of love in that in life situations love and faith cannot be separated. Faith leads to love, which is the goal and essence of salvation."[27]

In the focus of "faith expressing itself in love," both Wesley and Wynkoop added an ethical discussion to the forensic meaning of justification. Both saw faith as morally structured through love. Collins affirms this position as he captures the teleological nature of Wesley's position. He says, "For Wesley, saving faith ever points beyond itself to the love of God and neighbor. That is, faith is both instrumental to love and is ever active in love."[28]

FAITH'S RELATION TO GRACE

According to Harald Lindström, it was important for Wesley, in response to election, to show the human being as an independent subject of faith.[29] Wynkoop echoed this sentiment, "Wesley would agree with the Reformers that all of salvation is by the grace of God; however, he wasn't able to find scriptural support that salvation was for a select few only."[30] Wesley's emphasis on prevenient grace gave hope that all of humanity "is preserved for salvation."[31] Here, Wynkoop stood in full agreement with Wesley. Prevenient grace has been given to everyone, even the power to use it.[32] Wynkoop said, "No man, then, is now in a mere state of nature but is under the privileges and responsibilities of grace. Grace is not the irresistible power of God overcoming the will of man, but it is the loving hand of a Father enabling the child to use the resources given him in the first place by that Father."[33]

This means, as an initial gift, prevenient grace is irresistible; human beings cannot choose not to have it.[34] According to Maddox, Wesley believed prevenient grace restores a measure of freedom lacking in the bondage of original sin. Maddox interprets this "measure of freedom," as

---

27. Ibid.
28. Collins, *Theology of John Wesley*, 227.
29. Harald Lindström, *Wesley and Sanctification: A Study in the Doctrine of Salvation* (Wilmore, KY: Francis Asbury Press, 1946), 93.
30. Wynkoop, *A Theology of Love*, 154.
31. Ibid., 155.
32. Ibid.
33. Ibid.
34. Collins, *Scripture Way of Salvation*, 44.

understood by Wesley, to be a "partial restoration of man's sin-corrupted faculties."[35] Through these partially restored faculties, human beings are able to will God—or at least offer repentance, if not faith—toward their justification.[36] Maddox endorses Thomas Langford's recommendation that prevenient grace should not be seen as a gift *from* God but, rather, as a gift *of* God's activity in people's lives.[37] Maddox wants to make sure that grace is not seen as something that God gives us but, rather, as the way God gives us himself through the presence of the Holy Spirit.[38]

Noble indicates that there was a tendency in Wesley to view grace as an "impersonal infused substance," thereby replacing the personal action of the Holy Spirit.[39] This is what Wynkoop wanted to avoid. Given the focus on uncreated grace, it should be noted that Wynkoop made the same application to faith as well. She did not see faith as something given to human beings but as an inherent disposition that remained intact after the fall. She said, "The exhortations to exercise the faculty of faith were addressed mainly to unbelievers, obviously, and hence, to those who were in sin."[40] For Wynkoop, this is not a "partially restored faculty" but a faculty that remained fully intact after the fall, now expressed as rebellion or unbelief. The antithesis to saving faith for her, then, is not no faith but full, active rejection.[41] Wynkoop wrote, "The concept of the whole-man psychology in which all aspects of personality are seen to work as a unit—faith and will, heart and mind, love and obedience—preserves the integrity of personality without losing the idea of dependence on God's grace."[42] According to Wynkoop, this is especially true when viewed from the perspective of human beings' relationship to God. In this relationship faith seems to be an essential element in personality.[43]

However, she was cautious in describing this elusive faculty called faith. She wrote, "We ought not to be obsessed by the act of our faith. Faith in the New Testament sense describes the very reaching out of our most inner selves toward Christ, not conscious of faith as such, but con-

---

35. Maddox, *Responsible Grace*, 87.
36. Ibid.
37. Ibid., 89.
38. Ibid., 90
39. Noble, *Holy Trinity*, 100.
40. Wynkoop, "The Biblical Study of Man," file 1432-3, WC, 126.
41. Wynkoop, *A Theology of Love*, 232.
42. Ibid., 225.
43. Ibid., 227.

scious of the grasp of mutual love, a deep, profound resting and trusting and love in and for Christ. Faith is by definition obedience and love from the heart. Faith never appears unclothed and abstract. Faith is dynamic."[44]

It is then the activity of "someone" (the Holy Spirit) who helps human beings to change the direction of their affection. It is not the initiation of a new power. An "implanted" saving faith rising apart from human participation was not exactly what she had in mind when she reflected on Christian integrity in this divine-human interaction.

FAITH AND JUSTIFICATION

For Wynkoop, justification is by faith. Faith is turning from sin and walking in love and obedience. This faith becomes the foundation for the whole Christian life because, in her mind, "the just shall live by faith" (Rom. 1:17; Gal. 3:11; Heb. 10:38, KJV). Since love and obedience are the essence of sanctification, sanctification is just as important as justification for salvation. She said, "To refuse (or neglect) sanctification is to refuse (or reject) the very basis of justification." Sanctification preserves justification. She wrote, "The same love and obedience, which is implicit in maintaining justification, leads us invariably along the path of sanctification. Since faith (as turning away from sin and obeying God), leads us into definite crisis decisions regarding the sin of self will and pride which challenges the authority of God in our lives, we will inevitably be led by the Holy Spirit to the ultimate crisis."[45]

There is not much that separates Wynkoop and Wesley in their understanding of justification. Wesley would agree with the Reformers that justification is entirely God's work; however, Wesley saw a place for repentance prior to justification. "By repentance," wrote Wesley, "I mean conviction of sin, producing real desires and sincere resolutions of amendment; and by 'fruits meet for repentance,' forgiving our brother; using the ordinances of God, and in general obeying him according to the measure of grace which we have received."[46]

Since it is the law that the Spirit ordinarily uses to produce this conviction of sin, Wesley terms this "legal" repentance.[47] Collins indicates

---

44. Wynkoop, "The Problem of the Relationship between the 'First and Second Works of Grace'" (unpublished paper, undated), file 1434-13, WC, 3.
45. Wynkoop, "John Wesley's Doctrine," file 1432-3, WC, 6.
46. Collins, *Theology of John Wesley*, 157.
47. Collins, *Scripture Way of Salvation*, 69.

that this legal state goes hand in hand with the "spirit of bondage and fear," one who is "under the law," "the Jewish dispensation," as well as the "faith of a servant."[48] Collins says, "All of these phrases . . . are descriptive of those people who have a measure of faith and grace, but who yet fall short of the faith of those who are justified and born of God."[49] Legal repentance, however, becomes "evangelical" repentance as the convicted sinner begins to turn from sin toward God.[50] As human beings respond to God's awakening overtures, Wesley would say that repentance is only "remotely necessary," whereas faith is "immediately necessary " to justification.[51] Wesley then saw repentance as the holistic process of transformation, both on the inside and on the outside as the believer turns his or her life to God. Repentance and faith are thus seen to cover the whole trajectory of a believer's walk with Christ.

Collins draws our attention to the fact that the year 1738 marked a shift in Wesley's understanding of justification.[52] According to Collins, before 1738, Wesley often confused justification with sanctification. Wesley considered the holy life (with its works of piety and mercy) to be the basis for justification, instead of its fruit.[53] Collins references Wesley's comment to John Newton in 1765, "I think on justification just as I have done any time these seven-and-twenty years, and just as Mr. Calvin does. In this respect I do not differ from him a hair's breadth."[54] The breakthrough came as Wesley realized that the Christian's hope is not in his own righteousness but that righteousness which comes through faith in Christ.[55]

Maddox had already established this point. He wrote, "From 1739 Wesley was careful to distinguish justification from sanctification . . . for example, his most general distinction was between justification as a relative (i.e., relational) change in which God declares us forgiven by virtue of Christ, and sanctification as a real change in which the Spirit renews our fallen nature."[56] According to Collins, this shift allowed Wesley to confess, first of all, that true, salvific faith is in and through Jesus Christ, not some

---

48. Ibid., 72.
49. Ibid.
50. Ibid., 70.
51. Lindström, *Wesley and Sanctification*, 117.
52. Collins, *Theology of John Wesley*, 169.
53. Ibid.
54. Ibid.
55. Ibid., 174.
56. Maddox, *Responsible Grace*, 170.

general, rational belief in a deistic God. Justifying faith is not just mental assent but also a "disposition of the heart."[57] This realization meant to Wesley that his whole person should be involved in living out this faith. Wesley did not want to put the intellect aside but recognized that it cannot stand on its own or carry the full weight as a response of faith. It must be joined to a disposition of the heart. Collins further indicates that, for Wesley, true justifying faith had to go beyond the faith of the apostles, in that "it acknowledges the necessity and merit of Christ's death, and the power of his resurrection."[58]

In these three elements of justification by faith, we find a common bond between Wesley and Wynkoop. Wynkoop would endorse Wesley's position as described above. She quoted Wesley's summary with her approval, "This then is the salvation which is through faith, even in this present world: A salvation from sin, and the consequences of sin, both often expressed in the word, *justification*; which, taken in the largest sense, implies a deliverance from guilt and punishment, by the atonement of Christ actually applied to the soul of the sinner now believing on him, and a deliverance from the power of sin, through Christ *formed in his heart*."[59]

She affirmed what she saw as Wesley's position, when he describes his faith as directed to the *person* of Christ, describing this relationship as personal, rather than on an impersonal level. For her, faith was through and through personal. She was interested in the "lawgiver back of the law."[60] She wanted to protect the integrity of both parties, the personhood of Christ as well as the personhood of the one responding to the overtures of God's grace. "It is putting dishonesty in God," she said, "to say that a man is objectively righteous and subjectively unrighteous even by means of Christ's atonement."[61]

This "justifying faith" was very personal to Wesley, as is seen in his sermon "The Scripture Way of Salvation." Collins brings our attention to the personal nature of Wesley's testimony: "Faith is a divine *evidence* and *conviction*, not only that 'God was in Christ, reconciling the world unto himself,' but also that Christ 'loved *me*, and gave himself for *me*.'"[62]

---

57. Collins, *Theology of John Wesley*, 167.
58. Ibid.
59. Wynkoop, *A Theology of Love*, 236.
60. Ibid., 238.
61. Wynkoop, "A Theology of Depth," file 1431-15, WC, 170.
62. Collins, *Scripture Way of Salvation*, 134.

Wesley here was not only showing how personal this relationship is but also making reference to having an inner *spiritual sense* of the Holy Spirit working in his life.[63]

Wynkoop especially related to Wesley when he spoke of his faith as a disposition of the heart. Everything she proposed about "moral" becomes relevant at this point. As we have seen, "moral" to her is personal, dynamic, and communal. She would agree with Wesley that faith couldn't just be mental assent. Faith has to engage the whole person, not simply intellectual faculty alone or emotions or will. All of the personality has to act as a unit. Wynkoop wrote a thirty-page booklet called *John Wesley: Christian Revolutionary*, with a major portion of this booklet dedicated to an exploration of Romans 12:1. Paul's exhortation that we are to "present [our] bodies as a living sacrifice" (NRSV) in her mind confirms this holistic perspective. She said, "When one commits his body to something, the rest of what man is tags along pretty faithfully. . . . The body is the locus of 'me'—you."[64] She also reflected on "presenting" as not implying that persons inhibit themselves in presenting. To her, "'present' is active and 'whole personal.'"[65] Given her holistic approach, the idea of "accepting Christ" as a way of appropriating faith was to her a far cry from biblical teaching. She wrote, "Interesting enough, no New Testament passage gives the slightest hint that we are to 'accept' Christ or 'what he has done for us.' We are exhorted 'to believe in him.' In the occasions where 'accept' refers to a relationship of men and Christ (or God) it is man who is to make himself *acceptable*. The tremendous exhortation of Romans 12:1 is to the effect that we present ourselves 'holy and acceptable' to God."[66]

THE ASSURANCE OF FAITH

Even though Wesley and Wynkoop lived two hundred years apart, they both had to shift the focus away from grace being understood in metaphysical terms. Both worked to shift away from defining spiritual reality as supernaturally guaranteed independent of the knower, to defining it "as registering on consciousness, which includes the knower."[67] Run-

---

63. Ibid.
64. Mildred Bangs Wynkoop, *John Wesley: Christian Revolutionary* (Kansas City: Beacon Hill Press of Kansas City, 1970), 16.
65. Ibid., 19.
66. Wynkoop, "A Theology of Depth," file 1431-15, WC, 176. (Emphasis added.)
67. Runyon, *The New Creation*, 150.

yon describes the challenge Wesley faced to incorporate an experiential knowledge of God: "For Anglicans sacramental grace was imparted by the officially authorized administrators of grace, the clergy, in an event that takes place whether the recipient is conscious of it or not. An indelible status is granted by baptism, which is the product of God's grace independent of human consciousness. In Calvinism, God's election from eternity is what determines one's destiny, again independent of human consciousness."[68]

For Wynkoop, the struggle was further down the road. She was fighting the teaching or perception that the Holy Spirit imposes new character on the person metaphysically, without the involvement of the rational or moral capacities. This means that for both, salvation had to shift from a metaphysical status to an experiential knowledge of God that makes one a participant in what is known.

For Wesley, Scripture became the primary means through which he was able to judge the validity of a specific spiritual encounter. This was especially important to Wesley right after his Aldersgate experience, when he was very susceptible to the Moravian influence with its emphasis on feelings. Wesley realized that his feelings needed the accountability of the traditional means of grace, namely Scripture, the sacraments, public worship, and prayer.[69] In addition, "experience," according to Runyon, "functions for Wesley as a way to register the reality of a spiritual world that transcends the self."[70] The way it works, according to Runyon, is that "spiritual senses transmit sense impressions to the mind, where reason is used to interpret the impressions in the light of Scripture, the traditions of the church and the experiences of others in the community of faith."[71] Genuine experience of God is not the individual experience so much as it is "the experience of the other into whose life a person is taken by grace as a shared reality."[72]

However, the believer's "perceptible testimony" was still a strong indicator for Wesley that the Holy Spirit is at work in the life of the believer.[73] Wesley saw a progression in faith as the believer advances through

---

68. Ibid.
69. Ibid., 155.
70. Ibid., 161.
71. Ibid.
72. Ibid., 162.
73. Collins, *Theology of John Wesley*, 133.

different stages of assurance. This advancement in assurance is from one who has no fear or love (natural man) to one who has fear without love (the awakened) to one who has love and fear (babe in Christ) and finally one who has love without fear (a father in Christ).[74] When the justifying and sanctifying work begins in the life of the believer, a believer can have "a measure of assurance," but it is only in the experience of entire sanctification that the believer has the "full assurance of faith."[75] Wesley's key Scripture was Romans 8:16 (KJV), "The Spirit itself beareth witness with our spirit, that we are the children of God." Wesley wrote, "By 'testimony of the Spirit' I mean an inward impression of the soul, whereby the Spirit of God immediately and directly witnesses to my spirit that I am a child of God, that Jesus Christ hath loved me, and given himself for me; that all my sins are blotted out, and I, even I, am reconciled to God."[76]

Wynkoop echoed this sentiment. For her the Holy Spirit spotlights Christ, whereas what she calls the "**pseudo-spirit**" spotlights the person himself.[77] These sentiments are reflected in an article titled "The Holy Spirit and Pentecostalism." She affirmed the validity of feelings but warned against feelings that merely end in the self as an emotional experience. For her, feelings need to be connected to real life and cannot become substitutes for personal involvement and action.[78]

The following are a summary of reliable tests Wynkoop used in her paper to assess the validity of the presence of the Holy Spirit: First, since the Holy Spirit is "free," Wynkoop didn't believe that the activity of the Holy Spirit can be patterned. This is especially so, since human beings are unique and the Holy Spirit respects human individuality. Second, the Holy Spirit always maintains the unity of the Godhead. In other words, the Godhead cannot be divided into three separate Gods. This is essentially what underlay Wynkoop's concerns after hearing some students say, "I have found something better than Christ, I have found the Holy Spirit," or, "We, as Nazarenes, must leave behind the mere lordship of Christ and move up into the freedom of the Holy Spirit."[79] Third, the Holy Spirit does not decompartmentalize the divided heart in order to heal a broken relationship.

---

74. Ibid., 137.
75. Ibid., 136.
76. Ibid., 129.
77. Wynkoop, "The Holy Spirit and Pentecostalism" (article, 1974), file 1437-12, WC, 7.
78. Ibid.
79. Ibid., 11.

When the spiritual is separated from the rational and one equates the feeling part with the spiritual, Wynkoop believed a pseudo-spirit was at work. Fourth, the Holy Spirit always produces clear thinking, rational judgment, sharp self-awareness, the ability to discriminate, and the power to make contrary choices. The pseudo-spirit in turn lowers ego-consciousness, with the result that it relaxes the motor and thought control. Wynkoop said, "The false delight of blurred feelings wafting the consciousness into apparent freedom from restraint, is totally contrary to the work of the Spirit of God."[80] Fifth, the Holy Spirit encourages thinking and reasoning, since he is the Spirit of Truth. The pseudo-spirit, on the other hand, forbids questioning. The Holy Spirit stimulates a strong desire to learn, whereas the pseudo-spirit fears learning and only wants to tap the magic source of psychic power, which bypasses thinking. Finally, the Holy Spirit sheds the love of God in the heart. He is the source of love! This, to Wynkoop, was the most reliable test, since it is the fulfilment of the law.[81]

These cautions were not made in a vacuum. Wynkoop's observations came from the front lines as an evangelist in her own denomination. The tendency was to overemphasize the subjective and the immediate experience of the Spirit in the individual. In the absence of good exegetical work, experience itself became the source of understanding about experience.[82] Many times the only validation of the experience was the testimony itself.

The real concern for Wynkoop with this overemphasis on the emotional was that it tended to lead the mind away from the essential moral intent of biblical holiness.[83] In her mind, "the emotional focus tended to colour biblical exegesis so that proofs for holiness dogma were often psychologically determined."[84] As Wynkoop and her husband travelled in the United States as evangelists, what she encountered was the reifying of the experience of entire sanctification in such a way that the experience was disconnected from proper biblical exegesis and the person's existential realities of life.

Wynkoop did not stand outside these challenges as an independent observer. She tried to make sense of the encounters she had with the Holy

---

80. Ibid., 7.
81. Ibid., 7–10.
82. H. Ray Dunning, "Christian Perfection: Toward a New Paradigm," *WTJ* 33:1 (1998): 3.
83. Wynkoop, "A Theology of Depth," file 1431-15, WC, 44.
84. Ibid.

Spirit in her own life, as well as to give leadership to those who depended on her for spiritual guidance. As was mentioned earlier, when Wynkoop could not find assurance, even after forty altar experiences, her participation in the Episcopal Church helped her regain a freshness of the truth of Christ through the sacramental means of Holy Communion and small group meetings. These sacramental and communal experiences served as an important correction to her when her life tilted out of balance with its overemphasis on her own experience and feelings. There were certain checks and balances at work in Wynkoop to stabilize her relationship with Christ. The sacrament of Communion continued to be an important means of grace throughout her life. Dr. Jesse Middendorf commented, "Though advanced in years, Mildred was carefully attentive to every detail in a service. Her occasional notes of encouragement always spoke with appreciation for the music, the sermon, or some other element of the day. She especially loved Communion and would often send me notes of affirmation and appreciation for the service of the Lord's Table."[85]

On Sanctification

Wynkoop arrived at her understanding of sanctification by bringing together all the various building blocks we have examined up to this point. Her doctoral thesis on biblical interpretation, her master's thesis on the image of God, her philosophy of moral integrity, and her desire for a practical, existential understanding of holiness all merge together in her understanding of sanctification. The role of faith, expressing itself in love and obedience, also finds its place in her understanding of sanctification.

As Wynkoop followed her evangelist husband on the revival camp-meeting trails, she realized that not much time or consideration was given to theological anthropology. There seemed to be a disconnect between the high ideals of holiness theology and the fallible, imperfect human beings who were called to *be* holy. When preachers spoke about "growth in grace," something she seldom heard on the evangelistic trails, the question that plagued her was, "How can I be sanctified and human at the same time?"[86] Beyond her belief that grace is *received*, Wynkoop also believed

---

85. Written in the foreword of the republication of *Foundations of Wesleyan-Arminian Theology*. Dr. Jesse C. Middendorf, later a general superintendent in the Church of the Nazarene, was Wynkoop's pastor in her golden years.

86. Wynkoop, "Foundations," file 2227-11, WC, 10.

that grace is something that can be *experienced* in this world and that it has relevance for people's everyday lives. She wrote, "The ideal must be specifically related to the practical details of human life. Theology must become experiential. . . . The preaching of the gospel arouses so much hope in the sin-tormented human heart that care must be exercised lest it seem to become a one-step lift to heaven itself so that the actual practical steps of life seem to be a denial of the truth of the message."[87]

Wynkoop's existential reading of Scripture became the foundation for her formulation of sanctification. For her it was not so much the theological use of the dynamic words of the New Testament that ensured the doctrine of sanctification but, rather, a recovery of the existential meaning of these words and concepts. The doctrine of sanctification was, first and foremost for Wynkoop, an existential doctrine. Her approach was not to formulate formal doctrine by way of logic but, rather, to give voice to the faith and existential realities of ordinary people in daily living situations. Wynkoop believed that if she stayed close to the existential teaching of Scripture, she would be able to remain close to the common experiences of people everywhere in all times.[88] And, as we have already established, Wynkoop read Scripture with an eye for the living Word who became flesh and lived among ordinary people. The key teleological anchor point for Wynkoop was *Christlikeness*. This was the controlling principle of her doctrine of sanctification. Starting with this in mind, we can now look at some of the key postulates of Wynkoop's existential doctrine of sanctification. In "The Foundations of *A Theology of Love*," Wynkoop listed four categories that described her default position on sanctification. She described sanctification as Christocentric, relational, teleological, and socially oriented (ecclesiological).[89] These four categories provide a useful structure through which we can now take a closer look at her understanding of sanctification.

SANCTIFICATION IS CHRISTOCENTRIC

Wynkoop described Jesus as "the very first real Christian (religious) existentialist."[90] She made this provocative statement because, in her

---

87. Wynkoop, "A Theology of Depth," file 1431-15, WC, 15.
88. Wynkoop, "Sanctification Is Existential," *The Preachers Magazine* 33:7 (July 1958): file 1051-1, WC, 1.
89. Wynkoop, "Foundations," file 2227-11, WC, 9.
90. Ibid., 3.

mind, Jesus did not write anything—whatever he wrote in the sand was blown away by the wind—but lived a life full of grace and love so that people could get a picture of what it is like to be a true human being. She said, "Jesus was seen, heard, touched, loved and hated. He spoke to real people enmeshed in the web of real life experiences. Wherever Jesus went, he not only engaged people's intellect, but challenged people to the very core of their existential selves."[91] We pick up on this Christocentric focus in her quest to see how the normal usage of theological terms (sanctification) holds up in its biblical context. In "A Theology of Depth," Wynkoop undertook a study to understand New Testament words in their New Testament framework. Her stated interest in examining these words was not only to do better theology but also to be a better communicator of the truths of Scripture.

She said, "Holinesss theology is very dependent on the existential meaning of words, because holiness is precisely not an abstract thing but the very dimension of religion which relates it intimately with human experience. Salvation is *not* in 'principle and not in fact.' It is rather *in practical fact* before it can be reduced to principle."[92] Having said that, she believed that the biblical background of meaning could be the building blocks of a vital theology. It is therefore incumbent upon us to take a brief excursion into Wynkoop's *contextual study* of the term "sanctification." From her extensive research we may here reference a few examples:

First, she believed that sanctification is "in Christ." She supported this claim by showing that the Old Testament sacrifices point forward to Christ's work (blood sanctifies). She brought our attention to Hebrews 9:13–14, "If the blood of goats sanctifies to the purifying of the flesh, how much more shall the blood of Christ purge your conscience . . . to serve the living God?" In Hebrews 10:10, she saw the theme continuing, "We are sanctified by the offering of Christ's body once for all," and Hebrews 10:14, "By one offering Christ has perfected forever all who are being sanctified."[93]

Second, she showed that the purpose and results of Christ's sacrificial act are for the sanctification of the church. She brought our attention to

---

91. Ibid.

92. Wynkoop, "Biblical Definition of Theological Terms" (article, undated), file 1425-21, WC, 1.

93. Wynkoop, "A Theology of Depth," file 1431-15, WC, 199. Scripture quotations are Wynkoop's partial paraphrases from the KJV.

Ephesians 5:25–26, where Christ is presented by Paul as the one who "gave himself" for the church in order to "sanctify and cleanse it with the washing of water by the word" (KJV). In Hebrews 13:12 she saw the same idea expressed. Jesus suffered in order to "sanctify the people with his own blood" (KJV). In Hebrews 2:9–11 (KJV), we "see Jesus . . . suffering . . . crowned," made "perfect through sufferings. For both he that sanctifieth and they who are sanctified are all . . . one." Wynkoop showed that being made "perfect in suffering" is here equated with sanctification. Jesus's prayer for unity in John 17 solidified her conviction that our sanctification is anchored in Jesus Christ, especially vv. 16–19 (KJV): "They are not of the world, even as I am not of the world. . . . As thou hast sent me into the world, even so have I also sent them into the world. And for their sakes I sanctify myself, that they also might be sanctified." Wynkoop wrote, "In this text, Jesus made no reference to any defect or failure in the disciples. His concern was that they should be locked into the commission he had received from God and was laying down in his death."[94]

Third, Wynkoop indicated that there are no "inner distinctions" in the status of those who are sanctified. She referenced 1 Corinthians 1:2 (KJV), where Paul refers to the church as those "sanctified in Christ Jesus," or "saints." Wynkoop here emphasized the fact that all believers are referred to as "sanctified." Her commentary on 1 Thessalonians 5:23 is especially relevant: "May the God of peace sanctify *every one of you* (grammar sustains this). May your (each individual) whole spirit, soul, body (the entire self) be preserved blameless."[95] We notice again here that it is not sanctification from God's side that is moving to a higher level but Paul addressing the corporate body, expressing God's desire for the sanctification of everyone in that fellowship.[96]

Finally, Wynkoop concentrated on humanity's responsibility in appropriating sanctification. She referenced 2 Timothy 2:21 (KJV), "If a man . . . purge himself . . . he shall be a vessel unto honour, sanctified, and meet for the master's use," and 1 Peter 3:15, "Sanctify in our hearts, Christ as Lord" (paraphr. by Wynkoop).[97] Here Wynkoop believed that the context supports her assessment that sanctification is not something that should

---

94. Wynkoop, "Biblical Definition," file 1425-21, WC, 3.
95. Wynkoop, "A Theology of Depth," file 1431-15, WC, 211.
96. Ibid., 210.
97. Ibid., 213.

be sought after but, rather, an imperative command to appropriate what is already a reality in Christians' lives. The verdict is that Christians should *be* or *become* what they already *are*.[98]

Throughout this contextual study, Wynkoop was able to make several analytical observations regarding the usage of the term "sanctification." The following is a summary of her observations:

(a) She believed that it is only through Christ's blood that our sanctification is possible. This means that justification does not exhaust the meaning of the atonement. She wrote, "It cannot be merely said that Christ died to provide forgiveness for sin or for our justification only. Nothing less than our sanctification is sufficient to comprehend the mystery of the death of Christ on the cross."[99] Christ's atonement extends to our sanctification as well. However, Wynkoop was quick to remind us that sanctification can only be received in the Holy Spirit.[100]

(b) Wynkoop was convinced that human beings do not achieve sanctification on their own power. It is not based on the depth of their repentance or the power of their will. It is always given by God but must be appropriated by us. And to that she added, "We do not make him Lord, we enter the kingdom where he is Lord."[101]

(c) For Wynkoop, sanctification as a status was always related to a group. She wrote that, "of the two prayers for sanctification recorded in the New Testament, both were petitions in behalf of others and not for the one who did the praying."[102] Wynkoop was not aware of any individual in Scripture who received an experience called sanctification. She could not find any passage that specifically indicated that sanctification was ever to be sought. The focus, rather, was on keeping the sanctification one already had.[103]

(d) So far as the word itself is concerned, Wynkoop did not believe that entire sanctification was directly related to the baptism of the Holy Spirit, though the whole process of sanctification is in the presence and ministry of the Holy Spirit.[104] Wynkoop wrote, "A careful survey of the

---

98. Wynkoop, "Biblical Definition," file 1425-21, WC, 4.
99. Wynkoop, "A Theology of Depth," file 1431-15, WC, 227.
100. Ibid., 228.
101. Ibid., 230.
102. Ibid., 207.
103. Ibid., 219.
104. Ibid., 220.

biblical use of the word reveals that 'sanctification' is seldom if ever used to refer to a second crisis."[105]

In general, we can conclude that, for Wynkoop, the whole sweep of biblical teaching relative to sanctification centred on one major concern: human beings' practical relationship to God and their neighbours. Similar to Wesley, Wynkoop had a high view of justification and the concomitant experience of sanctification. According to Wynkoop, there is no comfort provided by the New Testament for any conformity to God's will less than the ultimate at any moment. There is no place to hide behind anything such as method, time sequence, and levels of grace, etc. There is no trace of a double standard for Christians—or for any kind of person, for that matter. Decision is always now.[106]

SANCTIFICATION: RELATIONAL AND TELEOLOGICAL

Some of the realities that Wynkoop had to deal with were expectations that a subjective change in the personality or a rearrangement of the DNA, below the level of consciousness, is the result of an encounter with God.[107] In her specifically Wesleyan circles, the questions were, "What does entire sanctification do for a believer?" "What kind of change does it produce?" These questions sound simple enough, yet Wynkoop knew that each of them revealed presuppositions that must be identified and criticized.[108] As an evangelist, pastor, and teacher, Wynkoop encountered many variations of the understanding people had of their encounter with the divine.

A. The Supernatural versus Nature

For some, the supernatural world, or "God's space," was perceived to be totally other than the realm or dimension called "our" space. Nothing of what God is can be comprehended by or contained in the created world. It is the complete inability to record or measure anything belonging to the supernatural world.[109] This view gets so stuck on the absolute transcendence of God that knowledge of God and revelation are impossible.

---

105. Ibid., 236.
106. Ibid., 235.
107. Wynkoop, *A Theology of Love*, 213.
108. Ibid.
109. Ibid., 214.

Wynkoop said, "In this view, Christ can be a symbol only, not the divine-human person of Christian faith."[110]

B. Mysticism

On the other end of the spectrum was mysticism. This view encouraged an unwholesome, cult-like detachment from life and critical thinking. Here, direct contact with the supernatural is anticipated, either to lower human consciousness to the point of oblivion or to replace the human will entirely. In this case the rational mind either gives way to the divine mind or is completely bypassed by it.[111] Wynkoop wrote, "In this view, human personality is ravished and rationality is destroyed. The will is surrendered to that which is imagined to be God, and what the person does is identified as the activity of God."[112]

C. Christian Conflict and the Supernatural

Wynkoop also encountered the extreme view that human nature could not be changed in this life; the Holy Spirit could only control it. The divine nature is imposed on the evil nature so as to control it.[113] Wynkoop wrote, "Suppression is a key word in such a position."[114] In this view, human nature is seen as an enemy to be conquered and the Holy Spirit sits as a slave master over human nature. In fact, the lifelong conflict between the Holy Spirit and human nature is seen as a badge of being a true Christian warrior.[115] Here Wynkoop wanted to protect human integrity and keep the real self intact as it engages the Holy Spirit. She warned of the dangers if this is not addressed: "In this view, a divided personality is the necessary evidence of the spiritual life. Man may, and should, will to contest the will of the flesh, acknowledging an essential and ontological dualism. Sanctification consists in a 'possession by' the Holy Spirit, who then subdues but does not—and cannot—'reform' the self. . . . It ends up being scarcely more than an armed truce."[116]

Again, this view is a subtle way of deflecting moral responsibility away from humanity. In essence, humanity is said to be incorrigible and unable

---

110. Ibid., 213.
111. Ibid., 214.
112. Ibid.
113. Ibid., 215.
114. Ibid.
115. Wynkoop, *Foundations*, 74.
116. Wynkoop, *A Theology of Love*, 216.

to respond to the overtures of God's grace. God is then placed in a position where his expectations that humanity should keep the law are viewed as unrealistic and out of touch with the "real condition" of humanity.

D. The Subconscious and the Supernatural

Here the spiritual nature of humanity was thought to be acted upon by the grace of God sub-rationally, where wrong impulses are changed to right impulses below the level of consciousness. In this scenario it is possible to expect that if sanctifying grace operated thoroughly, then all possibility of sin would be eliminated from the impulsive nature. The impulse is expected to change through a sort of "spiritual operation" by the Holy Spirit.[117]

Given the environment represented by these four examples, we can understand why Wynkoop took so much time to define "moral." In Wynkoop's existential world, for an act to be moral, it had to involve the whole person in responsible decision-making. This meant that every aspect of soteriology, from God's provision of grace to every step required by God of humanity in redemption, had to be in the interest of moral integrity.[118] This is not exactly what she experienced as an evangelist and teacher. What Wynkoop wanted to get across is that in humanity's encounter with the divine, it was not some*thing* that happens to us but, rather, some*one* who unites with us.[119] Given these distortions, one is more able to understand why Wynkoop placed so much emphasis on transformation not being "deeper down." Wynkoop wanted to safeguard the church from the gospel's being presented in non-personal categories and subjected to non-moral and even magical manipulation.[120] For her, the existential realities of Scripture dealt with real people, real relationships, and real struggles, and it was important to her to describe the interaction between God and humans in personal terms. She wrote:

> If God acts toward man apart from his thinking and choice; if salvation is "applied" to man by a supernatural alteration of his mind, body, psyche, "deeper down" than his conscious life, where he cannot be held responsible; if man can expect a "psychological mutation" so that he no longer needs to feel the full force of temptation, then—though

---

117. Wynkoop, "A Theology of Depth," file 1431-15, WC, 70.
118. Ibid., 81.
119. Wynkoop, *A Theology of Love*, 182.
120. Ibid., 166.

God is a personal being and man is a person—"personal relationship" is a fiction, biblical salvation is a myth. . . . God acts toward man in terms of personal relationship. If he did not, if he took advantage of his power and position by bypassing the integrity of man whom he made for love and fellowship, he would destroy man as man.[121]

However, Wynkoop's theology is left with the challenge to account for the research done on the subconscious in the behavioural sciences.[122] As will be shown, Wynkoop wanted to keep the conversation on the conscious level, which to her was the "moral" level. It was only on this level that she believed Scripture confronts the sinfulness of humanity.

Wynkoop was especially interested to see if there was any correlation between *crisis* and *process* (as expressed in the Holiness Movement) and the moral development of human beings. This caused her to look to the behavioural sciences to deepen her understanding of the normal moral development of human beings. Wynkoop observed that her own altar experiences, considered crisis experiences, were often disconnected from the existential process of her ordinary Christian life. She wrote, "The historical interpretation emphasized the continuity of events to provide the meaning of the present. The apocalyptic stressed the discontinuity of events, the breaking in on history of new, unrelated forces and events. The historical has to do with the ongoing, day-by-day, moral, responsible linking of human choosing into character. The apocalyptic is the intrusion of crises that force a change of direction which is not linked to any human choice. The historical is morally related. The apocalyptic is amoral."[123]

The apocalyptic paradigm especially manifested itself in what Wynkoop described as "distorted Wesleyanisms which were grafted on non-Wesleyan philosophical roots."[124] These distortions arose as a result of dualistic presuppositions. One was the extreme ontological distinction made between the persons of the Godhead with the resulting belief in tri-theism; the other was trichotomous anthropology. Tri-theism allowed

---

121. Ibid., 169.
122. Dr. Noble, in *Holy Trinity, Holy People*, differentiates between the conscious level and physiological level. The physiological level is where the basic drives such as sex, hunger, and aggression are based in the nervous system. At this unconscious level, the believer is still in the old, fallen flesh (107).
123. Wynkoop, "Theological Roots of the Wesleyan Understanding of the Holy Spirit," *WTJ* 14:1 (1979): file 2227-33, WC, 10.
124. Ibid.

one to say that Christ is Saviour and the Holy Spirit is Sanctifier. According to Wynkoop, this ushered in some strange doctrines: "(1) That there is something better than Christ—the Holy Spirit, (2) that this is the age of the Holy Spirit, not the age of Christ, (3) that the Bible is no longer our real final authority, because the Holy Spirit gives revelations not found in Scripture and that you get part of the Holy Spirit at the first work of grace and the rest at the second work."[125]

Trichotomy, on the other hand, made it possible to suppose that the multiple entities of human personality account for the need for multiple works of grace.[126] As a consequence, it became possible to study the doctrine of sanctification separate from Christian theology as a whole. "The result," she wrote, "was that the event of entire sanctification as a second work of grace began to absorb the whole meaning of sanctification so that no aspect of development could be included in it."[127] These dualistic presuppositions produced an extreme supernaturalism that served to weaken the moral interaction between God and human beings. Wynkoop wrote, "The historical Pentecost became the model for all personal experience, and the question was raised about how one would know when the baptism of the Holy Spirit would be received. There was in the baptism language no inbuilt mandate for discipleship and service. Obedience in terms of legalism and moralism and often emotionalism gained priority over *agape*."[128]

The challenge for Wynkoop was with those who wanted to standardize some of the psychological expressions as representing the heart of the doctrine of sanctification.[129] This led to what Wynkoop called a "reduction in terminology."[130] It was the attempt to limit the use of the word "sanctification" to a second work of grace, or what Stephen Lennox refers to as "reading Scripture with a perfectionistic hermeneutic."[131] The great irony, as Wynkoop reminded us, is that in the New Testament all Christian believers were called saints, or were referred to as "sanctified."[132] Wynkoop

---

125. Wynkoop, "The Holy Spirit and Pentecostalism" (article, 1974), file 1437-12, WC, 2.
126. Wynkoop, "Theological Roots," file 2227-33, WC, 5.
127. Ibid.
128. Ibid., 6.
129. Wynkoop, *A Theology of Love*, 309.
130. Ibid., 303.
131. Stephen J. Lennox, "Biblical Interpretation in the American Holiness Movement: 1875—1920," *WTJ* 33:1 (1998): 27.
132. Wynkoop, *A Theology of Love*, 304.

wanted to make sure that sanctification was not lifted away from justification. She wrote, "When the interrelatedness of justification and sanctification is severed and justification is slipped under sanctification as a sort of poor basement apartment under the luxurious upper-floor living quarters, or it is made to mark the difference between first- and second-class Christians, something essential is lost from the meaning of both these terms."[133]

Wynkoop was not against crisis experiences, but her caution is especially relevant when these moral decisive moments happened but could not be made to mesh with life prior to the experience. The recognition to balance *crisis, growth,* and *development* is especially evident in Wynkoop's own journey of faith. We witnessed previously Wynkoop's frustrations as she tried to make sense of the doctrine of entire sanctification, how she recorded forty altar trips and finally tore that page out of her Bible and ended up with an Episcopal group.[134] This all took place in 1934, when she was twenty-nine years old, but that experience was only recorded in writing on February 18, 1939, in an unpublished article titled "What Holiness Means to Me." Years later, at the age of seventy-six, she reflected back on this time of her life and gave us the rest of the story. In an article published in the *Light and Life Magazine,* she wrote about her realization that she was not the subject of the gospel but that God wanted her to be part of his team. There was a bigger story going on than just her individual journey of faith. Entire sanctification was no longer a merely isolated, unrelated blessing but a holistic integration of her whole life into the reign of Christ. She learned that special encounters with the Holy Spirit were not to be seen as ends in themselves but as means to an end. It was to get on with the business of being a servant and joining the mission of Christ. She came to realize that holiness is Christ*likeness* and that Jesus is the clue to holiness. She came to love John Wesley's practical theology of sanctification, which to her meant a "deeply personal and transforming relationship to God. A relationship that delivered from 'all sin,' 'filled the heart with the Holy Spirit,' and produced 'perfect love.'"[135]

Likewise, in the year 1725 at the age of twenty-three, after reading parts of Bishop Taylor's *Rule and Exercises of Holy Living and Dying,* Wes-

---

133. Ibid., 305.
134. See chapter 2, "Wynkoop's Journey of Authenticity."
135. Mildred Bangs Wynkoop, "Christian Celebrating Jesus Christ," *Light and Life Magazine* (June 1981): file 2223-30, WC, 13–14.

ley gave a personal testimony of his own journey with Christ: "Instantly I resolved to dedicate all my life to God, all my thoughts. And words, and actions; being thoroughly convinced, there was no medium; but that every part of my life (not some only) must either be a sacrifice to God, or myself, that is, in effect, to the devil."[136]

These testimonies are a reminder that the teleological journey for both Wesley and Wynkoop was not just a philosophical and rational development of new thoughts and ideas about the Christian life. Wesley and Wynkoop both demonstrated that their existential theology was developed on convictions deeply rooted in real-life experience, in which they included themselves. As we will see, for Wesley and Wynkoop, "life is greater than logic."[137]

Wynkoop saw crisis and process as essential elements in the Christian life. She did not view these elements as ends in themselves but, rather, as means to an end. As she already demonstrated, when the experience itself becomes the content of holiness, serious breakdown results between theological constructs and human nature. At this point, those in the behavioural sciences threw a lifeline to Wynkoop as they helped her broaden her own understanding of the natural moral development of human beings.[138]

In 1972, Wynkoop's book *A Theology of Love* came into the hands of Dr. Donald M. Joy and Catherine Stonehouse, who were both working in the field of education and moral development. These connections opened new doors and new ways of thinking. Wynkoop was invited by Dr. Joy to a three-day conference to address the ministry implications of the Piaget and Kohlberg findings pertaining to what they considered to be "the innate moral sense with which humans are born."[139] It is interesting to note that Dr. Joy, then professor of education at Asbury Theological Seminary, found the Kohlberg findings to parallel Wesley's writing and experience. What piqued his interest was the possibility of establishing a theological basis for moral development.[140] He published his findings in the *Asbury*

---

136. John Wesley, *A Plain Account of Christian Perfection* (reprint, Kansas City: Beacon Hill Press of Kansas City, 1966), 1.
137. Wynkoop, "The Whole Wesley in a Broken World" (unpublished article, undated), file 1426-4, WC, 4.
138. Mildred Bangs Wynkoop, "Wesleyan Theology and Christian Development," *The Asbury Seminarian* 31 (1976): 36.
139. Wynkoop, "Holiness Theology," file 1425-21, WC, 1.
140. Ibid.

Seminarian in 1976 as a monograph titled "Human Development and Christian Holiness," in which he presented a schema of the stages, or levels, of human development through which every human passes on the way toward moral thinking.[141] The Lawrence Kohlberg moral development theory postulates pre-conventional, conventional, and post-conventional stages of self-understanding, in which moral reasoning progresses from hedonism to high moral responsibility.[142] These levels are cognitive levels of moral understanding and are not to be confused with moral action.[143] The Joy insight, in Wynkoop's assessment, "gave a reasonable way to explain *process* in the Christian life on the way toward fulfilment."[144]

Catherine Stonehouse's studies in the same developmental field provided another dimension to the same human potential and procedure. Her adaptation of Jean Piaget's four causes, underlying the movement from one level to another, was of great interest to Wynkoop. Her findings provided a way to explain the function of *crisis* in the Christian life. Wynkoop explained, "In brief, it is the ever-recurring 'disequilibration' experienced as persons are forced into situations which demand resolution of some kind because a larger perspective is jarring the comfortable familiar world which cannot cope with the new experience. The creative trauma of this experience can be a most fruitful way of explaining *crisis*. (Crisis is not necessarily a clock-time measurement but a radical new step in commitment.)"[145]

Wynkoop was overjoyed with this introduction to moral development, but some of the theories about the relation of the theology of sanctification to moral development created uneasiness in her. After all, this was brand-new territory. She wrote, "But, now, the theologian in me sits up and takes notice. *What are you doing with your Wesleyan commitment?* it wants to know. Are you letting your attractive new friends lead you out of the narrow way? Are you substituting developmental theories for the 'two-ness' of Wesleyan theology? Is all this *apropos* of what Wesleyans mean by 'entire sanctification?' My answer is, yes and no, a judicious way of solving difficult problems."[146]

---

141. Wynkoop, "Wesleyan Theology," 36.
142. Ibid.
143. Wynkoop, "Holiness Theology," file 1425-21, WC, 1.
144. Wynkoop, "Wesleyan Theology," 36.
145. Ibid.
146. Ibid.

These crossroad questions went to the heart of Wynkoop's theology. Experientially, she knew there was a disconnect, but how was she going to reconcile this with her theology? The problem arose at the point where the similarities of the Kohlberg/Piaget models and the two-works-of-grace model in Wesleyan theology came together. What was the relationship between them? These and other questions kept knocking on Wynkoop's door. She asked, "We want to leap over human nature—from conversion to perfection in two jumps. We interpret immature moral sense as sin, and think moral maturity comes by a crisis event. How do we reconcile this?"[147] She posed another question, "Each 'work' is accepted as a sort of gift, on the basis of understanding it. We need to understand 'salvation,' to receive it. Where in life is this possible?"[148] Some of these questions were wrong questions, since Wynkoop had already posted signs along her theological journey, directing us to take the qualitative path rather than the quantitative. Applying the Piaget model required a recalibration in Wynkoop's thinking. As she tried her hand at this difficult task of doing theology at the ground level, where life happens, Wynkoop's first inclination was to make sure she stayed faithful to the moorings that had anchored her faith. This meant that these moral development theories had to pass the tests of Scripture, reason, and experience.

For Wynkoop, teleology implied *change* within *continuity*. Change, which simply leaps from one state to another with no essential link between, is not teleological. And yet Wynkoop recognized that change had to be an essential ingredient of teleology.[149] Moving into new territory required that Wynkoop rely on strong teleological anchor points. The first step was to go back over her Christian affirmations and look at them in a fresh and more penetrating way. Her first check was the foundation that *God is revealed in Christ*. God created the world and human beings for a purpose. This purpose requires a history to achieve.[150] This means that God is interested in what humanity does. God takes on our humanity. God's grace operates dynamically in the realm of our humanness, and it is only on this basis that love is possible. God is not a philosophical absolute but a personal being who can genuinely interact with us without losing

---

147. Wynkoop, "Holiness Theology," file 1425-21, WC, 2.
148. Ibid.
149. Wynkoop, *A Theology of Love*, 69.
150. Ibid.

his Godness.[151] As Wynkoop processed these developmental theories, her first impulse was to safeguard her belief in prevenient grace. This meant that God's grace not only preserves human beings "saveable" but also manifests itself as God's initiative or the grace that goes "before" anything humans do.[152]

Her second check was the fact that *Man is revealed in Christ*. This anchor point was nonnegotiable for Wynkoop. Jesus is the *imago Dei*. This truth was applied not only to the person of Christ but also to the way he lived his life. We can almost see the light going on in Wynkoop's thinking as her teleological understanding of the life of Christ now provided a vehicle for her to process this new information of moral development. In agreement with the Eastern fathers, she had already concluded that Jesus lived out the whole history of humanity. This belief she put to work as she ventured this hypothesis: "Jesus was born as a human being and he had to progress through physical growth with all the stages entailed in that. Through discipline he acquired wisdom and favor with God and man (religion and social interaction). This does not mean that badness, or humanness, had to be beaten out of him, but that he needed to go through all the stages all men must go through to come to maturity. . . . Jesus' pilgrimage says to us that the steps we must take are not primarily the result of sin, but because we are terribly and wonderfully human."[153]

Her third check was that *Love is revealed in Christ*. Jesus not only showed humanity how to be human, but he also demonstrated what true love is—*agapē* love, an *outgoing, giving* love. This, to Wynkoop, was the qualitative pathway of holiness.[154] It also provided a filter through which she could process the correlation between holiness and moral development. She wrote:

Life is probation. History is the workshop of moral development. Man was made to glorify God but he could not realize this "end" apart from an environment in which moral choice could confirm and develop love. No holiness is automatic or impersonal. It is both a quest and a relationship, a way and a quality of life. In the providence of God, the child becomes a man; the ignorant one by dint of effort becomes

---

151. Wynkoop, "Wesleyan Theology," 37.
152. Ibid., 39.
153. Ibid., 37.
154. Ibid., 39.

knowledgeable; the immature maturate; the seed dies, sprouts, grows, and bears fruit; innocence becomes holiness; holiness is perfected in love and faith.[155]

The teleological operation of God's grace and love is actively engaged throughout this journey of faith. This journey of faith required both crisis and process, yet Wynkoop did not see "two works of grace" as quantitative additions or as higher levels of grace. It was, rather, a moral relationship that included love, forgiveness, and discipleship.[156] Love, which was the fulfilment of the law, was not a "sort of commodity that could be implanted in the psyche, a 'works in the drawer' power source, but a relationship established with God in which the fulfilment of life and ministry could effectively proceed."[157] These affirmations not only anchored Wynkoop, but they also in a sense catapulted her forward into this new arena where integration is required without compromising the integrity of either school of thought.

On the other side of the fence were the findings of behavioural science with their postulations of moral development. Wynkoop realized that she could not just focus on that which is moral, with all that this concept brought to the table, but she also had to account for the cognitive developmental aspects of human beings. She learned that developmentalism identifies three levels of self-understanding. (1) The pre-conventional level is described as the child stage. This stage is about self-discovery, self-acceptance, and the development of personal identity. Here, self-interest is not to be seen as sinful. (2) In the conventional level, the person is placed in the world of others to whom he must learn to relate. Authority and the law are required to tell him what is right. (3) The post-conventional level motivation postulates a self who is able to do what is right on principle, not because of the pressure of social demand. Responsibility for others is a natural part of this level.[158] This over-simplified presentation suggests the adaptations the Christian must make in the pilgrimage from infancy to mature and responsible discipleship.

---

155. Wynkoop, *A Theology of Love*, 69.
156. Wynkoop, "Wesleyan Theology," 38.
157. Ibid.
158. Ibid., 39.

SOME CONCLUSIONS ON WYNKOOP'S DOCTRINE OF SANCTIFICATION

Navigating all these rapids brought Wynkoop to a place where she thought a synthesis was possible. Wynkoop was trying to place religious experiences in the context of history, while acknowledging the dynamic nature of human beings. This exercise required her to look at her basic Christian affirmations as a relationship with God, others, and herself. She also had to account for growth in grace and then relate this to the various stages of moral development. Given all this work, Wynkoop came to the following conclusions.

First, she was convinced that all of life and reality are in process, and change is in the very nature of reality. She believed that all redemptive procedure took place dynamically within the structure of God's grace according to the movement of human development. She was, however, cautious not to make it sound as if process is automatic in moral life. For her the crucial factor tying process and crisis together was faith. She wrote:

> The link between the two is faith, faith that opens the heart to God's justifying grace, and faith that unites the whole self around the lordship of Christ. Faith, that dynamic trust in God instead of self, is the continuity of the Christian life. In it, as essential ingredients, are the moment-by-moment reliance on the atonement of Christ and the continuing life of the obedience of love. As life deepens, widens, becomes more involved and complex the need to strengthen the cords of faith through many crisis decisions continues. Process/crisis defines moral quality.[159]

For Wynkoop, within process are crucial, decisive steps without which it cannot continue. At whatever human development level human beings begin their Christian pilgrimage, their religious experience will be interpreted according to the way they think at that level. This means that salvation can be entered into at any stage in moral development. Again, the focus for Wynkoop is on moral understanding, not to be confused with moral action. It is not how to behave but the development of a person's cognitive ability to make decisions about moral action.[160] As the psyche develops, it adds and deletes and chooses and raises questions and decides better alternatives. The salvation commitment must then follow the en-

---

159. Wynkoop, "The Wesleyans" (article, undated), file 1432-7, WC, 3.
160. Wynkoop, "Wesleyan Theology," 40.

larging psyche and put it in the service of the Lord.[161] In this process, the Holy Spirit plays a critical role to help people become aware of themselves as responsible individuals. The Holy Spirit also enables the individual to sustain responsible relationships. Wynkoop wrote:

> Too many people have never allowed the Holy Spirit to bring them face to face with their real selves—they never come to clear personal identification. . . . When one becomes a Christian, or is born again, the ultimate in self-awareness and self-consciousness and personal identity is reached. . . . The newborn person finds himself in a world of deepest responsibility. The inward look is no longer adequate. There must be the usually painful wrenching of self-interest from the self as centre to the two-focii perspective of love to God and others also.[162]

Second, "'full sanctification' does not leap over the developmental levels, transporting a person into [instant maturity] without the trouble of taking every step in between. One does not get 'sanctifieder and sanctifieder' as the levels are negotiated, but the life in Christ engages more and more of the self" and the interpersonal world of others.[163] In other words, salvation is not parcelled out in doses. A personal relationship is established and grows, as the person is able to share more deeply in that relationship. And, as Wynkoop wrote, "Since it *is* [a] religious relationship, it can become a genuine reality *at any stage in the development of human life*. Love is possible in any and all stages in life, but there are changes in love's contour through life that cannot be implanted, whole, anywhere. It must go through the grid of growth. Baby love is right for a baby but disgusting in an adult. Adult love is totally beyond the capacity of a child. Baby love is not defective, only immature."[164]

Third, Wynkoop embraced the idea that *crisis* can be seen as a recalibration. She wrote, "Each developmental level leads to crucial 'value' bar-

---

161. Wynkoop, "Holiness Theology," file 1425-21, WC, 1. The primary material indicates that these thoughts were not just a passing exercise in curiosity but need to be integrated into Wynkoop's overall doctrine of holiness. In the same year Dr. Joy published his monograph, Wynkoop followed suit with her own in *The Asbury Seminarian* titled "Wesleyan Theology and Christian Development." Two years later, in 1978, she introduced a new elective at NTS called Holiness Theology and Moral Development. These views also influenced those who taught with her. Rob Staples credits Wynkoop as the primary influencer of his article in *WTJ* 7 (1972), titled "Sanctification and Selfhood: A Phenomenological Analysis of the Wesleyan Message."

162. Wynkoop, *A Theology of Love*, 203.
163. Wynkoop, "Wesleyan Theology," 40.
164. Ibid., 39.

riers, which must be broken through. The expanding human perspective runs headlong into previous narrownesses, prejudices, undisciplined self-interests, blind spots, insensitivities and entrenched dogmas that must be squarely faced if progress is to be made."[165]

Wynkoop anticipated that new growth, moral conflict, and crises would be the hallmark of the sanctified life (the whole Christian life).[166] Progress from one stage to the next was anticipated to be dynamic. This meant that progress would not be evenly paced. Wynkoop also made allowance for "arrested development," which can be imposed by others or self-induced.[167] Nevertheless, the self now begins to function in a new environment with all the responsibility that comes in this new relationship, and the law that guides this relationship is the law of love.

All these strands of the analysed elements of the subject under discussion came together at this point and answered the question as to the relationship of sanctification to human nature. Wynkoop wrote:

God does not partially save and then fully save. Men do not respond with part of the personality and then later with the rest of it. Sin is not partially destroyed at one time and fully destroyed at another, nor is a second work of grace for the purpose of correcting the defects of the first. At least there is no biblical warrant for this kind of explanation. The *"second crisis" is different in kind, not different in degree, from the first.* The two represent two essential movements of the person as a person. They have respect for the double psychological aspect of selfhood in its freedom and responsibility.[168]

Here again, it is important to remind ourselves that Wynkoop was only showing the way in which human beings appropriate the sanctifying grace of God. She wrote, "Moral integrity is not merely self-realization as such but the self integrated with God, and in this way a realization of one's true self. This is a restoration of the sanctifying fellowship of the Holy Spirit. No one sanctifies himself, but is sanctified by the Holy Spirit."[169]

We can now ask, "What is 'entire' in relation to sanctification?" For Wynkoop, this did not mean a higher version of sanctification from God's

---

165. Wynkoop, "Wesleyan Theology," 40.
166. Wynkoop, "Holiness Theology," file 1425-21, WC, 4.
167. Ibid., 5.
168. Wynkoop, *A Theology of Love*, 207.
169. Ibid., 349.

side. It meant the total integration of the personality in its total commitment to Christ. It did not mean that the process of character building and spiritual development is complete, but it did mean that the whole person united himself or herself with the life of Christ. "Entire" can then be interpreted as full participation in the process of sanctification, commensurate with the stages of moral development. Wynkoop wrote, "God requires men to love him wholly. Sanctification is the moral atmosphere of that love. It has two movements, a total renunciation of the self-centred life and a total commitment to God. Everything sanctification requires is in keeping with wholesome personality. God accepts this living sacrifice and fills the 'heart' with the Holy Spirit. As religion, this is loving God with the whole heart, mind and strength; in psychology, it is an integrated personality; in theology, it is cleansing."[170]

THE PARALLELS WITH WESLEY

In Wesley's understanding of sanctification, we see similar patterns of teleology and development as observed in Wynkoop's theology. Wesley defined sanctification as the whole process of recovery, from justification to death, with the goal of restoring humanity to the image of God.[171] Wesley did not limit sanctification to entire sanctification. This is where Wynkoop strongly related to Wesley. Collins describes Wesley's 1765 sermon "The Scripture Way of Salvation" as representing the "heart of Wesley's theology."[172] The first part of the title shows, according to Collins, that for Wesley, Scripture served as the primary guide in the formulation of his theology. The second part of the title points, as Collins sees it, to the practical interest Wesley had in connecting his theology with real life.[173]

At this level we see the influence Wesley had on Wynkoop. We see the same pattern in Wynkoop. Her default theological stance always started with Scripture, within which she was particularly interested to find the spiritual sense and the existential *Sitz im Leben*. Wesley's sermon "The Scripture Way of Salvation" serves as a way to describe the primary *modus operandi* in Wynkoop's existential theology. In this sermon Wesley expounded the gradual nature of sanctification: "From the time we are born

---

170. Ibid., 208.
171. A. Skevington Wood, *Love Excluding Sin: Wesley's Doctrine of Sanctification* (Occasional Paper no 1. of the Wesleyan Fellowship. Ilkeston, UK: Moorley's Bible and Bookshop, 1986), 5.
172. Collins, *Scripture Way of Salvation*, 13.
173. Ibid.

again, the gradual work of sanctification takes place. We are enabled 'by the Spirit' to 'mortify the deeds of the body,' of our evil nature; and as we are more and more dead to sin, we are more and more alive to God."[174] In other words, something begins in regeneration that has no ceiling. In the same sermon, Wesley elaborates on this process: "We walk on from grace to grace while we are careful to 'abstain from all appearance of evil' and are zealous of good works, as we have opportunity doing good to all men; while we walk in all his ordinances blameless, therein worshiping him in Spirit and truth; in which we take up our cross, and deny ourselves every pleasure that does not lead to God."[175]

We can see that, similar to Wynkoop, Wesley's concept of regeneration was very high. Regeneration was not downgraded to make room for sanctification. Victory over the power of sin was possible right from the start. According to Lindström, Wesley believed that the power of sin is already broken at regeneration. Referencing Wesley's sermon "On Sin in Believers," Lindström wrote, "The regenerate man was already delivered from sin in the sense that he was no longer dominated by it. It could be said of him that he did not sin. This meant that he did not commit outward sins."[176] Lindström helped us to see that the absolution of removing the guilt of sin in an instant (normally at baptism) was placed over and against the therapeutic restoration and renewing of the corrupt nature.[177] Wesley thus placed much more emphasis on the developmental part of sanctification. God's therapeutic method of healing the soul played itself out in a practical way as Wesley talked about being a child, then a young man, and then a father in Christ.[178]

Here we see strong similarities between Wesley and Wynkoop. Both tie the process of sanctification to the development of natural life. The idea of a gradual advance in sanctification through stages and degrees of change is a natural part of Wesley's views of sanctification. However, Wesley also paid attention to the crisis aspect of the salvation journey. According to Maddox, Wesley had a comprehensive therapeutic view of spiritual transformation that included instantaneous encounters with the

---

174. John Wesley, Sermon 43, "The Scripture Way of Salvation," *Works*, 2:160.
175. Ibid.
176. Lindström, *Wesley and Sanctification*, 143.
177. Ibid., 103.
178. Ibid., 140.

Holy Spirit. The instantaneous aspect was, for Wesley, a way to point to the fact that justification and entire sanctification were unmerited gifts of God.[179] Maddox writes, "Wesley remained convinced of the importance of an instantaneous beginning of the Christian life . . . in controversial dialogue he ultimately admitted that his concern was not with matters of circumstance but of substance; that is, he was not so much defending a psychological model of conversion as a theological evaluation of it."[180]

According to Wynkoop, Wesley's perspective regarding circumstance was, as the term indicates, mainly circumstantial and not dogmatic. It was based on case studies of hundreds of people whose religious experience he examined. This gave him a general pattern and even the confidence to say, "It happens this way to Methodists," but never as a dogmatism.[181]

The process of salvation was, for Wesley, likened to entering a house. Through the operation of prevenient grace, "man walks onto the porch of the house," and through justifying grace, "he opens the door and walks into this house of grace going on from stage to stage as he makes progress in sanctification."[182] However, this forward movement in sanctification did not happen in a vacuum. For Wesley, progress and development in sanctification required a focus on repentance and compliance to the moral law of God. We shall look at this with particular reference to repentance and the law.

A. Repentance

Wesley believed that sin remained in the believer's life after the new birth that caused him or her to place particular emphasis on repentance within the Christian life.[183] Repentance in the life of the believer had to do with a kind of self-knowledge, knowing oneself to be a sinner.[184] However, according to Lindström, "even though the believer is aware of the continued presence of sin, sin is no longer supreme . . . this consciousness of sin is accompanied by consciousness of acceptance of God."[185] Repentance in the Christian life then acknowledges an utter helplessness to retain the benefits of salvation, much less deliverance from the root of sin, and it therefore depends on the continuing pardoning relationship to

---

179. Maddox, *Responsible Grace*, 154.
180. Ibid., 153.
181. Wynkoop, *Wesley and Sanctification*, 308.
182. Runyon, *The New Creation*, 27.
183. Maddox, *Responsible Grace*, 165.
184. Quoted by Maddox in *Responsible Grace*, 162.
185. Lindström, *Wesley and Sanctification*, 116.

Christ.¹⁸⁶ Repentance is also seen in its fruits, which Wesley divided into works of piety and works of mercy.¹⁸⁷ Here we see a direct correlation with the second table of the law, as he expressed the law of loving one's neighbour as oneself, to reflect the image of God. Wesley was convinced that if a believer did not practise this level of repentance, it blocked the way to sanctification. In his sermon "The Scripture Way of Salvation," Wesley wrote, "There is no place for repentance in him who believes there is no sin in his life or heart; consequently, there is no place for his being perfected in love, to which that repentance is indispensably necessary."¹⁸⁸ According to Maddox, Wesley took repentance one step further, insisting that even after entire sanctification there was still a need for repentance.¹⁸⁹ The believer never outgrows the need for repentance, no matter how much transformation occurs.

Wynkoop was in full agreement with Wesley on the ongoing need for repentance and faith in the life of the believer. Wynkoop wrote, "Repentance must be a settled life attitude toward sin, not a momentary emotional upheaval. In repentance we take God's point of view on sin—our sin. This isn't just past sin, but sin always, everywhere. Hatred of sin is to be a permanent element of our Christian lives. We do not graduate from this. The whole weight of moral life rests on this. When and if this is relaxed, the whole personal moral structure collapses from within. No work of grace subsequent in time can have meaning apart from the integrity of a repentant attitude that never ends."¹⁹⁰ And on the ongoing role of faith in the life of the believer, Wynkoop wrote, "Faith is a new direction of love and is as stable as the repentance that guards against a wrong center of affection . . . this repentance-faith complex is the atmosphere in which all other elements of grace are unfolded."¹⁹¹

B. The Law

According to Wynkoop, the moral law played a significant role in Wesley's understanding of sanctification. She referenced Wesley's emphasis on the moral law as he described the law as a "copy of the eternal mind, a

---

186. Ibid.
187. Ibid.
188. Wesley, "The Scripture Way of Salvation," *Works*, 2:166.
189. Maddox, *Responsible Grace*, 166.
190. Wynkoop, *A Theology of Love*, 345.
191. Ibid., 346.

transcript of the divine nature," as well as an "incorruptible picture of the Holy One."[192] Wynkoop believed that Wesley came close to equating the law with Christ. This is so, since, as Wynkoop saw it, Wesley considered "Christ in the heart as the law written on the heart."[193] Interpreting Wesley, she wrote, "A Christian is free from the law in that he does not keep it in order to be acceptable to God. But the law is written on his heart and he loves to do the things he should. His corrupt nature, being changed from enmity to love, no longer brings him under condemnation. He is no longer clashing with the law but finds himself so in harmony with it that he is almost unconscious of it."[194]

Lindström identifies three uses of the moral law in Wesley's system: "The first use is to instill conviction of sin. It unmasks man and reveals to him his real nature; that he is dead to God and devoid of all spiritual life. The second use is to lead man to Christ that he may live. Although in these functions the law acts as 'a severe schoolmaster,' love is operative behind it and uses the law for its own ends. The third use of the law concerns its place in the Christian life. The law does not only lead man to Christ; it also serves to keep the justified and the regenerated man alive and helps him to grow in grace."[195]

Lindström indicates that this third use of the law functioned in Wesley's mind as a way to promote sanctification. This, too, is threefold: "First it convinces the Christian of the sin that remains, secondly, it serves as a way to derive 'strength from Christ' for the believer, and thirdly, it provides hope as the believer receives 'grace upon grace,' till he is in possession of the fullness of God's promises."[196] This close association between the moral law and Christ in Wesley's understanding is best summarized by Lindström: "The law drives man to Christ, and Christ drives man to the law."[197]

As we saw in chapter 4, "Wynkoop's Theological Anthropology," Wynkoop believed the law played a specific role in keeping moral responsibility in check after the fall. The expectation that the law should and could be kept was evidence to her that the *imago Dei* remained intact after

---

192. Wynkoop, "John Wesley's Doctrine," file 1432-3, WC, 11.
193. Ibid.
194. Ibid.
195. Lindström, *Wesley and Sanctification*, 81.
196. Ibid.
197. Ibid., 82.

the fall. However, the law fulfilled in love was the main focus for Wesley. On this level, we will find much similarity in emphasis between Wynkoop and Wesley. This aspect of Wesley and Wynkoop's theologies will be addressed in the last section of this chapter, where we will come to see that, for both, love is the fulfilment of the law, and to express the law through love is to participate in the fullness of Christ.[198]

On Sin

Wynkoop's understanding of sin did not arise in a vacuum. When Wynkoop first entered the field of theology, she inherited Wiley's theological agenda. Her book *Foundations of Wesleyan-Arminian Theology* shows the deep influence of Wiley on her work as she recognized the Calvinistic inroads into the thinking of Nazarene pastors and laity. She referenced these inroads as coming in the form of "Calvinistic Wesleyanisms" and "Wesleyan Calvinisms." She explained this strange marriage of ideas: "Calvinism with a Wesleyan emphasis is the result of uniting Calvinism's doctrine of human depravity and unconditional eternal security to Wesley's doctrine of the work of the Holy Spirit. Wesley's teaching relative to victory over sin and dynamic power for service is fused to Calvin's concept of human nature, which says that it is antagonistic to grace and cannot be reformed in this life."[199]

Here human nature is viewed as so corrupted by sin that it cannot be changed, but only controlled, by the Holy Spirit. In this view the Holy Spirit is in conflict with human nature, and this lifelong conflict is ironically seen as the badge of the presence of the Holy Spirit.[200] Wynkoop described those who make a distinction between a carnal nature and the human nature. She wrote, "Calvinistic Wesleyanism conceives of a sort of dual human nature—almost two entities or selves. A familiar question is, 'What is the difference between human nature and carnal nature?' Eradication, then, is the removal of one of the natures, the carnal nature. And hereon hangs the problem relative to the use of the term 'eradication.'"[201]

Given this background, we have to examine what exactly Wynkoop meant when she described sin as "not farther back or deeper down than

---

198. Ibid., 107.
199. Wynkoop, *Foundations*, 73.
200. Ibid., 74.
201. Ibid., 78.

man's moral responsibility." What is evident is that her studies on the *imago Dei*, her doctoral work on biblical interpretation, as well as her studies of Greek and Hebrew, became the primary tools that she applied to reach a biblically authentic view of sin. In her handwritten articles "Observations on Sin and Holiness," "Sin as Relational Truth," and "What Sin Is," we get a clear picture that sin to Wynkoop was always a religious matter.

Wynkoop aligned herself with the Wesleyan movement and with the unique quest to understand how human nature can be free from sin. This is in contrast to other traditions that, in Wynkoop's mind, "choose to handle the sin problem in more simplistic ways—by either putting freedom from sin in the next life, by reinterpreting sin in the believer, or by neutralising sin by divine decree."[202] Wynkoop's major concern was to relate her theology to practical life. This, of course, raised the problem of human nature and how it interacts with God's grace in the face of its fallenness. As we have seen, this is especially relevant when we try to account for a person's imperfections and the various stages of maturation and moral development. The heart of her investigation into the nature of sin can be described as an existential exploration of the moral interaction between humanity and God. She understood the importance of formulating the doctrine of sanctification, but her real interest was to express the coherence between doctrine and life. In fact, holiness itself prevented her theology from becoming a mere intellectual exercise. For Wynkoop, holiness is life. She wrote, "As the incarnation of Christ is God's answer to speculation about God, so holiness is the answer to theological abstraction relative to salvation."[203]

It is critical to understand the filters Wynkoop used in order to construct her doctrine of sin. First, Wynkoop was convinced that holiness and sin must be considered each in light of the other. For her, they were absolute contrasts.[204] Second, her theological premise was that sin cannot be discussed in the abstract; that is why she limited herself to studying sin in the context of the biblical stories of real people. In other words, the terms "holiness" and "sin" referred to personal characteristics, never impersonal things. Third, the existential stories and context behind the words really grabbed her attention. Sin and holiness lie in the realm of relationships,

---

202. Wynkoop, "Our Presuppositions Are Showing," file 1426-2, WC, 2.
203. Wynkoop, *A Theology of Love*, 210.
204. Wynkoop, "A Theology of Depth," file 1431-15, WC, 305.

both with God and other people. When Wynkoop used the word "personal," she was referring to the whole Hebraic self. The self, to Wynkoop, is a "non-reducible reality lying within the framework of rationality."[205] The impersonal area in which the self functions, the non-rational, is not the "dwelling" of sin or holiness. Fourth, Wynkoop clearly wanted to make a distinction between Platonic dualism, namely, the separation of idea (abstract) and reality (actual), and the Hebraic concept of the unity of personality. She wrote, "The Platonic concept conceives of sin and holiness as 'idea,' absolute perfections, set in contrast to acts in human experience. The Hebraic concept distinguishes between self-commitment and that which flows out of the committed heart. The Platonic ideas are sub-rational; the Hebraic is moral to the core."[206]

In correspondence between Dr. Richard Taylor, professor of theology at Nazarene Theological Seminary from 1961 until 1977, and Wynkoop herself, it is evident that Wynkoop's biblical approach was a huge part of their dialogue on the matter of the sinful nature. In a letter dated November 10, 1970, Taylor shared with Wynkoop what his understanding of the sinful nature was, and he asked for her response.[207] In Wynkoop's response, dated November 28, 1970, she did not answer his questions but instead reacted to the method Dr. Taylor employed to arrive at his position on the sinful nature. The following is an excerpt from her response to Dr. Taylor:

> To categorize any view as Augustinian or Pelagian and accept or attack a view because it is one or the other narrows the field of theology far too greatly. . . . Sin has meaning only as a religious concept—man's relationship with God. And holiness is, in the Bible, a religious matter—relationship to God. Neither Augustine nor Pelagius thought in these terms. To call any biblical writer either Augustinian or Pelagian is to miss the biblical teaching wildly. When this is done, it is evident that a prior, prejudiced stance is considered more important than what the biblical writer is trying to get across. . . . Now, if you put what you say in a framework large enough to include what I have tried to outline—

---

205. Wynkoop, "Biblical Study on Holiness vs. Sin" (article, undated), file 1425-21, WC, 1.
206. Ibid.
207. Dr. Richard Taylor to Wynkoop (correspondence, November 10, 1970), file 1427-15, WC.

in other words, to interpret what you have said in the light of the biblical religious framework, I'll give you an A+ or better.[208]

Obviously, the correspondence did not go well. Years later, in an article called "Why the Holiness Movement Died," Taylor shared his belief that Wynkoop's book *A Theology of Love* contributed to the so-called demise of the Holiness Movement. He wrote, "She expressly repudiated any underlying sinfulness of birth nature . . . thus she effectively ruled out any inherited sinfulness of nature. . . . When we lose our grasp of the profound reality of original sin, we blunt the saving message of Jesus Christ and cut the rug out from under the doctrine of a second work of grace."[209]

The point here is not to take sides but to show how important Scripture was as Wynkoop's method to define the nature of sin.[210] If she could have responded to Richard Taylor's public comments about her (which happened two years after she passed away), she would surely have tried to remind Taylor that Scripture is silent on how sin is transmitted, or even whether it is transmitted.[211] She may have been tempted to quote some of what she wrote in "A Theology of Depth" on the matter of sin being inherited: "In Romans 3:23, Paul says that in sinning men have fallen short. He does not say, having fallen short, men sin."[212] She would surely have liked to remind Taylor that familiar theological terms like "original sin" and "carnality" are not biblical expressions.[213]

This may seem to be an overreaction to those who frame their definitions of sin within the field of systematic theology, but it is critical to understand that Wynkoop was responding to her environment. As a teacher and evangelist in a revivalist movement, she observed that the theological concepts and the term "holiness theology" had been abstracted from the

---

208. Wynkoop to Dr. Richard Taylor (correspondence, November 28, 1970), file 1427-15, WC.

209. Richard Taylor, "Why the Holiness Movement Died," *God's Revivalist and Bible Advocate* (March 1999): 27.

210. Given Wesley's treatise of Augustine's doctrine of original sin, particularly the notion of an "inherited sinful nature," Mark Olson believes that Richard Taylor is closer to Wesley at this point. Olson may have a point. Olson takes the position that Wynkoop reflects Charles Finney more than Wesley, since Wynkoop rejected anything "deeper down and further back" in the doctrine of original sin. See Mark K. Olson, "Strange Bedfellows: Reappraisal of Mildred Wynkoop's Book *A Theology of Love*," *WTJ* 45:2 (2010): 196–217.

211. Wynkoop, "A Theology of Depth," file 1431-15, WC, 304.

212. Ibid., 303.

213. Ibid., 304.

dynamic living situations.[214] The only way she thought to counterbalance this was through the existential use of Scripture. At this juncture, Wesley would not have supported Wynkoop. Collins indicates that initially Wesley was not concerned about how sin is transmitted from Adam to all humanity but later arrived at a traducianist perspective as he affirmed procreation to be the means through which a "fallen soul" is transmitted.[215]

In assessing Wynkoop's doctrine of sin, we need to pay attention to the placement of her study on sin in her overall theology. In "A Theology of Depth," her study of sin comes after her study on sanctification and Christian perfection, which is intentional. For her, sin is the antithesis of holiness, rather than holiness the antithesis of sin. She wrote, "Holiness is not the absence of sin, but sin is the absence of holiness."[216] Close scrutiny into the way she processed the sin problem reveals a movement from light to darkness, from the positive to the negative. She wrote, "A biblical theology must, of necessity, look at sin and grace through the eyes of the atonement in Christ."[217] In other words, sin can only be recognized for what it really is by seeing it against its opposite, holiness, or as a distortion against the normal. This can easily be overlooked in gaining an understanding of Wynkoop's view of sin. Holiness is prior and positive. Wynkoop also took the time to define in what way the human race stands in solidarity with Adam as the first corporate personality and in what ways the human race is in Christ as the last Adam.

"OLD MAN" VERSUS "NEW MAN"

Our understanding of Wynkoop's doctrine of sin will not be adequate unless we give some attention to the meaning of the Pauline terms "old man" and "new man," as well as the significance of Adam and Christ in relation to these terms. Wynkoop believed that the Hebrew idea of corporate personality was at work in the way Paul uses these terms and relates them to Adam and Christ. Her definitions of the old man and the new man in *A Theology of Love* are supported by significant biblical research in her main work, "A Theology of Depth." She did an in-depth study into the thinking

---

214. Wynkoop, "Breakfast Club," file 1426-2, WC, 1.
215. Collins, *Scripture Way of Salvation*, 33. The term "traducianist" refers to the belief that God created the soul once in Adam and Eve and that this soul is transmitted from one generation to the next by natural generation along with the body.
216. Wynkoop, "A Theology of Depth," file 1431-15, WC, 305.
217. Ibid.

of Paul in Romans 5—8 and also looked at Ephesians 4:22 and Colossians 3:9. From this study we can make several observations that would clarify Wynkoop's analysis of the condition of humanity after the fall.

First, Wynkoop interpreted the old man as used by Paul in Romans 6:6 to be a reflection of humanity's spiritual condition in Adam. The old man was not an individuation for her, describing some materialistic condition in the human self but, rather, a personification of a spiritual condition that characterized the whole human race.[218] This spiritual condition "has been crucified with Christ." Only when the benefits of Christ's death are understood on a corporate level can these benefits be applied on an individual level. This is the meaning behind the strange wording of Paul in Ephesians 4:22, 24 and Colossians 3:9. The "old man" is, according to Paul, to be "put off," and in its place we are to "put on" the "new man." Wynkoop understood "putting off" and "putting on" to be expressions of serving either in the kingdom of Adam or the kingdom of Christ.[219]

Second, Wynkoop was more prone to focus on the moral and psychological consequences of the fall. She understood the primary meaning of Paul's description of death in Romans 5:12 to be a reference to spiritual death, and only secondarily physical death. She said, "It may or may not include physical death, but it is almost universally agreed that spiritual death is most certainly the most significant fact of the condition of fallen man. . . . Whatever this death means, Paul says it is in the world because of one man's sin, from Adam on to every human soul (Romans 5:12). This death is co-extensive and concomitant with sin (Romans 5:21)."[220] Wynkoop's position here shows more affinity with Augustine than the Eastern fathers. (The Eastern fathers placed more emphasis on the ontological fallenness of humanity than the West.)[221]

Third, Wynkoop was prone to use the moral category of sinfulness, rather than the ontological category of fallenness, to describe the consequences of the fall. However, she did not want the fallibility of the human race to be confused with sin. For this reason, Wynkoop maintained

---

218. Ibid., 329.
219. Wynkoop, *A Theology of Love*, 161.
220. Wynkoop, "A Theology of Depth," file 1431-15, WC, 338.
221. Noble, *Holy Trinity*, 114. This is the idea expressed in Romans 5—8 (interpreting Genesis 3) that we are physically affected by corruption or decay (*phthora*) leading to death. Our bodies are therefore fallen, but this does not imply that they are sinful in the sense that physical life is inherently evil.

a strong distinction between that which is moral and that which is amoral. She wrote, "If sin is amoral and inheres in the human flesh then the Christian is subject to the impossible psychological condition of being the battleground on which is fought out the warfare of flesh and spirit—his flesh and God's Spirit. But Paul is never caught in the toils of this dualism. Paul never considers the body evil."[222]

Because life begins in an experience of grace, Wynkoop viewed fallen humanity as an abstraction never encountered. She wrote, "We know nothing about any sinful, depraved, eternally damned person. All men are born to human life under the universal influence of what is called prevenient grace."[223] We see Wesley's influence especially at this juncture of Wynkoop's theology. Wesley always started with free grace and then afterward proceeded to speak about sin. Lindström points out that Wesley's thoughts on original sin were saturated with the optimism of grace: "Although man is subject to guilt and punishment because of his relationship with Adam, he is nevertheless absolved from original sin because of the atonement of Christ."[224] So, human beings are after all not damned by the very fact of original sin.

Through the Arminian tradition, Wesley adopted the belief of conditional election. This meant that participation in the grace of God gives the human being the ability to choose and the ability to overcome the inclination of evil.[225] Wynkoop referenced this point in Wesley's sermon "On Working Out Our Own Salvation." Wesley wrote, "For allowing that all the souls of men are dead in sin by nature, this excuses no one, seeing that there is no man that is in a state of mere nature; there is no man, unless he has quenched the Spirit, that is wholly devoid of the grace of God . . . no man sins because he has not grace, but because he doesn't use the grace which he hath."[226]

Wynkoop echoed Paul's statement in Romans 3:23 that "all have sinned and fall short of the glory of God," but she remained optimistic that the possession of mind and will constituted human beings capable of redemption. She was not taking a position similar to Pelagius, who be-

---

222. Wynkoop, "A Theology of Depth," file 1431-15, WC, 335.
223. Ibid., 305.
224. Lindström, *Wesley and Sanctification*, 30.
225. Ibid., 37.
226. Wynkoop, *A Theology of Love*, 99.

lieved that fallen man is born with grace built into his basic constitution but, rather, sides with Augustine in her understanding that grace comes to man externally. She wrote:

> The truth in Augustine's teaching is that no man can, by the exercise of his highest faculties, and under the most ideal conditions, make himself righteous in the sight of God, for he is not morally autonomous but separated eternally from the source of righteousness. Standing, as he does, in the image of God, man is, yet, totally unlike his prototype, Christ. . . . Grace is the one word that makes the whole scheme of redemption intelligible. Through the atoning blood of Jesus Christ there is grace for everyone. The good in man is not the residue of man's original holiness but the preventing [prevenient] grace of God, which preserves the basic structure of man to savability.[227]

Special attention should be given to the phrase "the preventing [prevenient] grace of God which preserves the basic structure of man to savability." Wynkoop here called the grace of God as a witness to the response (ability) of human beings in their capacity to interact with and appropriate the favour of God. In saying this, Wynkoop wanted to avoid thoughts that the essence of the fall was merely personality disorientation. Rather, she saw the fall as man's immoral attempt at orienting his person about the self, as centre, instead of God.

Wynkoop also wanted to guard against the idea that the accrued depravity and personality defects lessen moral responsibility. She wrote, "Though man is born in spiritual death, that is, separated from ethical union with the Holy Spirit, yet every faculty of personality is active and free to prompt the acceptance of the provisions of grace which are extended to every man."[228] In order to understand what change, if any, occurred in the human being as a result of the fall, we now turn to Wynkoop's biblical analysis of sin.

SIN, "NOT DEEPER DOWN OR FURTHER BACK"

So far, we have confirmed that for Wynkoop, moral capacity and moral responsibility go hand in hand. Humanity created in the image of God, humanity as possessed of moral capacity, and humans as morally

---

227. Wynkoop, "The Biblical Study of Man," file 1432-3, WC, 88.
228. Ibid., 106.

responsible, all have to go together to make real intelligence possible.²²⁹ And yet, fallen humans, even though they are able to know and do the law and are held responsible in the choice of their response, are said to be "dead in trespasses and sins."²³⁰ Given that the moral disposition of human beings remained intact, even in fallen humanity, Wynkoop believed that the answer to this mystery lay elsewhere. She postulated that the operating centre for fallen humanity is in the realm of human personality where moral probation operates. She identified the primary locus for sin as the *nous* (mind). In this thinking, purposing faculty, she saw evil being introduced and sin manifesting itself as unbelief. It is then of vital interest to our subject that we understand the biblical terms Wynkoop used to describe human nature. These terms, as defined by Wynkoop, will create a foundation for her biblical analysis of sin:

> *Nous* (mind)—is the person as he is related morally to truth. It judges between good and evil and chooses between them. When it rejects truth it becomes reprobate and corrupt, and leads to sinful decisions. It needs renewal and transformation. When it is rightly related to truth it becomes like the mind of Christ. These are not different "minds" but the one mind acting according to its created and divinely supported capacity and obligation. *Dianoia*—This New Testament word for mind means the ability to understand, to feel and to desire. It is used to describe one's love for God and love for sin. It refers to the "bent" of the inner person's desire. In the unregenerate person it is the enemy of God, but may be turned toward the love of God so that the person may love God as wholly as he loved self and sin before. *Nouma*—This word gives us a direct clue to the nature and seat of sin. The *nouma* is the thinking purposing faculty where evil is introduced. Unbelief is the sin of this "mind." It is here that corruption resides. *Phronema*—This word means to purpose to do something, to direct one's mind and actions to a thing. Five times it tells us to have "the mind of Christ" and two times the reference is to earthly, sinful things. The most significant use and the one that points up the contrast possible in its use is in Romans 8. The mind that is dedicated to the flesh is at enmity with God but the mind that is spiritual has life and peace.

---

229. Ibid., 58.
230. Ibid.

These are not two minds in one person, but the person himself set in his affections toward sin or God.[231]

In her extensive biblical research of human nature and sin, she correlated these terms used by Jesus and Paul first, to describe the nature of sin; second, to show the faculty used; and, third, to show the holy outcome when these faculties are redirected in a holy manner. She also noted that Jesus and Paul did not speculate about the origin of sin or how it is propagated; they were content with recognizing sin as an existential fact.[232]

In Matthew 7:11 she showed that evil human beings have the capacity to give good gifts to their children but instead used the capacity for good in evil ways. In Mark 7:21, she observed that Jesus located sin in the heart. The same heart that should have been occupied with loving God now is shown to be the source of evil. In Ephesians 4:17–19, she showed that sin is a "darkened understanding," the faculty in operation is *dianoia*, and the possible redirection of this faculty is to "be renewed in the spirit of your mind" (v. 23, KJV). In 2 Corinthians 3:14 (KJV), she observed that sin is described as a "blinded" mind, the faculty referenced is *noema*, and the repentance needed is "to lead every thought captive to obedience to Christ" (2 Cor. 10:5, paraphr. by Wynkoop). In Romans 8:6–7, she saw sin described as the "mind of flesh not subject to God" (paraphr. by Wynkoop), the faculty referenced *phronēma*, and the possible redirection of this faculty was "to have the same mind that is in Christ" (Phil. 2:5, paraphr. by Wynkoop).[233]

These examples point to a relational, not metaphysical, description of sin. *Both sin and holiness have to do with the same responsible area of human personality.* Wynkoop wrote, "The biblical contrast between holiness and sin emphasizes the dynamic reacting character of the self as over and against any passive concept which could harbour a non-rational idea of sin . . . Sin must be interpreted in keeping with the 'existential' terminology of Scripture."[234] What is obvious is that she was totally against any impersonal or ontological interpretation of sin. Her Hebraic understanding of the unity of the person emerged at this point as she saw sin not as

---

231. Wynkoop, "Analysis of the Human Personality" (article, undated), file 1425-21, WC, 2.

232. Wynkoop, "A Theology of Depth," file 1431-15, WC, 319.

233. Ibid., 325.

234. Ibid.

a location in the person but, rather, the whole person taking a rebellious stance against God. She wrote, "When sin is put outside the rational and responsible nature of man, the thing sin is, is no longer the deadly moral and spiritual force that could occasion all that Christ found it necessary to do for mankind."[235]

We can then see that for Wynkoop the location of sin in the New Testament is always in connection with some responsible function of the person. She wrote, "The locus of sin is an area of responsibility because the wrong use of this function is roundly condemned. These areas are primarily the heart and mind, which is given direction by the self. Never is the body sinful, or the enemy of the Spirit, though it may become the slave of sin and is often the occasion of sin."[236] Here we find common ground between Wynkoop and Wesley. In agreement with Wynkoop, Wesley did not consider the body sinful in and of itself. Rainey brings our attention to Wesley's sermon "On Perfection II," where Wesley wrote, "A sinful body? . . . there is no authority for it in Scripture: the word 'sinful body' is never found there . . . for no body or matter of any kind, can be sinful—spirits alone are capable of sin . . . only the soul can be the seat of sin."[237] According to Rainey, in Wesley's understanding, the soul cannot be infected by sin without the body becoming corrupted as well. This corruption, however, is not to be confused with sinfulness.[238] He quotes Wesley's comments in *The Arminian Magazine* of 1783, "Yet is not sin so seated in the soul as that it should not infect the body also? For though it cannot dwell in the body alone, nor be propagated by it, yet together with the soul the body is infected and by them both sin is propagated."[239]

In line with Wynkoop, Rainey indicates that Wesley rejected the Augustinian tendency to see human physicalness in and of itself as sinful.[240] Wynkoop's research demonstrated that Scripture does not say that anyone *has* carnality but that something *about* him is carnal (as in a carnal mind).

---

235. Wynkoop, *A Theology of Love*, 153.
236. Wynkoop, "An Attempt to Put Biblical Content into the Key Terms and Theological Concepts Relative to the Doctrine of the Holy Spirit" (article, undated), file 1425-21, WC, 5.
237. David Rainey, "John Wesley's Doctrine of Salvation in Relation to His Doctrine of God" (doctoral thesis, University of London, 2006), 179.
238. Ibid., 175.
239. Ibid., 182.
240. Ibid., 179.

In correspondence with Rev. De Paul, dated November 19, 1980, Wynkoop answered his questions about carnality. She wrote,

> Being flesh (human, carnal) is not our problem. The problem is well indicated by Paul in Romans 8:6, 'To set the mind on the flesh is death (the carnal mind—not carnality), but to set the mind on the spirit is life and peace.' The whole passage, 8:1-9, helps us to see that carnal or flesh itself is not wrong, but 'setting the mind' on our humanness and rejecting the Spirit is the essence of sin—death. It is the set of the mind that makes the difference. The same mind can be set on itself as god (Romans 1:18-23) or on the Spirit.[241]

By contrasting the sinful and spiritual possibilities, Wynkoop showed that the Bible does not portray a human predicament that cannot yield to the grace of God. The extensive sample of texts used in her biblical research shows that the essence of depravity manifested itself first of all in the purposing faculties of human beings. She showed the intellect being darkened because the carnal person is no longer in contact with truth; second, she showed that a person's will was perverted because, believing a lie, he persisted in pursuing evil; and third, his affections were degraded because, loving himself, his whole life drive was perverted.[242] This biblical research demonstrates why Wynkoop believed that sin is "not farther back or deeper down."[243] She was not referencing the subconscious but her conviction that depravity is not placed outside a biblical solution or a biblical way out. She believed that Scripture kept the depravity of sin within the responsible capacity of human beings as they respond to the atoning provisions of the blood of Christ. Only on this basis did she speak of sin not being "farther back or deeper down." She wrote, "Any serious discussion of redemption with its clear biblical declaration that there is cleansing from all sin, *must relate itself to and limit itself by a biblical definition of the sin which can be taken away.* . . . This is just another way of saying that it is not sin that limits grace and our understanding of God's redemption,

---

241. Wynkoop to Rev. De Paul (correspondence, November 19, 1980), file 1427-19, WC.
242. Wynkoop, "A Theology of Depth," file 1431-15, WC, 312.
243. This is a phrase Wynkoop used to describe the tendency of some to depersonalize original sin. The principle of sin is sharply distinguished from committed sins. It is seen as a virtual substance with real existence in some way attached to the substance of the soul "farther back and deeper down" than the person or language can even describe. Its removal is taken out of the moral responsibility of human beings and divorced from a conscious response to the demands of grace. (*A Theology of Love*, 164.)

but God's revelation of grace and redemption that must help to define and interpret sin."[244]

We are then left to ask if Wesley's description of sinful human nature remained within the realm of the dynamic reacting character of the self, or if he allocated a passive non-rational idea of sin outside the realm of moral responsibility. According to Rainey, Wesley defined sin as both outward and inward.[245] Rainey wrote, "Inward sin refers to a disposition that is involuntary, prior to any action."[246] He brings our attention to Wesley's sermon "On Sin in Believers," where Wesley gave a description of inward sin: "By 'sin' I here understand inward sin: any sinful temper, passion or affection; such as pride, self-will, love of the world, in any kind or degree; such as lust, anger, peevishness; any disposition contrary to the mind which was in Christ."[247]

Here Wesley described a relational mind-set within the realm of the dynamic reacting character of the self. This mind-set needs to be renewed or redirected by the power of the Holy Spirit. Here again we find points of agreement between Wesley and Wynkoop. Wesley also described outward sin as an "actual, voluntary transgression of the known law of God."[248] Theodore Runyon believes that Wesley's emphasis on voluntary transgressions demonstrates Wesley's prime concern to link sin to a sense of responsibility. According to Runyon, responsibility to Wesley was only valid if it connected to conscious and willful sin.[249] Even though Wesley used substantival language at times, describing inbeing sin as an "evil root," Wynkoop believed that Wesley should not be viewed under the same umbrella as the Reformers.[250] Given Wesley's teleological view of Christian perfection as love excluding sin, Wynkoop believed that Wesley would have had trouble thinking of an individual who had become so sin-bound that God himself could not help him in his most urgent need. She wrote, "Any theory of man and sin that made a mockery of the death of Christ drew from Wesley the finest of his scorn. To him, when sin was put so far back and so deep down that the essential, rational, responsible

---

244. Wynkoop, "A Theology of Depth," file 1431-15, WC, 305. Emphasis added.
245. Rainey, "John Wesley's Doctrine of Salvation," 182.
246. Ibid.
247. Ibid.
248. Ibid.
249. Runyon, *The New Creation*, 87.
250. Wynkoop, *A Theology of Love*, 153.

nature of man was said to be destroyed to the point where man could not be restored to the image of God in this life, sin was no longer sin in the evangelical sense. It has lost its religious and ethical meaning. Sin which lay behind that which is personal was not the concern for Wesley, for to him in the religious sense it had no meaning."[251]

The real issue for Wesley and Wynkoop was not a substructure of some alien substance clinging to the human soul but the human's own alienation from God and neighbour. Sin only has meaning in the realm of the personal and historical context of humanity's relationship with God. Wynkoop would be more comfortable to speak about "inbeing sin" than "original sin." For her, sin should always be placed in a moral context in the New Testament and should not be confused with fallibility or imperfection. Never is sin said to inhere in a non-personal substance. It is moral, through and through. According to Wynkoop, sin as a moral defect is *in this life* possible of correction. Given the availability of grace, the verdict is not that humanity *could* not believe but that humanity *would* not believe. The biblical message is ethical to the core.

On Perfect Love

We have now come to the place where we focus on what Wynkoop considered to be the central integrating factor that is able to absorb all the various elements of her existential theology. I would consider this to be the holy grail of all her theological concepts. It is what she would consider to be the essence of Christian perfection, namely the simple yet profound concept called *love*. This will be the main subject of our investigation as we conclude this chapter on Wynkoop's theology. We will first explore Wynkoop's understanding of perfection and then conclude with an exploration of her emphasis that love, focused on the right object, is the essence of Christian perfection. Along the way we will be able to assess to what extent there is agreement between Wynkoop and Wesley in their understanding of Christian perfection.

BIBLICAL PERFECTION

For Wynkoop, perfection was teleological. Simply put, every step taken in the Christian life of holiness is a means to an end, a progress toward

---

251. Ibid., 156.

a goal, which we will come to find was, for Wynkoop, perfection in love. Wynkoop did not subscribe to an approach that can be called "philosophical perfection," where perfection is projected as something that is either ultimate in possibility or from which there can be no further development. Instead, Wynkoop preferred to discuss perfection in a specific context as it related to an end relative to a particular case or standard.[252]

Given the absolutistic understandings attached to the English use of the term *perfection*, Wynkoop believed that the source of trouble was in a failure to completely understand its biblical meaning.[253] It is, then, definitions derived from Scripture, as seen within its unique context, that safeguard the truth of Christian perfection.[254] The fact that this term has been unwisely and even erroneously used did not justify for her its disuse in biblical theology. She wrote, "Perfection is the central concern of the gospel and it cannot be deleted from it if the gospel is to remain the gospel."[255] She arrived at this conviction through her extensive research of the biblical use of the term "perfection." The words that particularly drew her attention were the New Testament words of the family of *teleios* (perfect). She noticed that the abstract use of the term "perfection" (*teleiōsis*) was in each case uniquely moulded by the author to a specific need. From her research we list here a few samples:

In Matthew 5:48 Wynkoop showed that Jesus's use of the word "perfect" (*teleios*) in the Sermon on the Mount was used to emphasize right attitudes, rather than simply right conduct, as a requirement for perfection.[256] In Matthew 19:16–21 Wynkoop illustrated that in Jesus's conversation with the rich young ruler, perfection (*teleiōsis*) was discussed in the context of "active obedience to Christ."[257] In 1 Corinthians 3:1 (KJV) Wynkoop showed that Paul played on the idea of the word "perfect" by contrasting those who are childish (immature) with those who are mature. Wynkoop also noticed the idea of arrested development in 1 Corinthians 13 as Paul described a man who was unable to "put away childish things."[258] In Ephesians 4:13–14 (KJV) Wynkoop showed that the "perfect man" (*teleion*), which in Paul's

---

252. Wynkoop, "A Theology of Depth," file 1431-15, WC, 245.
253. Ibid.
254. Ibid., 246.
255. Ibid., 245.
256. Wynkoop, *A Theology of Love*, 285.
257. Ibid., 286.
258. Ibid., 287.

mind was "the measure of the stature of the fulness of Christ," was contrasted with "children, tossed to and fro."[259]

In all these occasions Wynkoop noticed that the perfect Christian is responsible, and the idea of maturation is directly tied with moral development.[260] Wynkoop wrote, "The contrast is not the child who is growing up normally, but one of arrested development, of 'babyishness. . . .' In a word, it is moral integrity in whatever chronological age the possessor might find himself."[261] This study brought her to conclude that *teleios*, when used of persons, has to do with "physical development, ethical maturation and real goodness unrelated to maturity."[262] Yet, in spite of this primary emphasis, Wynkoop was cautious not to limit her understanding of perfection only to a developmental process. She used Philippians 3:15 to show that Paul understood maturation to be both a possession and a quest.[263] She wrote, "One not only can become mature but he must continue in maturation. It is proper to say, 'He is a mature person,' but maturity evaporates the moment it ceases to progress."[264] In other words, Wynkoop was saying that the one who is perfect has attained the goals set before him, such as maturity, and all this happens in the context of continuous development. Perfection is integrity and depth relative to one's spiritual capacity at any point along the line of maturation.[265]

It is also important to note that Wynkoop's view of "perfection" expanded beyond the individual. For her, the corporate aspect was the primary means through which Paul advanced his idea of perfection. She referenced Ephesians 4:12–13, where Paul referred to the fully matured body of Christ or the church.[266] The Greek word used in verse 12 is "perfecting" (*katartidzō*) and conveys the idea of unity as the community is knitted together as an expression of their responsibility to each other and all of them together as an expression of Christ. The call to perfection in this context is a call toward fellowship within the church. As Wynkoop saw it, it was "holiness in its interpersonal dimension."[267] She wrote:

---

259. Ibid., 288.
260. Ibid.
261. Ibid.
262. Ibid., 285.
263. Ibid., 290.
264. Ibid.
265. Ibid., 301.
266. Ibid., 289.
267. Ibid.

There is a corporate aspect to the fellowship of the Holy Spirit and this can no more be disregarded than the personal relationship. The extremely individual leading which is characteristic of the highly moral relationship which the Holy Spirit requires, is for the purpose of the highly responsible interrelatedness which the "fellowship of saints" requires. . . . A redeemed man is not an end in himself, absorbed in his own holiness, jealous of his own status, critical of his brethren, demanding in regard to his own interests, even spiritual interests. The redeemed man is now a "family man" whose eyes and heart and interests merge with those of the household of faith. We do not say, "my father" but "our father," not "give me bread" but "give us this day our daily bread."[268]

Wynkoop came full circle in showing that the one in whose image we were created also becomes the goal of our perfection. Christ himself comes to perfection through suffering and obedience. Christ brings humanity to perfection. This pathway of perfection provides the atmosphere in which probation has meaning. Wynkoop saw the process of ascending to the adoption as sons strikingly set forth in Hebrews 2:10 (KJV): "For it became him, for whom are all things, and by whom are all things, in bringing many sons unto glory, to make the captain of their salvation perfect through sufferings."[269] The fact that Christ passed through every age is a pledge of his ability to strengthen human beings at every stage of their journey. Wynkoop wrote, "As a man he was brought to perfection by normal development. In absolutely sharing in the experience of humanity even to death and the fear of it, he conquered death and fear. As 'God/man,' he, through suffering and death, perfected salvation and makes his people 'perfect.'"[270]

Given this biblical survey, Wynkoop observed that perfection has no meaning scripturally apart from an understanding of its "this life" relevance.[271] Perfection has meaning exactly in the realm of the moral existential realities of ordinary human life, with all its relational ramifications both to God and to fellow human beings.[272] The moment perfection is

---

268. Wynkoop, "A Theology of Depth," file 1431-15, WC, 150.
269. Wynkoop, "The Biblical Study of Man," file 1432-3, WC, 122.
270. Wynkoop, *A Theology of Love*, 291.
271. Ibid., 297.
272. Ibid., 298.

seen to bypass the moral element, Wynkoop believed perfectionism was at work. Here we find common ground between Wynkoop and Wesley. Wynkoop indicated that Wesley made a strong connection between the process of Christian perfection and the development of natural life. According to Wynkoop, Wesley viewed the Christian as going through several stages of maturity until he has grown up into what he would describe as "the measure of the stature of the fulness of Christ."[273]

In agreement with Wesley, Wynkoop brought our attention to Wesley's sermon "Christian Perfection," where he asked, "In what sense, then, are Christians perfect?"[274] It is significant to note that Wesley did not use philosophical definitions to answer his own question. Instead we see Wesley going to 1 John 2:12, where he observed a pathway of perfection in the way John described a growing-up process from a little child to a young man and from a young man to a father. When the stage of father is reached, a Christian can be described as having reached perfection. Having used the same process to describe sanctification, we can see that this developmental process overlaps with Wesley's understanding of Christian perfection. And even here Wynkoop brought caution if any idea was left in the reader's mind that Wesley considered a Christian to have reached a place of concluded development.[275] On this matter, Wynkoop endorsed Wesley's position as he gave a summary of his position on perfection in *A Plain Account of Christian Perfection*. Wesley wrote, "(4) It is not absolute. Absolute perfection belongs not to man, nor to angels, but to God alone. (5) It does not make a man infallible: None is infallible, while he remains in the body. . . . (8) It is improvable. It is so far from lying in an indivisible point, from being incapable of increase that one perfected in love may grow in grace far swifter than he did before. . . . (10) It is constantly both preceded and followed by a gradual work."[276]

Wynkoop observed that the most important characteristic of perfection was its positive nature. She wrote, "Perfection is not principally the absence of all that is less than perfect, but the presence of love with all the

---

273. Ibid.
274. Ibid., 299.
275. Ibid.
276. Ibid.

dynamic meaning of love."[277] We now turn to this emphasis as we explore Wynkoop's understanding of love.

LOVE AS CHRISTIAN PERFECTION

Wynkoop credited Wesley as the main catalyst for rediscovering and revitalizing the doctrine of perfection as the perfection of love. She wrote, "Wesley's concept of love is a more complete catalyst than any other that I know of; i.e., when both theology and life are considered together, love, as Wesley conceived it, solves more theological and religious problems than other concepts seem able to do."[278] Wynkoop continued, "Wesley's 'love' would belong to the same kind of thing that God's love is, because that is where Wesley got the idea."[279] Wynkoop believed that love was the theological key to Wesley's thinking. To support this claim, Wynkoop quoted from Wesley in *A Plain Account of Christian Perfection*:

> It were well you should be thoroughly sensible to this, "The heaven of heavens is love." There is nothing higher in religion; there is, in effect, nothing else; if you look for anything more than love you are looking wide of the mark, you are getting out of the royal way, and when you are asking others, "Have you received this or that blessing?" if you mean anything but more love, you mean wrong; you are leading them out of the way, and putting them upon a false scent. Settle it then in your heart, that from the moment God has saved you from all sin, you are to aim at nothing more, but more of that love described in the thirteenth of the Corinthians. You can go no higher than this, till you are carried into Abraham's bosom.[280]

The centrality of love in Wynkoop's existential theology can also be credited to the fact that she considered love to be the central truth of the gospel. In fact, love for her *is* the gospel message. She said, "Christian love, revealed by God in Christ, is the correction of man's limited, selfish, selective perverted love. It stands against any human concept of love projected into a theory of God's nature and his way with man."[281] Wynkoop's understanding of love was clearly not anchored in human philosophy but in God's heart as revealed in Christ. Similar to Wesley, Wynkoop believed

---

277. Ibid.
278. Ibid., 18.
279. Ibid., 17.
280. Ibid., 22.
281. Ibid., 18.

that the great commandment served as a primary anchor for her theology of love: "The first commandment is, Hear, O Israel, the Lord our God, the Lord is one: and thou shalt love the Lord thy God with all thy heart, and with all thy soul, and with all thy mind, and with all thy strength. The second is this; Thou shall love thy neighbour as thyself. There is no other commandment greater than these. (Mark 12:29–31 [paraphr. by Wynkoop of KJV])."[282]

Here in a few words Wynkoop found an existential interpretation of holiness that cut through all intellectual formulations and touched the very nerve of humanity's creational purpose. For Wynkoop, love was not a concept that could be discussed in the abstract. She observed that there are three key concepts that emerge from these biblical texts on love—namely *holiness, personal relationship,* and *dynamic.* At the point where these concepts intersect, Wynkoop believed a principle of interpretation was possible. It is especially the *dynamic* nature of humanity's relation with God and the unique nature of *agapē* as seen through the lens of Wynkoop and Wesley that will complete our understanding of her view of perfect love.

Since love operates in the context of personal relationships, it is important to revisit the foundations of Wynkoop's theological anthropology. For Wynkoop, the end as a goal should be in harmony with the nature and possibility of that which is to be brought to perfection. She wrote, "Perfection is something that ought to be the case, in any particular situation, and can become so under grace. That which, in man, is to be considered under the term perfection was endowed with the capacity for perfection and must proceed to that goal if one is not to repudiate the grace given to this end. This simply means that evangelical perfection is not only consistent with the human probationary status, but is essential to it in that it marks out the goal of probation."[283]

Special note should be taken of Wynkoop's reference to the capacity for perfection and the goal of probation. The reader is reminded that Wynkoop did not align herself with the West in its tendency to think Adam was created in an already-perfect state. Wynkoop, rather, sided with the Irenaean view that Adam was created with room for develop-

---

282. Wynkoop, "An Existential Interpretation of the Doctrine of Holiness" (unpublished article, undated), file 1432-12, WC, 4.
283. Wynkoop, *A Theology of Love,* 294.

ment and growth. Hence, Wynkoop's emphasis on Adam being endowed with the "capacity for perfection" should be read with an Eastern lens. As we have seen, the capacity for development and perfection is embedded in the concept "likeness" and is, according to Wynkoop, an essential part of the way God created Adam. Even the fall did not change this basic disposition. Since, in her mind, likeness is found in the realm of human personhood where moral probation operates, the potentiality for likeness remained, even in fallen humanity. It is then important to note that, for Wynkoop, the potential for Christian perfection is anchored in creation, not in the fall. This is so, since in her mind grace does not have to re-create or restore the moral disposition of humanity after the fall but, rather, operates to renew or redirect the disposition or faculties that remained intact. This pre-suppositional stance in Wynkoop's theological anthropology has a direct bearing on how she defined *agapē*.

AGAPĒ

For Wynkoop, the New Testament term *agapē* was not a "heart word," but a "will word." It conveyed the idea of a love that showed itself by helping its object rather than desiring to possess and enjoy it. She wrote, "No emotion or sentimentality is indicated by *agapē*. It rather indicates a principle by which one lives, a deliberate attitude of the will."[284] Wynkoop drew our attention to 1 John 5:3 (KJV), "This is the love of God, that we keep his commandments" and 1 John 3:17 (RSV), "If any one has the world's goods and sees his brother in need, yet closes his heart against him, how does God's love abide in him?"[285] In these passages Wynkoop believed *agapē* is related to a quality of love that reflects action, not emotion.[286] In other words, *agapē*, in Wynkoop's understanding, makes a demand on one's dedication. The focus is on an act of obedience.

Wynkoop not only studied the use of this term in Scripture but also read contemporary works on *agapē*. After reading Anders Nygren's *Eros and Agape*, Daniel Day Williams's *The Spirit and Forms of Love*, and Gene Outka's *Agape*, Wynkoop confessed that she gained fresh insight into the idea that *agapē* is a very human function by which every person operates,

---

284. Wynkoop, "Love" (unpublished article, undated), file 1432-7, WC, 2.
285. Ibid.
286. Wynkoop, *A Theology of Love*, 298.

and by which he or she sets the direction of his or her life.²⁸⁷ It was Wynkoop's assessment that *agapē* is basic to all human beings. No one is free not to love. She wrote, "The deviant person loves, the Christian loves, the non-Christian loves. At the point of loving there is no difference among human beings. All people engage in what the Bible calls *agapē*. By translating *agapē* by the English word 'love,' the meaning of the term is totally lost."²⁸⁸ Wynkoop's basic position was that *agapē* is defined by its object. It can describe either holiness or moral disintegration. She wrote:

> *Agape* is man's operational commitment to a centre which determines his lifestyle. By *agape* man erects his God and establishes the lordship under which he serves, consciously and responsibly, or blindly, almost by default. The startling fact emerges from the biblical usage that one may *agape* God and make him Lord, or he may *agape* "the present world" as Paul said Demas did, and forfeit God. *Agape* toward God opens up the whole person to the whole rich potential of existence as a human being that God intends for man—to discover his desirable will (Romans 12:2).²⁸⁹

In correspondence with Dr. Darrell Moore in 1981, Wynkoop connected her understanding of *agapē* with the royal law. She wrote, "Agape is the non-emotional drive in every person to find fulfilment. No one is neutral—all are seekers. The human self in its major drives as reflected in the royal law, is not separate entities but relations. Each of these can select either God or something else to satisfy that urge. The same heart that loves God can also be the heart of unbelief. It is to the self that God appeals. The legitimate—essential relationship of life, never to be eliminated but brought into harmony with the self, is to 'aim at God'" (Wesley).²⁹⁰ For Wynkoop, the dedication and total self-giving aimed at God describe the essence of Christian perfection. This *agapē* set on God will then also affect all other relationships, whether *erōs*, *philia*, or *storgē*, and find the fulfilment intended for each of them.²⁹¹

---

287. Wynkoop, "Quality, the Price of Love" (unpublished article, undated), file 1432-7, WC, 7.
288. Ibid.
289. Ibid., 8.
290. Wynkoop to Dr. Darrell Moore, (correspondence, September 3, 1981), file 1427-17, WC.
291. Wynkoop, *A Theology of Love*, 37.

With this background we come to understand Wynkoop's position that sin is love, but "love gone astray."[292] She wrote, "Sin is love locked into a false center, the self. . . . Holiness is love locked into the true center, Jesus Christ our Lord."[293] By placing sin in juxtaposition to love, Wynkoop opened the door to grasp what freedom from sin requires. It is the object that reacts back on and defines the quality of love. *Agapē* is not a higher kind of love but the basic faculty necessary to make relationships possible. Perfect love, or holiness, becomes possible when *agapē* is redirected to Christ by the enabling grace of the Holy Spirit, but *agapē* set on the self throws all human relationships into chaos and destruction. In an article written while she was in Japan, "What Is Holiness?" Wynkoop wrote, "It is of interest to notice that Jesus did not require an initiation of love but a criticism of the object of love. What one loves is one's god."[294]

This all leads to the major postulate in Wynkoop's theology: "Moral is structured by love." All the concepts of integrity and freedom converge into this word "love." Wynkoop believed that "love" and "moral" derive meaning from each other. She wrote, "Love is the moral integrity which gives commitment its stability. The essence of love is not emotion, not simply will, not sentiment, but man's full dedication to some object. A divided dedication is a divided heart and is the essence of an unstable moral life . . . to be moral is to love wholly. Love is the personalizing of moral integrity. . . . In a word, moral is single-heartedness by its very definition, and single-heartedness is love."[295]

At this juncture we come to see the connection Wynkoop made between *agapē* and the moral. Also at this point, we find common ground between Wesley and Wynkoop. When Wesley described the natural image of God in which humanity was created, he highlighted four faculties: understanding, will, liberty, and conscience. Randy Maddox reminds us that Wesley did not consider the will as "rational self-determination" but, rather, equated the will with the affections.[296] Maddox describes what he understood the affections to mean:

---

292. Ibid., 157.
293. Ibid., 158.
294. Wynkoop, "What Is Holiness?" *Herald of Holiness* (August 15, 1962), file 1432-1, WC.
295. Wynkoop, *A Theology of Love*, 179.
296. Randy L. Maddox, "Holiness of Heart and Life: Lessons from North American Methodism," *Asbury Theological Journal* 51:1 (1996): 153.

They are not simply "feelings," they are the indispensable motivating inclinations behind all human action. On the other hand, they are neither mere intellectual assent nor blind attraction; rather, in their ideal expression, the affections integrate the rational and emotional dimensions of human life into a holistic inclination toward particular choices or acts. While provocative of human action, the affections have a crucial receptive dimension as well. They are not self-causative, but are awakened and thrive in response to experience of external reality.[297]

As a starting point, one can see that Wesley's use of the term "affections" can find a connecting point with Wynkoop's description of *agapē* as "the basic set of a person's dedication." Maddox indicates that these affections "can be habituated into enduring dispositions," which Wesley referred to as "tempers."[298] In the context of holy tempers (habituated affections), Wesley was able to speak of the love of God and neighbour.[299]

In this same arena, Wesley talked about inward sin. Referencing Gregory Clapper, Collins brings our attention to the fact that these affections are transitive; that is, they inevitably take on "objects."[300] At this critical juncture we find much in common between Wesley and Wynkoop. When the aim shifts away from a relationship with God, these faculties disintegrate and become corrupt. According to Maddox, these weakened affections also have the potential to become "unholy tempers."[301] Renewal of the heart after the image of Christ would require the awakening work of the Holy Spirit that will reverse these unholy tempers to become holy tempers. Yet, according to Maddox, God does not infuse holy tempers instantaneously as part of his restorative work; rather, God works "to awaken the seeds of every virtue" in a cooperative way with believers as they grow in grace.[302] The hope for recovery in Wesley's theology would then be perfection in love. And this again is framed in the context of holy tempers. Maddox wrote, "Entire sanctification (or Christian perfection) is not an isolated reality, but a dynamic level of maturity within the larger process of sanctification, the level characteristic of 'adult' Christian life. We

---

297. Ibid.
298. Ibid.
299. Ibid.
300. Kenneth J. Collins, "John Wesley's Topography of the Heart: Dispositions, Tempers, and Affections," *Methodist History* 36:3 (April 1998): 163.
301. Maddox, "Holiness of Heart and Life," 154.
302. Ibid.

noted above that Wesley considered love to be the essence of Christian life. Thus, when he wanted to be more specific, he would define Christian perfection as 'the humble, gentle, patient love of God, and our neighbour, ruling our tempers, words, and actions.'"[303]

It is evident that love was the hub in Wesley's understanding of Christian perfection. Love intersected his understanding of deliverance from the root of sin. Love intersected his understanding of fulfilling the requirements of the law of God. Love itself toward fellow human beings and God brings us to the essence of Wesley's understanding of Christian perfection. Through several excerpts from *A Plain Account of Christian Perfection*, we get a feel for Wesley's broad understanding of Christian perfection. Wesley said:

> In its simplest form it is purity of intention dedicating all the life to God. It is that purity of affection and one desire ruling all our tempers. It is not being half a Christian but devoting all our soul, body and substance to God. In another view: it is conformity to the Master by having the mind, which was in Christ, enabling man to walk as Christ walked. It is the circumcision of the heart giving man that habitual disposition wherein he is cleansed from outward and inward sin. In yet another, it is the loving God with all our heart, allowing all our thoughts, words and actions to be governed by pure love.[304]

Wesley believed that mistakes and imperfections of our corrupt bodies were not contrary to love, and could not be called sin.[305] However, since these defects of various kinds are all a deviation from the perfect law, Wesley thought they still needed the atonement of Christ. Wesley said, "Not only sin, properly so-called (that is, a voluntary transgression of a known law), but sin, improperly so-called (that is, an involuntary transgression of a divine law, known or unknown), needs atoning blood."[306] He explained himself a little more on this matter: "I believe there is no such perfection in this life as excludes these involuntary transgressions which I apprehend to be naturally consequent on the ignorance and mistakes inseparable from mortality. Therefore sinless perfection is a phrase I never use, but lest I should seem to contradict myself. I believe a person filled

---

303. Ibid., 155.
304. Wesley, *A Plain Account*, 9–21.
305. Ibid., 54.
306. Ibid.

with the love of God is still liable to these involuntary transgressions. Such transgressions you may call sin if you please: I do not."[307]

Wesley went out of his way to make it clear that there is no perfection that does not admit of a continual increase. The believer never *arrives*. Runyon references Outler's point that for Wesley it was not "perfected perfection" but, rather, a process of "perfecting perfection."[308] We are then not talking of an achieved state of perfection but, rather, a never-ending aspiration after the fullness of love.

The whole Christian life is thus seen as a development in love, with the difference between the new birth and entire sanctification to be nothing more than a difference of degree in a continuous development.[309] The definition of perfection as perfect love, therefore, does not imply a different kind of love from that granted at the new birth, not a new kind of holiness but, rather, the same kind of love, only now expressed on a higher level, as that of a "father."[310] Being a father in love is to have love unmixed with sin, with the result being a pure love.[311] Wesley believed that this gradual development in love is interrupted in an instant (exclusively as God's own work). He said, "A man may be dying for some time; yet he does not, properly speaking, die, till the soul is separated from the body; and in that instant he lives the life of eternity. In like manner, he may be dying to sin for some time, yet he is not dead to sin, till sin is separated from his soul; and in that instant, he lives the full life of love."[312]

In Wesley's sermon "The Scripture Way of Salvation," he summarized this point: "It is love excluding sin; love filling the heart, taking up the whole capacity of the soul."[313] Here we see that Wesley regarded sin as excluded or expelled by love. For Wesley it was a relational reordering in such a way that love and sin couldn't live together.[314]

The conclusion of Wesley and Wynkoop's pathway toward perfection brought them both to a place where the love of Christ is the ruling temper in the life of the believer. The common ground is especially seen in

---

307. Ibid.
308. Runyon, *The New Creation*, 91.
309. Lindström, *Wesley and Sanctification*, 141.
310. Ibid., 142.
311. Ibid.
312. Wesley, *A Plain Account*, 62.
313. Wesley, "The Scripture Way of Salvation," *Works*, 2:160.
314. Wood, *Love Excluding Sin*, 18.

Wesley's use of language like "purity of intention" and "that purity of affection and one desire ruling all our tempers." Even though Wesley would lean toward *partially restored* faculties and Wynkoop toward faculties remaining *fully intact* after the fall, the only way any movement toward God is possible to either redirect, renew, or restore is through the prevenient and enabling grace of the Holy Spirit. Wynkoop wrote:

> Love, then, positively or negatively defines holiness or sin. Love, being dynamic and free, includes or excludes others in its search for fulfilment. When the object of love, that about which the total self centers, is God, holiness is described. When, in this process, love centers in the self, God is excluded and sin is described. Holiness and sin are quality evaluations having to do with the kind of relationship the self sustains to God. They have meaning in the locus of personal relationship, not otherwise.[315]

THE DYNAMIC OF LOVE

Wynkoop was especially interested to unpack the meaning of the terms "dynamic" and "freedom" in the context of Christian perfection. These terms were important to Wynkoop since love was, in her mind, a quality of a person, never a "thing." It had to do with persons in relationship. She wrote, "It is within the personal dimension of reality that revelation as God's self-exposure is given and received, that communication has meaning, that rationality and morality are encountered, that individual and society are significant, that holiness and sin have definition. Inanimate nature is a tool of revelation, but only persons can manipulate the tool to make it reveal, or bear, communicated meaning."[316]

Dynamic, then, characterizes the relation of persons, not mere entities to be manipulated. Simply put, according to Wynkoop, "the dynamic of personal relationship is love and love is a quality of response between persons."[317] This is especially relevant when we consider the fact that the New Testament writers presented love as that which characterizes holiness. Beginning with the promise of God's love for humanity as revealed in John 3:16 and the invitation to return this love in the great command-

---

315. Wynkoop, *A Theology of Love*, 25.
316. Ibid.
317. Ibid.

ment in Mark 12:28, it is clear that the test of humanity's relationship with God is both in receiving his love and responding to his love.

The implications of this biblical invitation in Wynkoop's understanding are that the New Testament does not present an absolute God who is unaffected and unable to relate to human beings.[318] She wrote, "The dynamic emphasis in relation to God, man, love, grace, nature, and salvation and interpersonal relations is crucial to the Christian faith."[319] For this reason she did not support the distinction Nygren made between divine love (*agapē*) and human social love. She instead endorsed D. D. Williams's understanding that the dualism between God and humanity can be overcome by uniting *agapē* and *erōs*. She wrote:

> Daniel Day Williams contributes what I believe to be a more biblical approach to *agape*. Nygren, in Williams's mind, has set *agape* and *eros* in irreconcilable opposition. Never the twain meet. From a very different metaphysical presupposition Williams finds it possible and more biblical to relate *agape* and *eros*, or to unite them without losing the specific character of either. "Process theology" makes a much-needed correction to the dualisms of a former day. It is my considered opinion that, though the metaphysical foundation of process thought is not the only solution to theological problems, its insights are inescapable in a biblical theology.[320]

Given Wynkoop's desire to speak of humanity's relation to God in dynamic rather than absolute terms, special attention should be given to Wynkoop's reference that "process theology makes a much-needed correction to the dualisms of a former day." What shall we make of this statement? Shall we associate Wynkoop with the process theology of Alfred North Whitehead, who, as Michael Lodahl noted, "tried to resolve the God/world dualism by postulating God and World as co-creators and co-eternal?"[321] Did her aforementioned positive position on D. D. Williams mean that she endorsed the rest of Williams's naturalistic philosophy that

---

318. According to Michael Lodahl, "The 'Absolute' is absolute because nothing can affect or influence or change it. It is that which is unchangeable: the impervious, impassible and timeless deity" (as defined in the second lecture of the *Rothwell Lectures*, "Wynkoop's Debt to Wiley and Williams," Southern Nazarene University, 2005), 8.

319. Wynkoop, *A Theology of Love*, 11.

320. Ibid.

321. Michael Lodahl, "Wynkoop's Whiteheadian Wesley" (Rothwell Lectures, Southern Nazarene University, 2005), 4.

"humanity can be redeemed by hope, but not as an actual reality in this life"?[322] Given our research up to this point, this case cannot be made. Perhaps it is more true to say that Wynkoop could relate to the process philosophers' postulations of reality being dynamic and relational, while holding true to her theological convictions at the same time.

From her 1981 correspondence with Dr. Darrell Moore, we get a perspective on D. D. Williams beyond her preface statements in *A Theology of Love*. Here we can sense her struggle. She wrote, "Darrell, the chapters in *The Spirit and Forms of Love* that I found especially helpful were, 'Love in our History' and 'Three Forms of Love' among others." She wrote, "in spite—or because of (?)—his process orientation."[323] Given our research on Wynkoop's overall stance on personalism, what shall we make of Wynkoop's position that she found process thought's dynamic concept of God helpful? The answer is found in her previously stated position on the Trinity as a divine society of love. She has stated that love is not only experienced but also made complete within the being of the Godhead. Here we can see that, for Wynkoop, love is unchangeable in the Trinity and can be referred to as both dynamic and absolute. The essential requirement of freedom that makes love possible is also provided within the Trinity. She wrote, "The social nature of the Trinity is the first step away from mechanistic determinism and into moral freedom. It is important to an understanding of the Christian God because precisely at this point a truly personal concept marks the boundary against the blind, causal, deterministic power of philosophy's god."[324] It is, however, the Holy Spirit that plays a critical role in shifting the dualistic perceptions of an absolutist, unaffected God to the perception of a tri-personal God who is affected as he enters into a relationship with humanity. Wynkoop wrote, "The Holy Spirit not only explains personality in God but also in man. He who permeates the Godhead with moral freedom and fellowship, which is the essence of love, also permeates the human spirit, enlightening it by truth and compelling decision on the basis of truth and in the presence

---

322. Mildred Bangs Wynkoop, "An Analysis and Criticism of Daniel Day Williams's Book, *God's Grace and Man's Hope*" (monograph written at Western Theological Seminary, fall 1951), 23.
323. Wynkoop to Moore (September 3, 1981), file 1427-17, WC.
324. Wynkoop, "A Theology of Depth," file 1431-15, WC, 137.

of a proper decision sheds the love of God abroad in the human heart (Romans 5:1)."[325]

It is, then, the "fellowship of the Holy Spirit" that protects our contact with God from falling into abstract determinism. The dualism is supremely overcome in the incarnation. Wynkoop wrote, "In Jesus the Son conjoined in himself God and man in human nature. The Spirit, in Jesus, took on human experience and became available to all men."[326] We now turn to that emphasis.

THE EXTENT OF LOVE

As we have shown, Wynkoop firmly believed that Christian sanctification stands for redemption of the whole person. Wynkoop also understood that her theology of love not only stood on biblical, theological and, psychological pillars but also needed to play out sociologically in the real world of society. As we bring our study on Wynkoop's theological development to a conclusion, we want to show what this theology looks like, not on paper, but on the streets as seen through Wynkoop's eyes.

It is Stan Ingersol's assessment that "the young Evangelicals" played a critical role in shaping Wynkoop's interest in social ministries. Ingersol describes those referred to as "the young Evangelicals" as "that generation that launched the post-fundamentalist project who came of age in the 1960s and 1970s."[327] Richard Quebedeaux, a sociologist of religion, gives us deeper insight into the social movement of the young Evangelicals in the 1960s and 1970s. Ingersol references Quebedeaux: "The young Evangelicals were not a monolithic lot. Some were longhaired Jesus freaks who pioneered new ways of witnessing and new styles of Christian music. Others were influenced by the social struggles over civil rights for blacks and the peace movement to end the Vietnam War and launched new magazines like *The Other Side* and *The Post American*."[328]

It is not a surprise to see Wynkoop aligning herself with several strains of the young Evangelicals' thought. It was her desire—along with her colleagues at Nazarene Theological Seminary, W. T. Purkiser, William Greathouse, Kenneth Grider, Rob Staples, and Paul Bassett—to move the

---

325. Ibid., 141.
326. Ibid., 149.
327. Ingersol, "The Woman," file 1561-32, WC, 6.
328. Ibid. Quoted from Richard Quebedeaux, *The Young Evangelicals* (New York: Harper and Row, 1974).

conversation beyond the narrow views of fundamentalism.[329] As sanctification became more and more limited to a certain kind of psychological experience and less and less an integral aspect of fellowship in the body of Christ with all that means in social relationships and practical holiness, the Wesleyan emphasis so powerful in Wesley's day faded.[330] Wynkoop wrote, "Without the 'control' of holy love to unify and empower all that holiness people stood for, the various segments of doctrine were grafted to a number of theological systems, which was rejected by Wesley himself. Social concern no longer was rooted in evangelical holy love. Spirituality came to mean detachment from life, rather than the deepest possible involvement in it. This was fertile ground for an alliance with dispensationalism and its suspicion of all social action."[331]

Such in her view were some of the distortions of American Wesleyanism as it failed to maintain the unity of the many-faceted architecture of holy love. However, Wynkoop did not believe that what Wesley stood for was dead. Her passion for holy love, to be lived out in society, was an enduring reality in her life. This passion is especially evident in her development, as theologian-in-residence at Nazarene Theological Seminary in Kansas City from 1976 until 1980, of such courses as Radical Christian Movements and Sanctification and Liberation.[332] In this general context Wynkoop wrote *John Wesley: Christian Revolutionary*, a collection of three chapel talks given at Trevecca Nazarene College (now University). She wanted to make sure that her motives were understood. She was not interested in a revolution that ends up in rebellion and destruction. She wrote, "Essential Wesleyanism is sanctified revolution. This is a young person's religion. There is life in it. It is revolution but not rebellion. It is the gospel for individuals and for society but not a social gospel. It is human nature set on fire by the indwelling of the Holy Spirit bringing Christ to bear on personal, church, social, national, and world life."[333]

"Revolution," according to Wynkoop, was a good way to describe the mood of the sixties and the seventies in North America. At the same time, she did not feel that Wesleyan theology was "turning the world upside

---

329. Ingersol, "The Woman," file 1561-32, WC, 6.
330. Wynkoop, "The Wesleyans," file 2227-12, WC, 29.
331. Ibid., 30.
332. Ingersol, "The Woman," file 1561-32, WC, 6.
333. Wynkoop, *John Wesley*, 6.

down." She wrote, "It must be granted, grudgingly, that Wesleyan theology as such is not disturbing society to any appreciable degree, nor, for that matter, is any other theology doing so. But it will have to be granted also that Wesley stirred up ancient, entrenched human evils to do pitched battle against them with some measure of success. And is not that what revolution is?"[334]

Wynkoop stood diametrically opposed to any theology that allows a person to be saved in principle but not in real-life experience. She stood in solidarity with Wesley, who was sceptical of any theology "that could put a man in heaven without any holiness coming between the new birth and heaven."[335] Not only are human beings to be indwelt by the Holy Spirit to fulfil their own spiritual lives, but also, as Wynkoop noted, the Holy Spirit needs people through whom and by whom his power can be released.[336] Wynkoop wrote, "The Holy Spirit cannot unite himself to a stick, a stone, a church pew, an organization or a building—he must have a man, in some ways like unto himself, in whom not only the power of fellowship can be experienced but from which fellowship can flow love."[337]

True to her theological methodology, one of the key features of *John Wesley: Christian Revolutionary* was Wynkoop's focus on Romans 12:1–2, which she considered to be foundational in her call for a "sanctified revolution." Particularly, Paul's phrasing "present your bodies as a living sacrifice" catapulted her forward in her search for the biblical underpinnings of a truly Wesleyan liberation theology.

Human Worth

The cry of society for equal rights and freedom placed the concept of freedom front and centre in Wynkoop's existential theology. Freedom was to her the undercurrent that gives meaning to the worth of human beings. It is the undercurrent in the struggle for freedom on all levels of society. It addresses the breakdown of social unity, especially as seen in the third world, the black community in America, and the women's movement. The reason freedom was so important to Wynkoop is that she was convinced that love could only exist in freedom. She wrote, "Love can exist only in freedom. It cannot be coerced. Freedom is the most fundamental

---

334. Ibid., 1.
335. Ibid., 9.
336. Ibid., 10.
337. Ibid., 11.

ingredient of love. When love is spoken of, freedom is presupposed and persons are involved. Love describes the kind of response that exists between persons. Love may link the persons into a fellowship or it may short circuit about itself and reject other persons."[338] Love, then, being dynamic and free, can either include or exclude others in its search for fulfilment.

Based on Romans 12:1–2, her assessment was that a proper regard for others starts with a proper self-love that is centred in God. "Present your bodies a living sacrifice" (KJV) to her was a call for holistic engagement of the self in all its relational dimensions. She wrote, "In this exciting passage, we see not only how to treat others but we see how we ought to regard ourselves. Self-regard is basic to a dedication to 'other regard.' Our obligations to others cannot proceed apart from a proper and virile self-love. Self-fulfilment is the result of the proper outward flow of energy. Self-fulfilment is never achieved without the outwardness of the flow of spiritual energy."[339] This revelation was very personal to Wynkoop. From this text have come some of the most soul-searching insights of her life. Her personal testimony on this matter is revealing. She wrote:

> I was looking for some magic instant salvation that would take my real humanity out. The problem with me was my human nature. I wanted new works, but through great tribulation I had to learn that my human nature was rather important to God and to me. I really couldn't get along without it. I thought I had to be humiliated before I could receive the Holy Spirit. I thought I had to get rid of myself, hate myself. Be a nothing, a no self. . . . However, I learned that God does not humiliate us, tear down our self-acceptance, embarrass or de-self us in order to whip us into line. He builds up our self-confidence and then approaches us as if we were worthy of his attention and love.[340]

The theological rationale for Wynkoop's understanding of freedom is, first, that a discovery of the self, not a rejection of the self, is the first work of the Gospels. Second, divine forgiveness and a person's trust in God's love enable a person to recover possession of his or her true self.[341] The struggle for freedom was, to Wynkoop, a struggle for identity, for self-

---

338. Wynkoop, *A Theology of Love*, 25.
339. Ibid., 15.
340. Wynkoop, "Staley Distinguished Christian Scholar Lectures," January 31–February 1, 1978, file 788-79, WC, 2.
341. Ibid.

respect, for full humanity, and for equality.[342] The "sanctified revolution" was, for Wynkoop, primarily a movement from the inside out, not the outside in. Wynkoop wrote, "The search for perfection through reformation of society has never produced satisfactory results. Not only did the so-called social gospel fail miserably, but [also] subsequent rigid social and moral controls of modern-day dictatorships and Communism fail[ed] to reform or remake human nature according to the naturalistic dream of progress."[343]

If, as has already been established by Wynkoop, full personhood can only be discovered through other persons,[344] then to be free implies the freedom of others as well. This realization dawned on Wynkoop as she began to connect the dots of the implications of the Great Commandment and Romans 12:1–2. Displaying great vulnerability, she wrote, "If I can't be free by myself, if I must bring my fellow oppressed human being along with me, and the same Holy Spirit that made me free makes him free, I find freedom looking a little less alluring."[345] And yet, Wynkoop realized that the renewal of the *imago Dei* involves right relation not only to God but also to other fellow human beings. Thus, from her point of view, social ethics needed to be an integral part of Wesleyan ethics. In the end, a Christian revolutionary, according to Wynkoop, is someone who is *involved* in the warp and woof of the life of one's neighbour. And this *involvement* was, to her, holiness expressing itself in love.

As Wynkoop saw it, Wesley's understanding of sanctification as love said something about the worth of individuals that many of the theologies of his day denied.[346] Placing love in the centre of the gospel had the powerful effect of raising awareness of the "other." Standing in solidarity with Wesley, Wynkoop wrote, "Love, requiring as it must, on the part of the individual, the exercise of personal responsibility, raised one's own self-esteem and therefore his estimation of his neighbour and put him under love's obligation."[347] Wynkoop was deeply moved by Wesley's interest in what she would call the "bread and butter problems" of life in Wesley's

---

342. Ibid., 3.
343. Wynkoop, *John Wesley*, 12.
344. See chapter 5.
345. Wynkoop, "Staley Lectures," file 788-79, WC, 4.
346. Wynkoop, "The Wesleyans," file 2227-12, WC, 23.
347. Ibid.

day.[348] She was inspired by the fact that Wesley gave away 98 percent of his income. She was inspired by the way he tackled labour problems, fair wages, fair prices, and the way he fought for healthy and honest employment for the people of his day.[349] Wesley, in Wynkoop's mind, applied Christian ethics to a corrupt society. She wrote, "Wesley knew as much about medicine as the physicians of his day and he operated a free clinic in his house every Friday he was in London. He treated with remarkable success the scores of people who came. Wesleyan doctrine would not permit him to rest content in biblical theology or religious experiences as such, instead, it pushed him into the social and economic and educational problems in the world outside his church."[350]

In this assessment, Wynkoop would find great support from Kenneth Collins. Wesley valued works of mercy as a genuine means of grace.[351] Works of mercy included such things as "feeding the hungry, clothing the naked, entertaining the stranger, visiting those that are in prison, or sick, or variously afflicted."[352] Works of mercy, according to Collins, created a way in which the exercise of holy tempers became channels of grace, not only for those who are served, but also to those who minister to them.[353] Collins wrote, "This soteriological circle of ministry suggests a dynamic relation of care, whereby changes in the tempers of the heart, the implanting and fostering of holy love, may be the consequence of such simple helps and quite ordinary activities."[354] Here we find a practical correlation between Wynkoop's understanding of a self-love that is anchored in the love of God and, on the other hand, lived out in the daily existential realities of life through the power of the Holy Spirit. Wynkoop's heart for liberation was synchronized with Wesley's.

Collins further indicates that Wesley used the structure of the class meetings to distribute such goods as food, clothing, and fuel. However, Wesley's work to abandon slavery takes us to the heart of Wesley's quest for freedom. Collins wrote, "What grounded liberty for Wesley, and what could overturn slavery, was once again natural law, that is, rendering to

---

348. Wynkoop, *John Wesley*, 24.
349. Ibid.
350. Ibid., 23.
351. Collins, *Theology of John Wesley*, 267.
352. Ibid.
353. Ibid.
354. Ibid.

all human beings what pertains to them as human beings. 'Liberty is the right of every human creature, as soon as he breathes the vital air.'"[355] The connection between the natural law and the moral law was foundational in Wesley's assessment that slavery was not only a sin against humanity but also a sin against God.[356]

This whole Wesley, not just the proof-texted Wesley, had a profound impact on Wynkoop. In 1977, while attending a conference on liberation theology in Oxford, England, Wynkoop stayed in the East End Mission in London. She wrote, "It is here where Wesley laboured among the poor 200 years ago." During her stay, Wynkoop was able to go to the Wesley Chapel. As she walked into the chapel, the first thing that struck her was the object carved in wood hanging on the wall behind the pulpit. She noted, "It was a sort of icon with the illusion of depth carved in wood and softly lighted. A bare foot hung down from above caught between two tender hands reaching up. In the centre, where the foot and the hands met, were a washbasin and a towel." Here was an image that said everything Wynkoop experienced just a few days before. At some personal risk to herself, she had gone with the director of the East End Mission to the place where homeless men and women were fed. It was, according to Wynkoop, "for people who have sunk below the level of recovery." She wrote, "It rained the night we were there so scores of these people, these real people, crowded into the small building for shelter. We did not shrink from touching. . . . Here it was before us, sanctification and liberation in a university town and sanctification and a dirty foot washed by loving hands in London's poverty and crime ghetto."[357]

In the Oxford meeting, Wynkoop was able to engage those who had come to look for answers that would bring freedom for those in the American black community, the women's movement, the American Indian, and the Mexican. She wrote: "As a whole, the conference served to stretch out my cramped little soul painfully at times, to understand better why others do things that have irritated me before. . . . It is a terrifying experience to see into the soul of others. I felt I had been put in the dark."[358]

---

355. Ibid., 269.
356. Ibid.
357. Wynkoop, "Staley Lectures," file 788-79, WC, 6.
358. Ibid., 4.

CONCLUSION

• ● •

We set out to examine the extent to which Wynkoop's version of Wesleyan theology of Christian holiness was a faithful, twentieth-century reinterpretation of John Wesley's doctrine of sanctification. This journey took us into Wynkoop and Wesley's theological worlds, where it became obvious that an understanding of their presuppositions and theological methods was essential in order to assess whether Wynkoop's theology was a faithful reinterpretation of Wesley's theology. This critical examination required that we travel on foot with Wynkoop as an evangelist, missionary, and teacher as she encountered not only the American Holiness Movement but the Asian culture of Japan as well.

As we have seen, Wynkoop's own altar experiences and her experiences as an evangelist in the 1930s and 1940s helped her realize that there was a definite, observable disconnect between the doctrines sincere Christians confessed and the existential realities of their daily lives. Going back to study in her late forties helped her identify this problem as a credibility gap, which she realized would need to be addressed at a presuppositional level, if change were to occur. Both her doctoral degree in biblical interpretation and her master's degree in theological anthropology gave Wynkoop some of the filters she needed to evaluate what she perceived as a breakdown of authentic, biblical holiness.

Of major significance in understanding Wynkoop is to know her theological method. What came as a surprise was that *holy love*, as the central core of her doctrine of sanctification, was the conclusion in Wynkoop's theological pilgrimage. It was not the premise upon which she built her theological system. The secret of Wynkoop's method was her biblical orientation. We can affirm with confidence that her foundations for *A Theology of Love* were not anchored in philosophy but in her existential reading of Scripture. The fact that Christ, the living Word, is the revelation helped her find her way through the treacherous landmines of fundamentalism.

It affirmed her call as a woman in ministry, but more than anything else, it helped her understand that the true nature and purpose of Scripture is its sufficiency for salvation. Her Christocentric, empirical reading of Scripture became a primary way in which she tried to overcome the credibility gap on a presuppositional level.

One cannot ignore the influence of Wesley. Wesley's theological judgments were based on Scripture, reason, experience, and tradition. Wesley's discovery of the existential meaning of redemption in his study of Scripture drew Wynkoop to Wesley. He understood God's grace as operating in the context of human experience—in history. It was personal, dynamic, and social. In agreement with Wesley, Wynkoop believed that the proper use of God's Word could become a bridge to life, to relevance, to involvement, and to holiness.

Wynkoop's position that Adam's faculties remained fully intact, in spite of the fall, is another key to understanding her attempt to reframe her doctrine of holiness at a presuppositional level. The role of the "moral" became a critical principle in Wynkoop's existential doctrine of holiness. Wynkoop was able to use "moral" as a hermeneutical key to determine whether a person's response to the awakening overtures of the Holy Spirit is healthy. As a key interpretive principle, "moral" also helped Wynkoop to process whether redemption proceeds along the lines of moral integrity and moral responsibility. Wynkoop concluded that to be moral is to love wholly and that love was the personalizing of moral integrity. Wynkoop's interest in the "moral" was then soteriological, not philosophical. This is critical to understand since Wynkoop was constantly tempted to frame her position on moral freedom through the filters of Boston idealistic personalism.

Her critical study of the *imago Dei* helped her make a clear distinction between "image" and "likeness" in reference to humanity's relationship to God. The surprising outcome was that she begged to differ with the West and followed the East in its Christocentric reading of creation. Wynkoop agreed with what is widely held to be the Eastern position—that Adam was not created perfect but was created incomplete in a probationary status with the potential to develop and mature into the very image of the Son, who is the *imago Dei*. The source of Wynkoop's thinking on human potential, freedom, development, and growth is then embedded in her biblical understanding of "likeness," as enabled by the work of the Holy Spirit. The divine-human interaction, as postulated in her existential theology, was not anchored in the metaphysical world of Boston personalism or relationalism but, rather, in the Hebraic biblical understanding of corporate personality, where the Holy Spirit serves as the primary relational connector through whom human beings are incorporated into the Trinitarian society of love. As we have demonstrated, even though Wynkoop and Wesley's theological anthropologies ran on different tracks, they both had Sonship as their goal.

These two hermeneutical tools, that which is moral on the one hand, and her Christocentric reading of Scripture on the other, gave her what she needed to construct an existential doctrine of holiness. This two-sided methodology became a pattern she consistently applied throughout her existential interpretation of Christian sanctification. These revelations helped her make other key foundational shifts in her understanding of Christian sanctification. We witnessed her shifting from pneumatological to christological in her understanding of sanctification. We also saw her taking a stand on free grace versus free will in the doctrine of salvation. These shifts can be directly attributed to the influences of Wiley and Wesley.

Her own journey toward "A Theology of Depth" opened her eyes to Wesley's dynamic, christological, relational, teleological, and socially oriented understanding of sanctification. Together with Wesley, Wynkoop understood sanctification to be an act and a life. The beauty of holiness was not seen primarily as beautiful words in a book but in a life lived out by the grace of God. It was a life lived in shoe leather on the streets by the enabling power of the Holy Spirit. Through her own struggle, Wynkoop realized that character does not come in a nice, neat bundle at an altar, but it clears the ground as a person begins the journey of learning to love God, neighbour, and self. These transformative encounters were viewed by Wynkoop not as some*thing* that happens on a metaphysical level but as the person encountering some*one* on a moral level. That someone is the person encountering Christ face-to-face, albeit by the Holy Spirit.

Both Wesley and Wynkoop took holiness seriously. They both believed it is a "this life" possibility. It requires someone to begin the journey by faith, but it also requires a continuing walk of obedience. To present oneself to Christ involves the whole person in a moral revolution. Wynkoop's conclusion was that holiness is not a withdrawal from society in a posture of indifference, isolationism, or exclusiveness. It is, rather, love locked into the true centre, who is Jesus Christ, now being lived out on both a vertical and a horizontal level. It is faith expressing itself in love that bears witness to the enabling grace of Christ and fulfils the royal law to love your neighbour as yourself. It is the blood and life of Christ that justifies and sanctifies Christians as they follow Christ in the real, existential challenges of normal life. It is about growing up in Christ as part of a larger community to become mature followers of Christ. It means a constant enlargement of love commensurate with the daily growth and development of human personality.

The conclusion is that, while Wynkoop employed concepts and methods from twentieth-century thought, she presented a valid interpretation of John Wesley's theology of Christian sanctification. In addition, Wynkoop was not only a historical theologian but also a systematic thinker who was able to recast Wesley's doctrine in twentieth-century terms. For at least these reasons, the Wesleyan tradition shall remain in her debt for many years to come. Her critical importance cannot be overlooked or denied! Thanks a lot, Mildred!

GLOSSARY OF TERMS

Accommodation: The context in which this word is used is to convey the idea that God accommodates himself to us in vehicles that will make his revelation accessible to us. This would mean that God works within the cultural thought forms and milieu of the audience to whom he is communicating.

Aeons: This is in reference to eras or ages of time.

Altar call: The altar was the mourners' bench used to invite people to come forward and pray at the conclusion of the pastor's message. Robert Coleman in an article called "The Origin of the Altar Call" places the beginning of this practice in the year 1789, in a Methodist church in the southern United States, overseen by Francis Asbury.

Analogy of faith: This term, as used by Wesley and Calvin, describes a connecting chain of biblical truths that serve to unify Scripture as a whole. It allows scripture to interpret scripture.

Aristotelian bifurcation: To make a division between that which is seen and that which is beyond the realm of physics. Aristotle liked to ascribe reality to an abstract idea and make it more real than what can be seen and empirically verified.

Boston personalism: As proposed by Borden Parker Bowne, its main focus is theistic personalism. It is the attempt to describe ultimate reality in personal categories rather than impersonal. One example would be that, instead of trying to describe ultimate reality as an impersonal mind, Bowne would describe ultimate reality as a person. This person is not to be confused with human beings; it is a metaphysical reference point. As Wynkoop pointed out, it is not real but, rather, belongs to the realm of ideas.

Concomitant: A theological concept used to describe how several theological concepts can happen to a Christian simultaneously or concurrently. In other words, when a person becomes a born-again Christian, he or she is at that moment justified, sanctified, adopted, sealed by the Holy Spirit, and regenerated—this all happening concomitantly, or at the same time.

Epistemology: A branch of philosophy that investigates the origin, nature, methods, and limits of human knowledge. In other words, it is a theory of knowledge.

Existential/ism/ist: Wynkoop used the concept in a very general sense. She sought to emphasize the essential, vital involvement of a person in his or her theological affirmations. It is Christian truth incarnate in the dynamic flow of everyday, ordinary, human life. This existential focus is primarily anchored in the way she interpreted Scripture, especially demonstrated in her exegetical interest in the *Sitz im Leben*. However, Wynkoop also had much in common with existentialist philosophers like Buber and Heidegger. They share the ideas of human freedom and responsibility and equally reject the abstract ideals that ignore the *situatedness* of human life. However, Wynkoop rejected the atheism and lack of moral standards common in some of the contemporary existentialist philosophers of her day.

Free grace: The idea used by Wesley that God's grace is free for all and free in all. Basically, it conveys the idea that God's prevenient love preserves all people for salvation.

Fundamentalism: This phenomenon is seen among those who have a very strict view of doctrine, supported by a preference for a literal interpretation of the Bible. As experienced in the American Evangelical landscape, it sees itself as at war with science to preserve the miraculous and supernatural nature of the Bible. This battle is often accompanied with a militant spirit.

Gnosticism: Typically, Gnostic systems are loosely described as being dualistic, making a sharp distinction between the material world and the spiritual world. Those who adhered to this second-century belief system saw the material world as created by a lesser deity than the God who created the spiritual world. The outcome of this philosophical system is that the material world is viewed as evil and the spiritual world as good. For the human person this meant that the flesh was seen as evil and the soul as good. It didn't matter what the body did, as long as the soul was good.

Greek fathers: The fathers of the church were great, holy men of history who lived in the early centuries of Christianity and made a significant impact on the church and society by their lives and their teachings and writings. The early fathers who wrote in Greek are referred to as the Greek fathers.

Hermeneutics: The discipline or science applied to the interpretation of texts. This discipline is critical when dealing with biblical texts. It informs the student of the genre, the context, and the language in which a text is written. This in turn helps the student to gain an understanding of the intent of the original writer.

Hypostases: In early Christian writings, hypostasis is used to denote being or substantive reality and is not always distinguished in meaning from *ousia* (essence). This is normally used as a way to describe the Trinity as three *hypostases* in one *ousia*.

***Imago Dei*:** Literally, the image of God.

Immanent Trinity: Immanent, meaning "essential," speaks of the internal life of the Trinity. Some refer to the Trinity as a social society, where the very being is community. This focus is different than to speak of how the Trinity relates to creation.

Immutable: This concept is used as a way to describe God's nature over time. In this case, immutable would describe God as unchanging over time, or unable to change.

Impassible: Comes from Latin *in-*, "not," *passibilis*, "able to suffer, experience emotion," and describes the theological doctrine that God does not experience pain or pleasure from the actions of another being.

Imputation theory: Used to describe how the righteousness of Christ is *ascribed* or *imputed* to people as a way to make atonement for humanity. Usually in the form of substitution, in that Christ's righteousness covers our sin.

Ineffaceable: Unable to be erased or forgotten.

Justification by faith: In Protestantism, Luther came to understand justification as being entirely the work of God. Against the teaching of his day that the righteous acts of believers are done in *cooperation* with God, Luther asserted that Christians receive that righteousness entirely from outside themselves; that righteousness not only comes from Christ but also actually *is* the righteousness of Christ, imputed to us (rather than infused into us) through faith.

Metaphysical: This relates to things that are thought to exist but cannot be seen. It is beyond physics. The Greek philosophical understanding of the soul that can exist separately from the body would be a good example of a metaphysical concept. Wynkoop, of course, would not endorse a metaphysical understanding of the soul. She would say that the soul describes what a person is, not something that a person has.

Monadology: Gottfried Leibniz first developed the idea of a "monad" in 1898. It was his way to make sense of what is the essence of reality. So he used the idea of a monad, which to him was nothing but a simple substance. By "simple" is meant "without parts." These monads are the real atoms of nature and, in a word, the elements of things.

Monarchianism: A set of beliefs that emphasize God as being one person, in direct contrast to Trinitarianism, which defines God as three persons coexisting as one in being.

Nestorianism: Nestorianism is basically the doctrine that Jesus existed as two persons, the man Jesus and the divine Son of God, rather than as a unified person.

Niphil and Piel: As seen in chapter 4, these are the names given to two of the seven major verb stems in biblical Hebrew. *Niphil* would be used to indicate intensity and *piel* as causative.

Ontological: The philosophical study that examines the nature of being or asks questions about the very existence of reality. As an example, we can ask: What is the ontology of sin? In this case the object is to ask questions about the very existence of sin, such as: Does sin have substance, or is it a relational category like love?

Perichoresis: A Greek term used to describe the triune relations between each person of the Godhead. It can be defined as co-indwelling, co-inhering, and mutual interpenetration. An image often used to express this idea is that of a "community of being," in which each person, while maintaining its distinctive identity, penetrates the others and is penetrated by them.

Philosophical idealism: The metaphysical doctrine that ideas or thoughts make up fundamental reality. Essentially, it is any philosophy that argues that the only thing actually knowable is consciousness (or the contents of consciousness), whereas we never can be sure that matter or anything in the outside world really exists.

Philosophical pantheism: The belief that all of reality is identical with divinity, or that everything is god. Pantheists do not believe in a distinct personal god that is separate from everything that is. Pantheists would not talk about a god who creates.

Platonism: The philosophy of Plato, stressing especially that actual things are copies of transcendent ideas and that these ideas are the objects of true knowledge. In other words, Plato would describe us as human beings as copies of the real us. The real us preexisted in the form of human souls. When we are created, these preexisting souls come to live within our bodies and look forward to the deaths of our bodies so our souls can go back to where they came from. For Plato, the idea is more real than the actual, material object.

Presuppositions: Wynkoop defined "presuppositions" as mind-sets derived from personal temperament, cultural background, early training, and experiences that are formative for the way humanity responds to all the experiences and decisions made in life.

Prevenient grace: A theological concept that describes divine grace as that which precedes human decision. It exists prior to and without reference to anything humans may have done.

Process theology: The philosophical and theological position that God is changing as is the universe. Therefore, our knowledge of God must be progressing as we learn more about him, and it can never rest in any absolutes, which is why process theologians deny the absolutes of God's immutability and truth.

Provincialisms: The way of life or mode of thought characteristic of the regions outside the capital city of a country, especially when regarded as unsophisticated or narrow-minded.

Pseudo-spirit: Wynkoop used this term to describe a spirituality that is not genuine. It is a way of pretending or mimicking.

Recapitulation: In its simplest form, it refers to the repetition of themes, as seen in Irenaeus's belief that the incarnate Son of God, as the last Adam, recovered what was lost in the first Adam. Irenaeus saw recapitulation to be the summing up of all history and humanity in Christ Jesus as the conclusion of the drama of redemption.

Reification: A fallacy that manifests itself when an abstract belief is treated as if it were a concrete, real event or physical entity. In other words, it is the error of treating something that is not concrete, such as an idea, as a concrete thing.

Relational theology: Defining theological concepts through relational rather than substantival categories. Relationship is at the heart of the Christian faith, reflecting the fact that we as humans have been made for relationship. Jesus identifies the central message of the Law and Prophets relationally (Matt. 22:36–40).

Sabellianism: Also known as modalism, the non-Trinitarian or anti-Trinitarian belief that the heavenly Father, resurrected Son, and Holy Spirit are three different *modes* or *aspects* of one, monadic God, as perceived by the believer, rather than three distinct persons within the Godhead—that there are no real or substantial differences among the three, such that there is no substantial identity for the Spirit or the Son.

Sacerdotal: A doctrine that ascribes sacrificial functions and spiritual or supernatural powers to ordained priests. This is seen when only ordained elders are allowed to oversee the sacrament of Communion. It describes a tendency to elevate clergy above the laity.

Sanctification: In its verb form, "sanctify" literally means "to set apart" for special use or purpose—that is, to make holy or sacred. Therefore, sanctification refers to the state or process of being set apart, that is, made holy.

Scholasticism: From the Latin word *scholasticus*, "that [which] belongs to the school." The school of philosophy taught by the academics of medieval universities circa AD 1100—1500. The primary purpose of scholasticism was to find the answer to a question or to resolve a contradiction. It is not a philosophy or theology on its own but a tool and method for learning that puts emphasis on dialectical reasoning.

Septuagint: The Septuagint (from the Latin *septuaginta*, "seventy") is a translation of the Hebrew Bible into Greek. As the primary Greek translation of the Old Testament, it is also called the Greek Old Testament.

***Sitz im Leben*:** A German term making reference to the "situation in life," which is a primary way to discuss context.

Soteriology: Comes from two Greek terms, *soter* meaning "savior" and *logos* meaning "word." It is a concept used to describe the doctrine of salvation.

Syllogistic holiness: Involves a type of rationalism. Faith is seen as believing a proposition. Thus, the working definition of faith moves from personal trust to intellectual assent. In the theological case that is made, there is usually a major premise and a minor premise, which logically moves to a conclusion. Given the context in which this phrase is used, namely Phoebe Palmer's phrase, "the altar sanctifieth the gift," the conclusion can be described as sanctification by syllogism.

Teleological: From the Greek *telos*, meaning "end" or "purpose." This term attempts to describe things in terms of their apparent purpose or goal. Wynkoop's understanding saw teleology as a way to describe change within continuity as it moves toward the goal, which in this case is Christlikeness.

Tri-theism: The teaching that the Godhead is really three separate beings forming three separate gods.

BIBLIOGRAPHY

Primary Published Sources

Augustine. *On the Trinity*. Aeterna Press, 2014. Kindle publication.
———. *On the Trinity*. Book XIV, Chapter 12. Edited by Paul A. Boer. Veritatis Splendor Publications, 2012.
———. *A Treatise on Nature and Grace*. Aeterna Press, 2014. Kindle publication.
Bowne, Borden Parker. *The Essence of Religion*. Boston: Houghton Mifflin, 1910.
———. *Personalism*. Boston: Houghton Mifflin, 1908.
———. *Studies in Theism*. New York: Phillips and Hunt, 1879.
Calvin, John. *Institutes of the Christian Religion*. Volume 1. Translated by John Allen. Philadelphia: Presbyterian Board of Christian Education, 1932.
Schaff, Philip. *Ante-Nicene Fathers*. Online: Christian Classics Ethereal Library, I:28.
Wesley, John. *The Bicentennial Edition of the Works of John Wesley*. Edited by Frank Baker. Nashville: Abingdon Press, 1984—.
———. *A Plain Account of Christian Perfection*. Kansas City: Beacon Hill Press of Kansas City, 1966.
Wynkoop, Mildred Bangs. *Foundations of Wesleyan-Arminian Theology*. Kansas City: Beacon Hill Press of Kansas City, 1967.
———. "A Hermeneutical Approach to Wesley." *Wesleyan Theological Journal* 6:1, 1971.
———. *John Wesley: Christian Revolutionary*. Kansas City: Beacon Hill Press of Kansas City, 1970.
———. "John Wesley: Mentor or Guru?" *Wesleyan Theological Journal* 10:1, 1975.
———. *The Occult and the Supernatural*. Kansas City: Beacon Hill Press of Kansas City, 1976.
———. "Theological Roots of the Wesleyan Understanding of the Holy Spirit." *Wesleyan Theological Journal* 14:1, 1979.
———. *A Theology of Love*. Kansas City: Beacon Hill Press of Kansas City, 1972.
———. *The Trevecca Story: 75 Years of Christian Service*. Nashville: Trevecca Press, 1976.
———. "Wesleyan Theology and Christian Development." *The Asbury Seminarian* 31, 1976.

Primary Unpublished Resources from the Wynkoop Collection, Nazarene Archives, Global Ministries Center (Lenexa, Kansas)

Ingersol, Stan. "The Woman behind the Words." File 1561-32. Undated.
Wiley, H. Orton. "A Study of the Philosophy of John Wright Buckham." Nazarene Theological Seminary Lecture Series. File 1087-34. Kansas City, 1959.

Wynkoop, Mildred Bangs. "An Analysis and Criticism of Daniel Day Williams's Book *God's Grace and Man's Hope*." File 2227-35. 1951.
———. "Analysis of the Human Personality." File 1425-21. Undated.
———. "Appreciation Dinner at NTS." File 1426-5. Undated.
———. "An Attempt to Put Biblical Content into the Key Terms and Theological Concepts Relative to the Doctrine of the Holy Spirit." File 1425-21. Undated.
———. "The Authority of Christian Scriptures." File 2227-3. Undated.
———. "Biblical Definition of Theological Terms." File 1425-21. Undated.
———. "The Biblical Study of Man in His Relationship to the Image of God." Master of Theology Dissertation. Western Evangelical Seminary, 1952. File 1432-3.
———. "Biblical Study on Holiness Versus Sin." File 1425-21. Undated.
———. "Biography." File 1427. Undated.
———. "Birth and Marriage." File 1427. Undated.
———. "Breakfast Club." File 1426-2. Undated.
———. "Christian Celebrating Jesus Christ." *Light and Life Magazine*. June 1981. File 2223-30.
———. "Christian Words Incarnated." *Herald of Holiness*. January 18, 1968. File 1237-28.
———. "A Critical Analysis of Calvin's Doctrine of Scripture." File 2227-35. 1954.
———. "A Critique of Japanese Thought." File 1440-18. Undated.
———. "Educational Problems in Japan." File 1387-74. Undated.
———. "An Existential Interpretation of the Doctrine of Holiness." File 1425-21. Undated.
———. "The Foundations of *A Theology of Love*." File 2227-11. 1975.
———. "A Historical and Semantic Analysis of Methods of Biblical Interpretation as They Relate to Views of Inspiration." Doctorate of Theology Dissertation, Northern Baptist Theological Seminary, 1955. File 1237-27.
———. "Holiness Theology and Moral Development." File 1425-21. 1978.
———. "The Holy Spirit and Pentecostalism." File 1437-22. 1974.
———. "John Wesley's Doctrine of Perfection in the Light of His Whole Theology." File 1432-3. 1963.
———. "Life." File 1427-2. Undated.
———. "Look Out, Our Presuppositions Are Showing." File 1426-2. Undated.
———. "Love." File 1432-7. Undated.
———. "Mid-Course Corrections." File 1427-2. Undated.
———. "My Heritage and I." File 1427-2. Undated.
———. "My Life." File 1427-2. Undated.
———. "My Life—1961." File 2223-24. 1992.
———. "Notes on Irenaeus." Kansas City: Nazarene Theological Seminary. File 222-2. May 10, 1976.
———. "Notes on My Life." File 1427. Undated.
———. "Papers Presented at the Mildred Wynkoop Career Celebration." File 1561-32. Kansas City, February 27, 1992. File 1561-32.
———. "The Philosophy of Idealism and Its Influence on Religion in America." File 2227-35. 1953.

———. "The Problem of the Relationship between the First and Second Works of Grace." File 1434-13. Undated.
———. "Protestant Theology and the *Imago Dei*." File 1432-7. Undated.
———. "Quality, the Price of Love." File 1432.7. Undated.
———. "Recent Developments in Holiness Theology." File 1304. Undated.
———. "The Relation of Justification and Sanctification." File 1437-22. Undated.
———. "Sanctification Is Existential." *The Preachers Magazine* 33, July 1958. File 1051-1.
———. "Satisfactions and Regrets." File 1561-32. Undated.
———. "School, 1911—13." File 1427-3. Undated.
———. "Some Implications of the Existential Doctrine of Holiness." File 1432-7. Undated.
———. "Staley Distinguished Christian Scholar Lectures." File 788-79. January 31–February 1, 1978.
———. "Tendencies of Japanese Thought." File 1440-17. Undated.
———. "Theology of Depth." File 1431-15. 1958.
———. "This Is Mildred Bangs Wynkoop." File 1427-3. Undated.
———. "The Wesleyans." File 2227-12. 1980.
———. "What Holiness Means to Me." File 2227-14. Undated.
———. "What Is Holiness?" *Herald of Holiness*, August 15, 1962. File 1432-1.
———. "The Whole Wesley in a Broken World." File 1432-5. Undated.
———. "Why the Gospel Has Failed." File 1440-16. Undated.
———. "The Word Became Flesh." File 1425-21. Undated.

Secondary Sources

Alexander, Linda. "A Rebel in the Ranks: A Biography of Mildred Bangs Wynkoop." PhD thesis, University of Kansas, 2003.
Bangs, Carl. *Phineas F. Bresee: His Life in Methodism, the Holiness Movement, and the Church of the Nazarene*. Kansas City: Beacon Hill Press of Kansas City, 1995.
Barr, James. *The Semantics of Biblical Language*. London: Oxford University Press, 1961.
Bassett, Paul M. "The Fundamentalist Leavening of the Holiness Movement: 1914—1940." *Wesleyan Theological Journal* 13:1 (Spring 1978).
———. "The Holiness Movement and the Protestant Principle." *Wesleyan Theological Journal* 18:1 (Spring 1983).
———. "A Study in the Theology of the Early Holiness Movement." *Methodist History*, April 1975.
———. "The Theological Identity of the North American Holiness Movement: Its Understanding of the Nature and Role of the Bible." *The Variety of American Evangelicalism*. Edited by Donald W. Dayton and Robert K. Johnston. Knoxville: University of Tennessee Press, 2001.
Bassett, Paul M., and William M. Greathouse. *Exploring Christian Holiness*, vol. 2, *The Historical Development*. Kansas City: Beacon Hill Press of Kansas City, 1985.
Bassett, Paul M., et al. "A White Paper on Article X." *Didache: Faithful Teaching* 10:19 (June 2010).

Berg, Daniel. "The Theological Context of American Wesleyanism." *Wesleyan Theological Journal* 20:1 (1985).

Berkhof, Hendrikus. *The Doctrine of the Holy Spirit*. Richmond, VA: John Knox Press, 1964.

Bertocci, Peter A. "Borden Parker Bowne and His Personalistic Theistic Idealism." *The Boston Personalist Tradition*. Edited by Paul Deats and Carol Robb. Macon, GA: Mercer University Press, 1986.

Brightman, Edgar Sheffield. "Personalism." *A History of Philosophical Systems*. Edited by Vergilius Ferm. New York: Philosophical Library, 1950.

Buckham, John Wright. "An Outline of a Philosophy of Personalism." *The Personalist*, 3:4 (October 1922).

Burrow, Rufus, Jr. *Personalism*. St. Louis: Chalice Press, 1999.

Chiles, Robert E. *Theological Transition in American Methodism: 1790—1935*. New York: Abingdon Press, 1965.

Clapper, Gregory S. *John Wesley on Religious Affections*. Metuchen, NY: Scarecrow Press, 1989.

Collins, Kenneth J. "John Wesley's Topography of the Heart: Dispositions, Tempers, and Affections." *Methodist History* 36:3 (April 1998).

———. *The Scripture Way of Salvation: The Heart of John Wesley's Theology*. Nashville: Abingdon Press, 1997.

———. *The Theology of John Wesley*. Nashville: Abingdon Press, 2007.

Cox, Leo George. *John Wesley's Concept of Perfection*. Kansas City: Beacon Hill Press of Kansas City, 1964.

Cunningham, Floyd. *Our Watchword and Song: The Centennial History of the Church of the Nazarene*. Kansas City: Beacon Hill Press of Kansas City, 2009.

Dayton, Donald W. "Asa Mahan and the Development of American Holiness Theology." *Wesleyan Theological Journal* 9 (1974).

Deats, Paul. "Introduction to Boston Personalism." *The Boston Personalist Tradition*. Edited by Paul Deats and Carol Robb. Macon, GA: Mercer University Press, 1986.

Deschner, John. *Wesley's Christology: An Interpretation*. Dallas: Southern Methodist University Press, 1985.

Donovan, Mary Ann. *One Right Reading? A Guide to Irenaeus*. Collegeville, MN: Liturgical Press, 1997.

Dunning, H. Ray. "Christian Perfection: Toward a New Paradigm." *Wesleyan Theological Journal* 33:1 (1998).

Flewelling, Ralph Tyler. *Personalism and the Problems of Philosophy*. New York: Methodist Book Concern, 1915.

Kirkemo, Ronald B. *For Zion's Sake: A History of Pasadena/Point Loma College*. San Diego: Point Loma Press, 1992.

Knudson, Albert C. *The Philosophy of Personalism*. New York: Abingdon Press, 1927.

Koyama, Kosuke. *Water Buffalo Theology*. Maryknoll, NY: Orbis Books, 1929.

Lennox, Stephen J. "Biblical Interpretation in the American Holiness Movement: 1875—1920." *Wesleyan Theological Journal* 33:1 (1998).

Lindström, Harald. *Wesley and Sanctification: A Study in the Doctrine of Salvation.* Wilmore, KY: Francis Asbury Press, 1946.

Lodahl, Michael. *All Things Necessary to Our Salvation: The Hermeneutical and Theological Implications of the Article on the Holy Scriptures in the Manual of the Church of the Nazarene.* Monograph Series 4. San Diego: Point Loma Press, 2004.

———. "Wynkoop's Whiteheadian Wesley." Rothwell Lectures, Southern Nazarene University, 2005.

Maddox, Randy L. "Holiness of Heart and Life: Lessons from North American Methodism." *Asbury Theological Journal* 51:1 (1996).

———. *Responsible Grace: John Wesley's Practical Theology.* Nashville: Abingdon Press, 1994.

Marsden, George M. *Fundamentalism and American Culture.* New York: Oxford University Press, 2006.

———. "Fundamentalism and American Evangelicalism." *The Variety of American Evangelicalism.* Edited by Donald W. Dayton and Robert K. Johnston. Knoxville: University of Tennessee Press, 2001.

Minns, Denis. *Irenaeus.* London: Geoffrey Chapman, 1994.

Noble, Thomas A. *Holy Trinity, Holy People.* Eugene, OR: Cascade Books, 2013.

Oden, Thomas C., ed. "The Way of Holiness (1843)." *Phoebe Palmer: Selected Writings.* New York: Paulist Press, 1988.

Olson, Mark K. "Strange Bedfellows: Reappraisal of Mildred Wynkoop's Book *A Theology of Love.*" *Wesleyan Theological Journal* 45:2 (2010).

Osborn, Eric. *Irenaeus of Lyons.* Cambridge: Cambridge University Press, 2001.

———. "Irenaeus of Lyons." *The First Christian Theologian.* Edited by G. R. Evans. Oxford: Blackwell Publishing Ltd., 2004.

Pelikan, Jaroslav. *The Christian Tradition*, vol. 4: *Reformation of Church and Dogma.* Chicago: University of Chicago Press, 1984.

Price, J. Matthew. "We Teach Holiness: The Life and Work of H. Orton Wiley (1877—1961)." D.Ed. diss., Online: Holiness Data Ministry Digital Edition, 2006.

Quanstrom, Mark. *A Century of Holiness Theology: The Doctrine of Entire Sanctification in the Church of the Nazarene, 1905 to 2004.* Kansas City: Beacon Hill Press of Kansas City, 2004.

Quebedeaux, Richard. *The Young Evangelicals.* New York: Harper and Row, 1974.

Rainey, David. "John Wesley's Doctrine of Salvation in Relation to His Doctrine of God." PhD thesis, University of London (Kings College), 2006.

Ramsey, Paul. *Basic Christian Ethics.* Chicago: University of Chicago Press, 1980.

Rodes, Stanley J. *From Faith to Faith.* Eugene, OR: Pickwick Publications, 2013.

Runyon, Theodore. *The New Creation: John Wesley's Theology Today.* Nashville: Abingdon Press, 1998.

Shelton, Larry. "John Wesley's Approach to Scripture in Historical Perspective." *Wesleyan Theological Journal* 16:1 (Spring 1981).

Staples, Rob L. "John Wesley's Doctrine of the Holy Spirit." *Wesleyan Theological Journal* 21:1, 2 (Spring, Fall 1986).

Steenberg, Matthew C. *Of God and Man: Theology as Anthropology from Irenaeus to Athanasius.* New York: T&T Clark, 2009.

Taylor, Richard. "Why the Holiness Movement Died." *God's Revivalist and Bible Advocate*, March 1999.

Telford, John. *Life of John Wesley*. London: Epworth Press, 1930.

The Thirty-Nine Articles of Religion of the Church of England. Online: Christian Classics Ethereal Library.

Trotter, F. Thomas. "Boston Personalism's Contributions to Faith and Learning." *The Boston Personalist Tradition*. Edited by Paul Deats and Carol Robb. Macon, GA: Mercer University Press, 1986.

Truesdale, Al. "Reification of the Experience of Entire Sanctification in the American Holiness Movement." *Wesleyan Theological Journal* 31:2 (1996).

The Westminster Confession of Faith. Christian Classics Ethereal Library. Published AD 1647.

White, Charles Edward. "Phoebe Palmer and the Development of Pentecostal Pneumatology." *Wesleyan Theological Journal* 23:1 (1988).

Wiley, H. Orton. *Christian Theology*. 3 vols. Kansas City: Beacon Hill Press of Kansas City, 1943.

Wood, A. Skevington. *Love Excluding Sin: Wesley's Doctrine of Sanctification*. Ilkeston, UK: Moorley's Bible and Bookshop, 1986.

———. "Luther's Principles of Biblical Interpretation." http://www.biblicalstudies.org.uk/article_luther_s-wood.html.

www.ingramcontent.com/pod-product-compliance
Lightning Source LLC
Chambersburg PA
CBHW070800230426
43665CB00017B/2434